After the Orgy

THE SUNY SERIES IN

POSTMODERN CULTURE

Joseph Natoli, editor

After the Orgy

Toward a Politics of Exhaustion

Dominic Pettman

STATE UNIVERSITY OF NEW YORK PRESS

Published by
State University of New York Press, Albany

Printed in the United States of America

Cover art courtesy of Merritt Symes

For information, address State University of New York Press,
90 State Street, Suite 700, Albany, NY 12207

Production by Diane Ganeles
Marketing by Patrick Durocher

Library of Congress Cataloging-in-Publication Data

Pettman, Dominic.
After the orgy : toward a politics of exhaustion / Dominic Pettman.
p. cm. – (The SUNY series in postmodern culture)
Includes bibliographical references and index.
ISBN 0-7914-5395-2 (alk. paper) – ISBN 0-7914-5396-0 (pbk. : alk. paper)
1. Millennialism. 2. Civilization, Modern–1950- I. Title. II. Series.
BL503.2.P47 2002
306–dc21

2001049417

10 9 8 7 6 5 4 3 2 1

This book is dedicated to Merritt, who is my only answer to Baudrillard's question, "With whom would you share this end?" She is my partner in time, and regularly had to weather the effects of dead, crazy European men, as channeled through myself. I dedicate this book to her — I hope it was worth it.

Contents

Preface / ix

Acknowledgments / xiii

Introduction: After the Orgy / 1

The Dating Game / 10
The Coming of the Lord / 14
Technological Revelation / 17
A Note on Methodology / 21

1. **Panic Merchants: Prophecy and the Satyr** / 25

The Goat in the Machine / 31

2. **The Rapture of Rupture** / 37

Sade and the Death of God / 40
Avoiding the Void / 42
Eroticism and the Thanatic Asymptote / 48
Nietzsche's Dionysus / 52
Nihilism and the Thirst for Annihilation / 57

3. **The Virtual Apocalypse** / 63

Virilio's Accident / 67
Bacchanical Man and Ballard's *Crash* / 71
Technol-orgy: From Autogeddon to Infocalypse / 78
Snow Crash and Scopophilia / 82
Cyborgies in the Dionysian Landscape / 88
Carmageddon / 97

4. Decaying Forward: Satiety and Society / 99

De-fragging the Self / 106
Technologies of the Flesh / 110

5. Cosmic Architects / 117

Immaculate Contraception / 120
Sexless Hydrogen: The *Frisson* of Fission / 124
Dionysus in '69 / 130
The Politics of Play / 137

6. Playing at Catastrophe / 141

Prêt-à-Mort: Necrophilia and Death Fashion / 141
Close Encounters of the Third Kind: The Joachite Structure of Baudrillard's Philosophy / 144
"A Biocybernetic Self-Fulfilling Prophecy World Orgy I": or Surviving the Necropolis / 152
Temporary Autonomous Zones and the Archaic Revival / 157
Civilization and Its Discotheques / 162
After the Orgy (But Before the Test Results) / 168

Conclusion: The Revelation Will not be Televised / 171

Y2Care: Debugging the Millennium / 171
The Owl of Minerva Versus the Millennium Falcon / 178
Means to an End / 180

Notes / 183

Works Cited / 187

Index / 199

Preface

We currently find ourselves in the strange position of living in the future itself. Since Arthur C. Clarke and Stanley Kubrick combined to make the quintessential science fiction movie, 2001 has signified "the future" for several generations, and it is now a matter of some significance that we have passed this date. To what extent our present moment resembles the 2001 of 1969 is best left to the specialists in astrophysics, artificial intelligence, xeno-theology, and interior design. My interest in this temporal telescoping is the phenomenon of cultural exhaustion that Clarke and Kubrick worked so hard to counter (through the millenarian figure of transcendence). We have passed the year 2001, and no monolith has visited us to help guide us to the next evolutionary upgrade. We experienced the inevitable anticlimax of the "unofficial" millennium of 2000, and barely noticed the "technical" changeover a year later.

Such cultural malaise, of course, is not new: certain Western European minds felt they were living after the orgy over one hundred years ago, as I explore in the next section. Fatigue, I would argue, like boredom, is one of the fundamental notions in response to modernity, and yet is often dismissed as out of kilter with the exigencies of progress. ("Get with the program.") That such fatigue is directly linked to the notion of progress, along with all of the technological leaps and bounds it demands, is somehow often lost in the translation to languages designed specifically to facilitate this progress (bureaucratic, instrumental, and scientific). The assumption is that cultural exhaustion may have an impact (via such figures as "future shock," "chronic fatigue syndrome," and "screen fatigue"), but that somehow humanity has limitless resources to counter the entropic aspects of the postmodern, postindustrial world. Hence the current emphasis on human resources in the public sector, the presumption being that each generation of graduates is the equivalent of a new major oil find. And technology itself provides the tools to counter the enervation that technology produces.

("Sick and tired of the urban grind? Take these slow-release immunity-boosting pills.")

This book argues that the phenomenon of cultural exhaustion has shadowed the perceived progress of modernity itself since its staggered inception, and that the set of symptoms often designated as "postmodern" signal the eventual (and qualified) acknowledgment of this symbiosis. The fact that the second half of the twentieth century was always semiconscious of the imminent millennium only served to redeploy those discourses stemming from millenarianism itself, including apocalyptic anticipation, salvation, redemption, renovation, and revenge.

If the human race was an Olympian marathon race mapped out by the ancient Greeks, then the twentieth century often saw itself as staggering exhausted toward the finish line. Paradoxically and simultaneously, however, it was attempting to turn society into a perpetual-motion machine. The triumph of the technological drive underscored and underwrote the teleological project of modernity, prompting a variety of reactions based on the recuperation of organic innocence. In this sense F. T. Marinetti and Marshall McLuhan are the logical dance partners of the Luddites and Jean Jacques Rousseau, for they all recognize the irreversibility of technology. Cultural exhaustion moves center stage the moment dialectical or cyclic solutions become untenable. A "revaluation of all values," therefore, confronts the core narratives of the West the very moment these narratives are allegedly dissolving in the harsh light of relativism, pluralism, and an ethically precarious will-to-knowledge.

One symptom of this temporal crisis is the "psychology of belatedness" so explicitly rendered by the nineteenth-century decadents: the sense that while society flourished around us, we—as world-historical subjects—were somehow left behind by the acceleration of history. Such a perspective maintained that in our race to reach the millennium, something crucial was overlooked, so that the human race has become simply the after-effect of an event we would never even comprehend, let alone witness. "History is the shockwave of eschatology," says Terence McKenna (1991), capturing the proleptic logic of millenarianism, and the inbuilt obsolescence that it smuggles inside its narratives of salvation and revelation.

Another more meticulous scholar, however—namely, Giorgio Agamben—provides us with a metaphysical model for the "before-during-after" economy of our relationship to duration and endings, both immanent and imminent. Incorporating both the insights of Martin Heidegger and the Japanese psychiatrist Kimura Bin, Agamben introduces the notion of *post festum* (after the celebration), "which indicates an irreparable past, an arrival at things that are already done" (1999: 125). This *post festum* speaks of a kind of ontological belatedness "which is always late with respect to itself," and that probably needs little historical prompting before showing its melancholy face. Certain epochs may encourage the sense of missing the party more than others (in a collective reverence for the achievements of past ages designated "golden") but there may be something even more fundamental that nurtures such historical rubbernecking (see, e.g., Walter Benjamin's *Angel of History*).

Such a state of mind is difficult to endure, since in order to navigate time we need something to look forward to. Here we have the essentially *ante festum* outlook of the utopian and the schizophrenic; a "temporality [that] corresponds to the primacy of the future in the form of projection and anticipation" (ibid.: 126). The paradox of such a proleptic orientation is that "it always risks missing itself and not being present at it's own 'celebration'" (ibid.). Agamben goes on to say that

> One might expect the temporal dimension of *intra festum* to correspond to a point . . . . in which human beings would finally gain access to a full self-presence, finding their *dies festus* [feast day]. But it is not so . . . . [As witnessed by epilepsy] the point in which the "I" is about to adhere to itself in the supreme moment of celebration, the epileptic crisis confirms consciousness' incapacity to tolerate presence, to participate at its own celebration. (ibid.: 126-127)

The orgiastic "farewell to flesh" that is *carnival* always already contains this paradoxical economy, an economy that I view as chiefly libidinal.

Post-2001, we wake up with a historical hangover and ringing ears, but have no recollection of being at the party—a new dawn seems somehow less symbolic through bloodshot eyes. It then becomes significant how we answer Jean Baudrillard's question: "What are you doing after the orgy?" Do we start by cleaning up the deflated balloons and tattered streamers? Or does "cleaning up" lead to the sinister logic that turned the twentieth century into a global museum of horrors? Do we tentatively act on our New Year's resolutions to flush our systems, discipline our bodies, renounce our addictions, and sharpen our minds? Or do we succumb to the historical urge deeply rooted in linear conceptions of time, and start planning another party? Do we look *forward* to a time when things will be better (again)?

In such retroactive and repetitive compulsions does the neurotic history of the present *produce*—and *re*produce—the future.

The future, then, is the unexplored territory of potentiality. However, if we look *too* far into the future, there is no future (at least not for us, as the punks affirmed so noisily). The nervous exhaustion of being too late, and waiting for something that may have already left the building (Elvis, Godot, God) informs each passing moment, for the very reason that they are registered as passing. ("It is impossible to pass from linear to spatial consciousness, since passage is a linear concept" [Odell, 2001: 126].) It is this kind of fractured thinking—along with technological "advances" such as nuclear power—that led to books with titles like *Looking Back at the End of the World.*

And it is deep within this exhaustion that I glimpse the outline of a politics that barely resembles the movements that have historically been associated with such a category. This book does not claim to identify and deploy concepts on which we would somehow "build" such a politics, but rather follows the contours and exchanges of an economy that created the conditions for imagining "an otherwise," uncompromised by the ransom demands of Hegelian time. Such a politics recognizes the fundamental flaw with contemporary utopian agendas, precisely that they presume that we have the energy and will to try to realize them, a more than dubious premise these days. In order to unravel such a conceptual blockage, we must examine how we got here in the first place by following the red thread of libidinal millenarianism.

Acknowledgments

I would like to thank numerous people who contributed to this book, directly or indirectly, whether during its previous life as a doctoral thesis, or throughout its lengthy metamorphosis into a manuscript. Simon During, Ken Gelder, Mark Dery, David Bennett and Catherine Gallagher all guided my gauche enthusiasm into useful directions. I reserve special thanks for Steven Shaviro and Wlad Godzich, who both went out of their way to help some schmo they didn't know from Adam. Thanks also to Dan Ross, whose coffee and comments were far too intense to cope with, and to Justin Clemens and David Odell, who have both only begun to influence and intrigue. A host of other people gave support – moral or otherwise – including Eddie Maloney; Paul and Alia Dash; Kim Armitage; Kylie Matulick; Greg Duff; Adam Rainczuk; Adam Sebire; Brittany Dufty; Brigid Magner; Khass and Bianca Yianni; Ben Deacon; John Matthews; Nick Heron; Isabelle Wallace; and the Symes clan. Special thanks goes out to Tash, Saul, Ralph, Mike, and Jindy, who provided support on all fronts.

This book would be a totally different – and inevitably inferior – artifact, if it wasn't for Ken Ruthven, whose insights, suggestions, patience, stamina, and attention to detail are truly a wonder to behold. The Australian Network for Art and Technology provided an invaluable travel grant, as did Melbourne University's School of Graduate Studies. Earlier versions of certain sections have previously appeared in the *Tamkang Review* (Summer 2000), the *Journal of Millennial Studies* (Winter 1998/99) and *Zeitsprünge* (1999).

And finally, many thanks to Joseph Natoli and James Peltz, who both had a big impact on the (much improved) final product.

In the midst of the orgy, a man whispers into a woman's ear: "what are you doing after the orgy?"

Jean Baudrillard (1983: 46)

. . . and the beast will be huge and black, and the eyes thereof red, with the blood of living creatures, and the Whore of Babylon shall ride forth on a three headed serpent, and throughout the lands there shall be a great rubbing of parts . . .

Monty Python's *Life of Brian*

Introduction: After the Orgy

> It may comfort you to know that I am still not participating in any sexual acts.
>
> From a letter by Heaven's Gate cult member Gail Maeder, to her parents in 1997 (Adler 37)

> These monks that just took their heads in San Diego; they're way behind the times.
>
> Charles Manson to his parole board at Corcoran State Prison (Gleick 26)

On March 26, 1997, thirty-nine members of the Heaven's Gate cult were found dead in Rancho Santa Fe, San Diego, their Nike shoes sticking conspicuously out of their purple shrouds. They had taken their lives in the belief that the Hale-Bopp comet was shielding an alien space craft that was to take them to the Level above Human. The ensuing media frenzy focused on several angles, separating what was unique about the cult's mass suicide from what it shared with other extremist apocalyptic groups. The followers of Marshall Herff Applewhite (aka "Do") were almost uniformly portrayed as deeply repressed and gullible innocents who had trouble distinguishing science fiction fantasies from "reality." Editorials around the world could not resist puns involving these "alienated" individuals and their particular brand of *X-Files*-meets-Revelation rhetoric. In the following weeks, media commentators became obsessed with the voyeuristic revelation that six members, including Applewhite himself, had voluntarily castrated themselves in a surgical procedure designed to eliminate sexual urges—a serious offense to the neognostic ambitions of the sect. In the process,

Heaven's Gate became one more hyperreal coordinate on the psychosocial map of millennial America, where John Wayne Bobbitt was re-membered only to be instantly forgotten by a public whose hunger for the extreme devoured news of Aum Shinrikyo, Waco, Ruby Ridge, the Order of the Solar Temple, and the Oklahoma Bombing, in a globally expanding feast of apocalyptic proportions.

Motivation, as usual, was the question that gave this story such momentum; Why did they do it? Applewhite was presented as being tortured by "sexual demons." His idiosyncratic religion was viewed as the psychological escape route from his earthly desires, and more specifically from those homosexual impulses that compromised his career as a music teacher (Chua-Eoan 36). His followers were paired off in a surveillance strategy which, when combined with various hormones, bolstered the cult's doctrinal policies on the need for celibacy. (Indeed, at one point the group founded "The Anonymous Sexaholics Celibate Church.") Such rigorous libidinal constraints are commonplace among both fringe and established religions. The media, however, seized on its unprecedented intersection with popular culture, high technology, and voluntary mass-suicide.

In a sense, Heaven's Gate inhabited Bill Gates' slipstream by using the Internet as its major informational vector to spread its gospel of ascension to the Level above Human. They were described as an "Internet Death Cult" (Levy 46), adding to the already prevalent fear that the World Wide Web is populated by insidious spiders just waiting for children to stumble across their path. While the hysteria surrounding sexuality and the Internet is not unrelated to my topic, at this early stage I wish merely to spotlight the way in which certain metaphors and discourses were mobilized in support of moral panics exacerbated by the liminal temporal space of the year 2000. (Prophecy has often been attracted to round numbers.) *Newsweek,* for instance, finds answers to the Heaven's Gate riddle in not only Applewhite's charisma and the "uncertain times we live in" but also in the "*pull* of millennialism through the ages" (Editorial 35—my emphasis).

In its most general and abstract sense, this "pull" is the focus of this book, especially as it relates to the interpretation of twentieth-century millenarian movements and moments. Assuming the libidinal connection between messianic figures and their followers, I explore the seductive power of the millennial concept, and its capacity to "pull" people out of their normal lives and into that highly charged psychic space that Frank Kermode fleetingly refers to as "the erotic consciousness" inscribed within the moment of crisis (1975: 46). In this sense my study represents an inquiry into the magnetic properties of a transcendent "floating signifier," and the way in which prophecy and eschatology have filtered into our daily consciousness.

The years 2000, 2001, and 3001, the Millennium, the Eschaton[1], Utopia, Heaven, and the Level above Human: however we describe the object that lies at the end of history, it inevitably becomes the focus for intense cathexis—the libidinal transference of value. We project our most powerful fantasies onto the symbolic logic of these utopian artifacts. Just as the black monolith is stroked by early simians in Stanley Kubrick's version of *2001: A Space Odyssey,* so too the apocalypse is invested libidinally with a neo-Freudian reconfiguration of desire and transcendence. The millennium has become the ultimate seductive model, beckoning us toward the exquisitely elusive process of *revelation.*

In the days following the morbid discovery in California, *Time* magazine's Richard Lacayo identified two developments that have fostered the spread of apocalyptic cultism. One is the "strictly free-market and technological" phenomenon of communications technologies (what could be referred to as the "modem world"), while the other is the "end of communism": "Whatever the disasters of Marxism, at least it provides an *outlet* for utopian longings. Now that universalist impulses have one less way to expend themselves, religious enthusiasms of whatever character take on a fresh appeal" (34—my emphasis). *Newsweek* also warned that rampant millennialism will seek other outlets for its cathartic expenditure. It seems that Sigmund Freud's notion of the "return of the repressed" is alive and well, given the media's continued reliance on the established formula of accumulation and release.

The Janus-face of what I call "libidinal millenarianism" is thus produced by morphing images of Freud and Karl Marx. Twentieth-century developments unfolded in the shadows of these two (largely) utopian thinkers, including various poststructuralist attempts to transcend them, so that everything up to and including Heaven's Gate continues to be popularly conceived of in terms of *repression, liberation, transgression,* and *transcendence.* While I do not pretend to operate outside these conceptual coordinates, I intend to demonstrate—through a genealogically informed rereading of certain apocalyptic moments—that such terms are part and parcel of the apocalyptic dynamic. My argument begins, therefore, with the premise that notions such as "transcendence" bog us down in the tragicomic history of utopianism, unable to achieve "escape velocity" from the gravity of Marxist-Freudian ideas. This is not intended as either a jeremiad or a warning. It is merely a position from which to assess ideas about the future of a future, conceived of as "the beginning of the end."

Another canonical name should be invoked at this point: that of Charles Darwin, whose notion of the survival of the fittest has become (in an ironic twist) the model for the natural selection of ideas. In his article on "Viruses of the Mind," Geoffrey Cowley appeals to the new "science" of memetics; loosely defined as the viral transmission of ideas through language. Cowley speculates that the actions of the Heaven's Gate cult members could be put down to a virulent strain of millenarian ideas:

> Medical epidemiologists can sometimes predict the scope and course of a disease outbreak just by analyzing the structure of a virus. Memetics hasn't achieved such precision, but that is its mission: to explain how beliefs gain currency, and to predict their ebb and flow . . . . Unfortunately, as the Heaven's Gate tragedy reminds us, hosts who swallow both the heaven-is-ours and the end-is-near memes may conclude the end is theirs to hasten—and hasten it.
>
> But a virus that kills its host doesn't always kill itself. If the fluids flowing from a dying Ebola-virus victim infect a half-dozen nurses, the bug still comes out ahead. Likewise, if even a small minority of the TV viewers now following the Heaven's Gate story responded to the cult's message, the message might survive.[2] (14)

Such a metaphor speaks volumes about current obsessions with mental hygiene and its breakdown into cultural euthanasia. The viral rhetoric of the cold war has increased since the dissolution of the Soviet Union, intensifying the paranoia that the enemy is not only within, but unknown—an amorphous enigma.

Daniel Dennett describes the brain as a "meme nest" (Kingwell 177), and in his panic text, *The Hot Zone*, Richard Preston writes that, "[w]e live in a kind of biological Internet in which viruses travel like messages, moving at high speed from node to node, moving from city to city" (1995: 18). The key image here is "message," which evokes the appropriation by genetics of terms like *code* and *messenger* from communications theory. The suggestion here is that the body can understand its vulnerability only through the vocabulary of technology (a notion I explore further in chapter 3—especially in relation to *Snow Crash*). Despite its ideological crudity then, the viral model prompts us to trace the "memetic" genealogy of libidinal millenarianism.

The New Age messiah-prophet and fringe scholar, Terence McKenna—who attempts to occupy the problematic position of both mystical prophet and scientific rationalist—has much to say on the topic of libidinally inscribed end-of-time scenarios. That the "end is nigh" is taken for granted by messianic figures who preach transcendence, and McKenna (like Applewhite) is no exception. However, he *is* canny enough to couch his own UFO-related agenda in pseudosociological terms. And indeed his oracular predictions bear a striking resemblance to the "machinic desire" of the Heaven's Gate cult. "One dimension of the culture crisis," McKenna notes, "is a collective erotic desire for a connection with the other." And while this could be seen as a universal constant, "it is as though the Father-God notion were being replaced by the alien-partner notion" (73).

This observation is borne out not only in the realm identified by Malcolm Bull as the "popular secular apocalyptic" (1995b: 4)—including the *The X-Files* and countless other sf-inflected texts—but also in the metamorphosis of angels into aliens. In the case of Heaven's Gate, sexual sublimation was transferred on to the sublime alien, so that salvation was figured as a chaste version of St. Theresa's rapture. ("Beam me up!" chirped one recruit on the videotaped suicide note.) Although the sublime Other remains a genderless creature from the Kingdom of Heaven, it now looks more like something from Steven Spielberg's design department than from the brush of Botticelli. Indeed, in the popular mind it has usurped the role of Walter Benjamin's exterminating angel, overseeing the progressively unfolding catastrophe which we call "human history".

In considering the pulp-fictional futurism of modern American pseudo-religions, McKenna goes on to say that

> [t]he previous concerns of salvation and redemption are shifting into the background for the great majority of people, and what is driving religious feeling is a wish for contact—a relationship to the Other. The alien then falls into place in that role; the alien fulfills it. I believe that if religion survives into the long centuries of the future, this will be its compelling concern—an attempt to define a collective relationship with the Other that assuages our yearning and our feeling of being cast out or, as Heidegger says, "cast into matter, alone in the Universe." (73)

However, it seems to me that McKenna dismisses the drive for redemption a little too early, considering that it can still inspire thirty-nine people to kill themselves.

The collective desire for fusion is identified by Georges Bataille as the base-note of eroticism (see chapter 2), a sharp irony in the case of Heaven's Gate. McKenna completes a psychosocial feedback loop by stating that "the appetite for this fusion . . . is propelling global culture toward an apocalyptic transformation" (74). In dismissing the social and political stratifications of everday experience (i.e., in employing sweeping generalizations that conflate the destiny of an out-of-work coal-miner and a Silicon Valley executive) McKenna is guilty of peddling reductionist explanations and psychobabble solutions. Heaven's Gate, however, is an unsettling testimony to the possibility of such a shared destiny: people of different ages, sexes, and economic backgrounds swallowed applesauce and barbiturates in a final act of solidarity.

Freud saw Eros (the god of love) as a social binding-agent, feeding the appetite for construction. But he also sensed the destructive potential of its symbolic exchange with Thanatos (the god of death) in a yin-and-yang process. McKenna fudges the ambiguity of Eros, seeing it as the catalyst for an apocalypse that banishes Thanatos in favor of the benign Alien, who shepherds us in the manner of a Jew who roamed the earth two thousand years ago. It is thus important to identify libidinal millenarianism as the result of a constant interplay between the ur-myths of Armageddon and their rewriting in the present.

One word that perfectly encapsulates this "atavistic versus futuristic" dynamic is *panic.* "When the shaman's song fails," McKenna notes,

> his world erupts into a situation of weakened psychic constitution that contains an element of "panic" in the mythological sense that evokes Pan bursting through from the underworld. The equivalent panic in our society is the emergence of the UFO as an autonomous psychic entity that has slipped from the control of the ego and approaches laden with the "Otherness" of the unconscious. (60)

This leads to what McKenna calls succinctly "the revelation of the UFO" (61).

When Charles Manson heard about Heaven's Gate, he remarked, "These monks that just took their heads in San Diego; they're way behind the times" (Gleick 26). Any attempt to decipher this convicted killer's edicts is automatic conjecture. However, his statement could be read as an acknowledgment of his own allegorical role in the millenarian climate of the 1960s. Like McKenna, Manson finds the emphasis on redemption now outdated. Or perhaps, as I suggest in the next section, it has merely altered its form.

The genealogy I trace—from Sade through Friedrich Nietzsche to Bataille and J. G. Ballard (to name only a few)—represents the "dark side" of libidinal millenarianism, the one that acknowledges and embraces the Thanatic aspect of Eros. According to their "dionysian" perspective, Thanatos is never far behind.[3] This point is illustrated by the Select Followers of Oklahoma, who were prevented by police from sacrificing a virgin to Haley's Comet in 1910 (Lacayo 34). Heaven's Gate occupies an ambivalent space in the dionysian scheme of things. Rejecting its essential panic, they executed themselves with methodical discipline, rather than with the traditional gesture of sacrificial excess.

The police officers who discovered the bodies of Applewhite and his followers were immediately overcome by the stench of the corpses inside the giant mansion. Despite the anal-retentive ways of cult members, the organic basis of their existence (which weighed on their spirits so heavily) leaked out in the absence of Apollonian muscle control. The seventy-four members of the Order of the Solar Temple who have killed themselves since 1994 in Canada, Switzerland, and France are also sacrificial offerings to Bataille's "solar anus" of excremental nihilism. So long as humanity is an embodied entity, Dionysus will have the last laugh.

Heaven's Gate is thus the ideal cult for an age that Jean Baudrillard has described as coming "after the orgy"—the orgy being the specific moment when "modernity exploded upon us" (1993: 3). Unlike Shoko Asahara's lascivious evenings in the Aum Shinrikyo compound, or David Koresh's alleged satyric ceremonies in "ranch apocalypse," Applewhite's sublimation represents a rejection of the nihilistic-orgiastic dynamic of heretical history. As Damian Thompson notes in his pop-study, *The End of Time,* "[t]here is a pronounced tendency . . . for millenarian groups to veer toward extreme attitudes to sexual behaviour, in which sex is either forbidden or to be enjoyed indiscriminately" (1996; introduction—n.). Both options, however, partake of libidinal millenarianism, representing two sides to the same coin.

Neal Stephenson's post-cyberpunk novel, *The Diamond Age,* contains an extended section that plays on the literary motif of the pagan orgy. In this scene, the protaganist Hacksworth watches the mysterious behavior of the underworld.

> In a cavernous dark space lit by many small fires, a young woman, probably not much more than a girl, stands on a pedestal naked except for an elaborate paint job, or maybe it is a total-body mediatronic tattoo. A crown of leafy branches is twined around her head, and she has thick voluminous hair spreading to her knees. She is clutching a bouquet of roses to her breast, the thorns indenting her flesh. Many people, perhaps thousands, surround her, drumming madly, sometimes chanting and singing. Into the space between the girl and the watchers, a couple of dozen men are introduced. Some come running out of their own accord, some look as if they've been pushed, some wander in as if they've been walking down the street (stark naked) and gone in the wrong door. Some are Asian, some European, some African. Some have to be prodded by frenzied celebrants who charge out of the crowd and shove them here and there . . . . Hackworth notes that all of them have erections, sheathed in brightly colored mediatronic condoms—rubbers that actually make their own light so that the bobbing boners look like

> so many cyalume wands dancing through the air.
>
> The drumbeats and the dancing speed up very slowly. The erections tell Hackworth why this is taking so long: He's watching foreplay here. After half an hour or so, the excitement, phallic and otherwise, is unbearable. The beat is now a notch faster than your basic pulse rate, lots of other beats and counterrhythms woven through it, and the chanting of the individual singer has become a wild semi-organized choral phenomenon. At some point, after seemingly nothing has happened for half an hour, everything happens at once: The drumming and chanting explode to a new impossible level of intensity. The dancers reach down, grip the flaccid reservoir tips of their radioactive condoms, stretch them out. Someone runs out with a knife and cuts off the tips of the condoms in a freakish parody of circumcisions exposing the glans of each man's penis. (1995: 231-232)

The fact that such a familiar trope as the pagan orgy can fit so comfortably into the postindustrial, postmodern, and late-capitalistic narrative of a science fiction novel says much about historical cycles and the resilience of archetypal myths. In this voyeuristic scene the dionysian clearly continues to play an important role in the literary landscape. Far from dissolving into the haze of nineteenth-century recycled romanticism, the phallic god of lust has once again demonstrated his irrepressible nature by informing much of today's cultural zeitgeist.

This time, however, Dionysus must negotiate new foes and new forces that seek to restrict the irrationality and violence of his instincts. The Pan-like creature must adapt to the silicon valleys of the information revolution. Consequently Dionysus' traditionally pastoral context has been displaced by the cybernetic, resulting in what has been called—somewhat oxymoronically—the "cyber-dionysian" (Dery, 33).

The fifth issue of *Mondo 2000* (n.d.) has a photo-spread of naked women covered only by electronic circuitry and computerized gadgets. They are described as maenads (priestesses of Bacchus) and cavort alongside a text whose rhythms are ritualistic:

> Groaning, moaning, on your knees
> panther, Niger, come to me
> blood and milk together feed the pleasure
> carmine, throbbing, senses reel
> fleshy mystery, pagan meal
> Dionysus screams as we give pleasure
>
> (Springer 52)

Much of 1990's para-literature (articles, ads, reviews, comics, and rock lyrics) defines itself against or toward an assumed dionysian orientation. Moreover, this "attitude" is a crucial compass for identity-based politics both within and against the monolithic and abstract categories of modern existence: society, economy, nation, class, race, gender, life, and death.

The dionysian impulse is further aggravated by the dynamic, reciprocal, and symbiotic connections of millenarianism. I argue that the dionysian is paradoxically the desire to reinvoke the sacred while simultaneously embracing the nihilistic license of the Free Spirit in the face of imminent extinction. In Raoul Vaneigem's terms, such a strategy valorizes *life* over, above, and against, *survival*.

In describing the pervading aura of the *fin de millénium* as life "after the orgy," Baudrillard spotlights a general sense of entropy, depletion, and decadence, all factors contributing to a possible slow-motion apocalypse. Indeed, harnessing such a post-coital ambience is, I shall argue, the task of an emerging politics of exhaustion, a "radical passivity" that threatens the prevalent ethos of relentless productivity.

And yet despite Baudrillard's aphorism, an echo of the orgy survived in the erotic imagination of the 1990s. On January 22, 1995, an Asian-American porn starlet, Annabel Chong, (real name, Grace Quek) decided to perform "The World's Biggest Gang Bang" by having sex with 251 men in one day. This event took place

> in a Hollywood soundstage. Doric, Ionic and Corinthian columns decorated the set, along with various statues, urns, vases and fountains in an attempt to recreate an ancient Roman orgy. There was even a bust of what looked like Caligula . . . . The pretense of a Roman orgy seemed awkward at the very least. (Hallock 82)

When interviewed as to her motives, Chong replied that "she simply had to do it 'because it was such a daring idea.' She imagined it would embody the decadence with which she could end the century" (ibid.).

To couch such a stunt in these terms merely strengthens the dionysian genealogy—no matter how tacky the Roman replicas—of the happening in which she is such an enthusiastic (though problematic) participant.[4] Just as Chong's world record of 251 men was surpassed a few months later by Californian stripper Jasmin St. Claire, so too Baudrillard's orgy is supplanted by another, in a simulated *mise-en-abyme* effect extending into the future.

The Dating Game

> Another Millennium. Another Bestseller.
>
> Blurb for Arthur C. Clarke's novel *3001*

> Only the brain of a child or of a savage could form the clumsy idea that the century is a kind of living being, born like a beast or a man, passing through all the stages of existence, gradually ageing and declining after blooming childhood, joyous youth, and vigorous maturity, to die with the expiration of the hundredth year, after being afflicted in its last decade with all the infirmities of mournful senility.
>
> Max Nordau, *Degeneration* (1993 [1892]: 1)

> The future's uncertain and the end is always near.
>
> *The Doors,* "Roadhouse Blues"

At this point it may be useful to ask what exactly this "Millennium" *is* that I'm talking about. The answer may be that it isn't anything, *exactly,* but rather a "free-floating framework" (as Philip Lamy calls it), or a giant sliding signifier that hovers ahead of us like a carrot in front of a donkey; no matter what the "actual" date. Norman Cohn, the traditional authority on these matters, notes how the word *millenarianism* has "in fact become simply a convenient label for a particular type of salvationism" (1993: 13), which is indeed how I employ the term.

Thus in trying to pinpoint some kind of working definition, we must concede that the millennium is a symbolic concept tied to a symbolic measurement of time, which potentially is as contingent as the human population itself. It is a blank screen on which we project our own fantasies for the future, present anxieties, and regrets about the past. Yet the images that flicker across its surface have a thematic consistency and coherence that belie the randomness of calendrical fetishism. In simpler terms, *how* it is represented as occurring, and with what effects, are far more significant than *when* it happens.

Throughout history, prophets have predicted the very day of the dawning millennium, each date both a reflection of current events and a Magic-Marker cross on Henri Focillon's "perpetual calendar of human anxiety" (Kermode, 1975: 11). Although the debate continues as to whether or not the year 1000 A. D. bore witness to feverish millennial activity, the common feeling is that it passed almost unnoticed. The fact that significant millennial eruptions occurred in the seemingly irrelevant years of 1260, 1420, and 1666, indicates the dominance of sociological over astronomical patterns.

The frequency of prophetic failure, however, seems only to inflame the desire for new estimates of the impending existential terminus, thus confirming Wallace Stevens's observation that "the imagination is always at the end of an era" (ibid.: 31). As Kermode notes, "Apocalypse can be disconfirmed without being discredited. This is part of its extraordinary resilience" (ibid.: 8). And indeed the regenerative resources of the Japanese Aum Shinrikyo sect—after the disgrace of subway gas attacks, failed prophecies and legal prosecution—is but one recent case of this phenomena.

In a passage that forms the epigraph to this section, the nineteenth-century anti-Decadent Nordau affirms the random nature of temporality, and chastises those who impose a metaphysical system onto its mathematical branches. He goes on to make the important point that

> [T]he arbitrary division of time, rolling ever continuously along, is not identical amongst all civilized beings, and that while this nineteenth century of Christendom is held to be a creature reeling to its death presumptively in dire exhaustion, the fourteenth century of the Mahommedan world is tripping along in the baby-shoes of its first decade, and the fifteenth century of the Jews strides gallantly by in the full maturity of its fifty-second year. (2)

Throughout the Christian era, a timeless and cyclic infrastructure has lurked beneath the progressive, linear superstructure. Cohn attributes the initial emergence of a linear chronological mode to a figure whose name would come to represent the mortal pinnacle of historical evolution: the Iranian prophet Zarathustra, who is more commonly known by his Greek name, "Zoroaster", which means "he who has active camels."

Zoroaster's is the first recorded instance of a narrative that tells of a "coming consummation," in which an unhappy situation will be replaced by a utopian one. This positive apocalyptic scenario, known as "the making wonderful," was certainly something to look forward to in times of strife. Cohn thus identifies Zoroaster as "the earliest known example of a particular kind of prophet—the kind commonly called 'millenarian'" (1995: 27). These prophets then represent a promised paradise, their name becoming a signature of guarantee. (e.g., "Jesus Christ").

Nietzsche reintroduced the transcendent legacy of Zarathustra, just as his modern spin on the myth of Dionysus redefined its philosophical usage while maintaining its linguistic roots. Zarathustra is indeed a curious choice to represent the circular logic of the "eternal return," considering his traditional role as the inventor of linearity. It is equally ironic that the twelfth-century monk responsible for much of the Roman calendar (and its attendant chronological confusions) was called "Dionysius Exiguus". But such provocative coincidences fall outside the scope of this book.

The important point is that this tension between linearity and circularity, which is often taken to be a fundamental historical dialectic, continues to inform current millennial behavior. According to Camille Paglia, the linear model of history—being a metaphysical projection of the phallus—is patriarchal, whereas cyclic history reflects a more "female" perspective. Millenarian moments are thus characterized as the teleological thrustings of Pan (experienced as "panic") rather than the wandering "womb-madness" known as "hysteria". Because Paglia models temporal consciousness on the body, genital destiny informs historical destiny, and the apocalypse itself is interpreted as a masculinist genre:

> Man is sexually compartmentalized. Genitally, he is condemned to a perpetual pattern of linearity, focus, aim, directedness. He must learn to aim. Without aim, urination and ejaculation end in infantile soiling of self or surroundings. Woman's eroticism is diffused throughout her body. (19)

> The western idea of history as a propulsive movement into the future, a progressive or Providential design climaxing in the revelation of a Second Coming, is a male formulation. No woman, I submit, could have coined such an idea, since it is a strategy of evasion of woman's own cyclic nature, in which man dreads being caught. Evolutionary or apocalyptic history is a male wish list with a happy ending, a phallic peak. (10)

If we look past the essentialist trappings of Paglia's formulation, we see an antiphallic critique of Western metaphysical models shared by poststructuralist feminists such as Lee Quinby (1994). According to such a critique, the majestic parabola of human History—from cadence to decadence—follows the bell curve of male urination. This golden arc which, on its downward trajectory, has the apocalyptic connotations of annihilation, is traced by Thomas Pynchon in *Gravity's Rainbow* (1975), as well as by Bob Dylan in his Cuban Missile Crisis song, "A Hard Rain's a Gonna Fall" (1963).

Baudrillard agrees that history is witness to the final moments of this curve toward a terminus:

> All we have left of the millenarian dateline is the countdown to it. For this century—which can do nothing more than count the seconds separating it from its end without either being able, or really wanting, to measure up to that end—the digital Genitron clock on

> the Beaubourg Centre [aka, the Pompidou Center in Paris] showing the countdown in millions of seconds is the perfect symbol. It illustrates the reversal of the whole of our modernity's relation to time. Time is no longer counted progressively, by addition, starting from an origin, but by subtraction, starting from the end. This is what happens with rocket launches or time bombs. (1997)

As Paglia has implied, the orgasmic model of history enjoys a profound hold over the Western imagination. The eternal *jouissance* of polymorphous "female" sexuality is contrasted with that genitally focused male "quickie" that lasts merely a millennium. However, things are never as black and white as Paglia's crude distinctions imply. Ernest Lee Tuveson tells us that, in response to the prophet Joachim, St. Thomas "concludes in effect that the Church is static, as is history. No purposive change, no climax in a historical plot is to be expected" (20). This edict would have suited the Adamites, an heretical Christian sect that "sought to recapture in this life the innocent eroticism of Adam before the Fall, [and] practiced *coitus reservatus,* intercourse without orgasm, that is to say, pure forepleasure" (Brown, 1970: 30).

At this point I submit another extended extract, to be read alongside Stephenson's, as evidence for the prevalence of libidinal millenarianism in Kermode's "modern demythologized apocalypse" (1975: 133). In this Internet newsgroup posting by a raver known only as "Kitten", we can see a miniaturized version of history's erotic deferral:

> When i was at Organic recently, there was one point when the music was just pumping i kept waiting for the "vibe" to hit, because i wanted the place to explode with the ENERGY that keeps everybody coming back for more. OH MAN, just thinking about that energy gives me chills. But what happened was that the dj . . . kept tweaking with the audience and bringing the climax *ALMOST* there and then bringing everyone back down. I was absofuckinglutely out of my mind, i was near tears, all i wanted was the climax, i didn't care what the fuck else happened. All of a sudden i realized that it was similar to when you're having sex and for whatever reason, you can't come and all you are doing is FUCKING YOUR BRAINS OUT, exerting every ounce of brain energy trying to make yourself come so that you have your orgasm and go to sleep. That was how i felt on the middle of the dance floor. And I realized that the dj had POWER over me. I was basically prostituting for the dj: i was a slave to what he had (the promise of the climax) and he was flexing his power and tweaking with me to see how much i could stretch myself out for it. It really scared me. I mean, it worked out okay, i'm not emotionally damaged or anything, i didn't fall into pieces, actually right after it

> happened, i went and had a cigarette with my brother and pretty much forgot about it), but every now and again, i think of that feeling, that split second where I would do anything for the dj to give me that climax.
>
> So, when I hear people talking about rave as religion, I just want to put $.02 in and say that some religions are more cult than religion, and i think some dj's definitely hold the power of a cult in their turntables and in their speakers, and it's really not something that i want to get down on my knees for. Just a thought, I'm not bagging here. I still think that rave is one of the best things the 20th century has to offer, but i think that if left unchecked, it could turn on us. (alt.music.techno April 19, 1996)

But as this techno-maenad testifies, what "could turn on us" is what turns us on.

The Coming of the Lord

> Q: What's white and hangs off telephone wires?
>
> A: The Second Coming.
>
> Old School Joke

> If therefore thou shalt not watch,
> I will come on thee as a thief,
> and thou shalt not know what hour I will come upon thee.
>
> St. John's *Book of Revelation* (3: 3)

> So it is a matter of the secret and the *pudenda*.
>
> Jacques Derrida (1984: 4)

Apocalyptic rhetoric, from the book of Daniel through John's *Revelation* to present-day adaptations, is saturated with sexuality. Beginning with the allegorical Whore of Babylon and her violent destruction, Eros and Thanatos have persistently stalked narratives of the End:

> I saw a woman sitting on a scarlet beast, full of blasphemous names, having seven heads and ten horns. And the woman was clothed in purple and scarlet, and adorned with gold and precious

> stones and pearls, having in her hand a gold cup full of abominations and of the unclean things of her immorality, and upon her forehead a name was written, a mystery, "BABYLON THE GREAT, THE MOTHER OF HARLOTS AND OF THE ABOMINATIONS OF THE EARTH." (*Rev.* 17: 15-16)

> And he said to me, "The waters which you saw where the harlot sits, are peoples and multitudes and nations and tongues. And the ten horns which you saw, and the beast, these will hate the harlot and will make her desolate and naked, and will eat her flesh and will burn her up with fire." (ibid.: 19: 2)

The sexual subject matter here makes explicit the usually obscured erotic subtext of eschatological fables.

The word *apocalypse* derives from the Greek *apokalupsis* and *apo-calyptein*, meaning to "uncover," "unveil," or "reveal": hence *Revelation*. In this sense the breaking of the Seven Seals anticipates a hymeneutic dance of the Seven Veils, choreographed around the deferred promise of disclosure. In his essay on "An Apocalyptic Tone Recently Adopted in Philosophy," Derrida teases out the libidinous logic of Armageddon: "Apokalupto, I disclose, I uncover, I unveil, I reveal the thing that can be a part of the body, the head or the eyes, a secret part, the sex or whatever might be hidden . . . man's or woman's sex" (4). He goes on to argue that "the gesture of denuding or of affording sight . . . [is] sometimes more guilty and more dangerous than what follows and what it can give rise to, for example copulation" (5).

Leaving aside for the moment the voyeuristic aspect of libidinal millenarianism (which I return to in chapters 3 and 6), here I wish merely to draw attention to the assumption that copulation is a logical, or at least possible, consequence of striptease and/or Revelation. Both follow the same highly ritualistic pattern. In this context, even the smutty schoolboy joke that introduces this section plays on those early millenarian myths that conflate—or rather *recognize*—the libidinal logic of apocalyptic prophecy.[5]

By exposing the sexualized subtexts and historical agendas that lie curled within the apocalyptic tone, Derrida returns to the metaphoric motif of ejaculation:

> What effect do these noble, gentile prophets of eloquent visionaries want to produce? . . . . To seduce or subjugate whom, intimidate or make whom come? These effects and these benefits can be related to an individual or collective, conscious or unconscious speculation. They can be analyzed in terms of libidinal or political mastery, with all the differential relays and thus all the economic paradoxes that overdetermine the idea of power or mastery and sometimes drag them into the abyss. (23)

In revealing the innuendo concealed in one of prophecy's key-words—*come*—Derrida inspires my own attempt to conduct a libidinal analysis of the political amplifications of apocalyptic thought (or, alternatively, a political analysis of the libidinal amplifications of apocalyptic thought).

In this respect Derrida further scatters the seeds of panic and their consequent sociohistoric repercussions. He refers the reader to the biblical scene in which the Christ-Lamb opens each of the Seven Seals, one of the "four living" responding with the pronouncement, "Come." In true deconstructionist fashion, Derrida notes that "'Come' does not announce this or that apocalypse: already it resounds with a certain tone; it is in itself the apocalypse of apocalypse; *Come* is apocalyptic" (35).

The prophetic tone is thus analogous to the arrogant confidence of sexual mastery: "The end is soon, it is imminent, signifies the tone. I see it, I know it, I tell you, now you know, come" (24). The very vocal vibrations of certainty ("I am unveiling the truth") solicit desires bound up inextricably with transcendence, rapture, and orgasmic extinction. The *petite mort* of the individual is inflated to include the entire human race teetering on the edge of oblivion. As Derrida observes, "*I am coming* means: . . . We're all going to die, we're going to disappear" (24-25).

There are, of course, exceptions to this somewhat pornographic interpretation, however these only serve to illustrate moral reactions against the *already* perceived libidinal tenor of Judgment Day. Take this biblical passage, for instance:

> Love not the world, neither the things [that are] in the world.
> If any man love the world, the love of the Father is not in him.
> For all that [is] in the world, the lust of the flesh, and the lust of the eyes, and the pride of life, is not of the Father, but is of the world.
> And the world passeth away, and the lust thereof: but he that doeth the will of God abideth for ever. (1 John 2:15-17)

Echoing these sentiments in the sixth century, Gregory the Great wrote; "Let us despise with all our being this present—or rather extinct—world. At least let worldly desires end with the end of the world; let us imitate what deeds of good men we can" (ibid. : 69-70). This is indeed an optimistic wish, considering the fact that the liminal structure of premillennial time serves to privilege nihilistic sexual license over the puritanical ideals of purity and chastity. Neville Shute's *On the Beach* (1956) is only one of countless representations of erotic excess in the Last Days; another being St. Augustine's observation that "as the end of the world approaches . . . infidelity increases" (Kumar 204).

In the pages that follow I trace—in an almost dot-to-dot fashion—that dionysian genealogy that links Revelation and the Romano-Greek myths of Pan, through the apocalyptic fantasies of Sade and Nietzsche, to the Bataillean millennium unconsciously mimicked by both mass and alternative medias of the 1990s. However, any study that seeks to emphasize historical and philosophical continuities must also take into account the different conditions and assumptions that inform each context. For this reason it is important to acknowledge the radical impact of technological development on subjective experience and expression. By following Martin Heidegger we can discern the telos of technology as yet another form of apocalyptic unveiling.

Technological Revelation

> The question concerning technology is the question concerning the constellation in which revealing and concealing, in which the coming to presence of truth, comes to pass.
>
> Martin Heidegger (33)

> Technology is no longer an aid in the perfection of being, but rather being is now an aid to the perfection of technology.
>
> Theodore John Rivers (10)

Heidegger's enormously influential essay, "The Question Concerning Technology," discusses the metaphysical status of technology as both the subject of history and the raison d'être of History itself. He sees technology less as a sophisticated tool, than as the name we give our propulsion towards a kind of quasi-mystical *revelation* of the Truth.

Heidegger goes on to unpack the ancient Greek notion of *techné*, that mode of "bringing-forth" into the world that transcends the contemporary banality of "manufacture." *Techné* is steeped in classical perspectives on the genesis of craftsmanship, which did not polarize "craft" and "nature" to the extent that we do today. For this reason, Monty Python's "machines that go ping" are merely the latest in a long line of human artifacts shaped through the highly nuanced constellation of skill, knowledge, and environment. Technology is consequently rooted in Hellenic notions of materialization through revelation.

"What has the essence of technology to do with revealing?" asks Heidegger. "The answer: everything":

> Instrumentality is considered to be the fundamental characteristic of technology. If we inquire, step by step, into what technology, represented as means, actually is, then we shall arrive at revealing. The possibility of all productive manufacturing lies in revealing. Technology is therefore no mere means. Technology is a way of revealing. If we give heed to this, then another whole realm for the essence of technology will open itself up to us. It is the realm of revealing, i.e., of truth. (12)

As we have seen, the Heideggerean definition of technology is not restricted to electrical hardware, but embraces any human activity that incorporates a mode of revealing in relation to truth. All of which begs the question, What kind of truth does technology point us toward?

According to Heidegger, this truth rests on the destiny of the human race, viewed in the Nietzschean neoclassical term *destining*. Technology is thus an ontological compass, inscribed within the secular, nihilistic view of history: "[D]estining is never a fate that compels. For man becomes truly free only insofar as he belongs to the realm of destining and so becomes one who listens and hears, and not one who is simply constrained to obey . . . . The destining of revealing is in itself not just any danger, but danger as such" (25-26).

The political subtext of Heidegger's analysis has been commented upon exhaustively elsewhere, but here I would merely observe that *destining* can be a code word for an existentially risky route to transcendence, intimately linked with the messianic attraction of Revelation. It is consequently problematic for those who detect an inherent conservatism—even fascism—within narratives that "foreshadow" the future.

Thus, both Heidegger and—by retroactive association—Nietzsche, stand accused of negating the potential freedoms of a godless universe. In contrast to the existentialist school of thought, Heidegger reinvents eschatology by practically deifying technology (along with its hidden agenda). In a direct polemic against Heidegger's essay, Rivers explores the time-bound nature of technology, believing it has succumbed "to the Christianization of time".

> [T]hat is, it has adopted Christianity's linear perception . . . . Since [technology] is built on the premise that there will be progress, it follows that we absolutely must be inclined toward its successful conclusion. It tells us that there is no salvation unless we side with technology because beyond its protection is damnation. Whereas Christianity's idea of linearity moves on to a final

> and decisive end from which there is no appeal, conceptualized in the Second Coming and the Last Judgment, technology's concept never reaches its end, since it is composed solely of means. (116)

Technology has "acquired Christianity's notion of inevitability" (115), an onto-theological ruse to rob humanists of their freedom to alter and control the future. Thus according to Rivers, the danger of destining is not (as Heidegger would have it) an incarnation of a tragic "bringing forth" of "primal truth," but rather the means by which mortality is deprived of any meaning:

> We experience time because we are aware of mortality. As for death, it is also influenced by technology's rationality, but negatively, because technology deprives death of meaning and robs it of any significance as an eschatological condition. Technology distorts death so as to give it a new qualification. Although it cannot disregard death as the termination of life, technology removes the death of the individual from one's own prerogative. The modern age dares to sustain life, when on the verge of death, by machines; it has the power to induce us to inhabit a body which is only technically alive. Life is prolonged not because we love it, but because we love technology more, and perceive it as a life-giving force. Not only have we cheated death of its meaning, but we have also degraded life by refusing to let it go. (64)

All apocalyptic philosophies must acknowledge and respond to this technological paradox—a secular eschatology merely unveils a void.

Eros and Thanatos must therefore permit a third term: *Techné*. This addition turns the former dialectic into something of a love-triangle. According to the French sociologist, Michel Maffesoli, admitting a third term also represents the beginning of society, and therefore, of all sociology—"infinity begins with the third person" (1996: 105). It is my contention that, in the spirit of Roland Barthes' *Lover's Discourse* (1978) and D. H. Lawrence's *Women in Love* (1920), this third term is also the libidinal catalyst for a constellation formerly devoid of metaphysical momentum. In other words, sex and death become recharged through technology. As the decadent writer Gabriele D'Annunzio maintains, "Love, like all divine powers, is not truly exalted except in a trinity" (Praz 293). The construction of history as a ménage-à-trois, brings me full circle back to Baudrillard's *post festum* philosophy of the orgy.

In short, this book endeavours to do two things, which—like its subject matter (transgression and transcendence)—run parallel, touching at several points, and ultimately dissolving into each other. One of its main aims is to trace the dionysian ambience of contemporary culture, while another is to weave different historical strands into a pattern defined by libidinal millenarianism. It is the nature of weaving not to reveal the full pattern immediately, but gradually, although my own Revelation may not be as earth-shattering as its subject and model: *apokalupsis*.

Geoff Waite maintains that "since *temporal* causal relationships" are often "less important than *logical* causal relationships, it is necessary to cut away from all *simple* teleologies . . ." (95) In order to establish a genealogy, then, I navigate between particularly distinct periods: Sade's 1790s, J. K. Huysmans's 1890s, the baby boomers' 1960s, and the period linking the held breath of the 1990s to the tentative exhalation of the new millennium. When investigating a subject as complex as libidinal millenarianism, it is not merely a matter of following a red thread sequentially through time, but realizing that the footsteps of the genealogist become caught up in this red thread as soon as the notion of causality is introduced. "[T]o be concerned with the questions of postmodernity is to be concerned with questions of temporality and sequence," writes Diane Elam. Since "cause and effect do not [necessarily] keep their temporal sequence; the original is not located as the 'source' that precedes the derivation" (9). And yet it can be useful to superimpose the diachronic onto the synchronic, if only to delineate the ways in which we recount certain histories that make up our imperfect understanding of the present. Accordingly, my research consistently plugs into what Mark Kingwell has called "the intricate feedback loops of popular culture" (343); these findings are then employed to reflect on his observation that "we appear to have no way of coping with uncertainty about the future that transcends the dichotomy between hope and dread" (166).

Chapter 1 focuses on the crucial notion of panic as an ubiquitous libidinal-millenarian phenomenon, and explores the relationship between sexuality, technology and image-addiction in movies such as *Cherry 2000* and *Strange Days.* Chapter 2 details the seminal Dionysian writers Sade, Bataille, and Nietzsche, introducing and defining their terms and key concepts within the context of my argument. It also incorporates a section on their contemporary adaption by more receptive and extreme elements of the academy. Chapter 3 investigates the explicit association of Eros, Thanatos, and technology in J. G. Ballard's autoerotic equation: sex plus technology equals the future. Ballard's novel *Crash* (1975) is then read against its own revision in Stephenson's cyberpunk thriller *Snow Crash* (1993). Chapter 4 reads nineteenth-century notions of artifice as a precursor to such twentieth-century discussions of technology, and does so through the decadent classic *A Rebours* (1884) by J-K. Huysmans. Chapter 5 identifies the contraceptive pill and the atomic bomb as two technological catalysts of the political, aesthetic, and literal orgy in the 1960s, and argues that this era was far more "thanatical" than current nostalgia would have us believe. Chapter 6 revolves around a reappraisal of Baudrillard's works as symptomatic examples of postorgy (and premillennial) tension. This reading then informs my analysis of certain popular cultural examples of the dionysian, including "rave culture," "death fashion," and other apocalyptic expressions of youth culture.

Pan, I conclude, is the goat in the machine, cavorting—like us—in the miraculous clearing between the *(always almost)* apocalypse and the *(always after)* orgy. Libidinal millenarianism thus blossoms in that psychically and politically charged space between anticipation and anti-climax.

A Note on Methodology

From the outset I would like to apologize for coining such an unwieldy phrase as *libidinal millenarianism.* Having spent the last five years trying to eloquently introduce this concept to friends and colleagues, I am only too aware of its capacity to glaze previously receptive minds. Unfortunately, I have found no alternative that does the concept justice, despite many public requests for a less academic phrase. *Erotic apocalypse,* doesn't quite capture the theoretical and historical overtones that I address, and *aphrodisiacal chiliasm* is no better than the term I started with.

I should also note that, considering the enormity of a topic like millenarianism, this book will inevitably be riddled with holes. Many important individuals and schools of thought will go unacknowledged simply because the field extends off into the horizon. AIDS and the Shoah are two apocalyptic phenomena, which have become such important components in discussions of millenarianism that they now constitute separate disciplines. While my study constantly engages with those forces that surround and produce these defining moments of the twentieth century, I have chosen to situate them "off stage," as it were, in my own story. The Holocaust and the HIV epidemic should be considered "structuring absences" which, at a later date, I hope to relate more rigorously to my dionysian genealogy. (See James Berger's *After the End* [1999] for a sustained reading of the Shoah as postapocalyptic trauma, and Richard Dellamora's work on the apocalyptic amplifications of AIDS.)

Medieval heretical sects, such as the Cathars and the Movement of the Free Spirit, would also belong in an exhaustive exploration of libidinal millenarianism, as would the Dadaists, Surrealists, and Situationists, to name only the most commonly invoked avant-garde movements. Nor would a closer study of Charles Manson and his particular modern brand of Saturnalia be out of place in such a study. All these "cults," however, have been written about extensively elsewhere. (See especially Greil Marcus's *Lipstick Traces* [1993], Norman Cohn's *Pursuit of the Millennium* [1993], and Bernstein's *Bitter Carnival* [1992].) They should not be considered, however, the only possible "paths not taken," as these are potentially infinite.

The End of the World is a vast topic, and I do not pretend to answer every question I raise concerning its traces and effects. Indeed I would consider my work justified if it were to provoke different questions in the reader concerning symbolic models of completion or exhaustion as they relate to time, finitude, redemption, and other related phenomena. Ready answers to such questions are more characteristic of prophets than of analysts.

All academic labor is intrinsically hypertextual, in that it results in a dialogue between writer and readers, who identify aporias, excesses, wrong-turns, and underdevelopments. The confluence of two such charged concepts as "the libidinal" and "millenarianism" provide coordinates for countless idiosyncratic interpretations. Each word brings with it the baggage of tradition, which we would do well to remember when tackling—or even merely identifying—the issues involved. These traditions, however, divide and multiply at a rapid rate the moment we attempt to locate the point of intersection between "the libidinal" and "millenarianism." The same is true also of "Eros" and "Thanatos," "transcendence" and "transgression," and "Apollo" and "Dionysus." In other words, to map libidinal millenarianism is a more fraught and subtle enterprise than merely juxtaposing Freud with Cohn, or Marx with Kermode. As with the orgy itself, it is not always clear who is connected to whom.

Heidegger, Nietzsche, and Bataille provide indispensable apertures into discussions about technology and transcendence. That is why they define the contours of my argument. Had I decided to take a different tangent, the names could easily have been Freud, McLuhan and Cioran; or Marx, Artaud, and Deleuze. Nontraditional primary sources point the readers in new directions. In this respect, the testimony of a technomusic fan or cult member can sometimes be as relevant and illuminating as a quotation from Marx or Freud. I am not conducting a philosophical history of ideas, but sifting through a cultural palimpsest in which every perspective has as much weight as the next. I thus draw from a heterogeneous array of sources in order to simultaneously provide, and deconstruct, examples of political exhaustion. I have endeavored to balance this synthetic approach with my own coherent commentary. The kind of criticism I am attempting, then, is closer to cultural studies than to philosophy or history.

This orientation leaves me open to criticisms regarding a perceived neglect of "real" political, social, and economic issues. It makes little sense, however, to adopt the valuable approach of Eric Hobsbawm or David Harvey in a study that focuses on the symbolic (general) economy as opposed to the political (restricted) economy. Such an approach would not only fall outside the scope and concerns of this project, but blind me to the libidinal economies which, to a significant extent, drive the political ones (although this can lead to chicken-and-egg questions). *After the Orgy* zooms in on a particular discursive response to globalization—the orgy itself, in Baudrillard's terms—which eschews rhetorical calls to acknowledging "reality."

Similarly, this study deals with a particular kind of language; one employed by, and addressed to, a certain kind of subjectivity and demographic. Given the authors who constitute my particular genealogy, it should be clear that this demographic is predominantly white, male, American, or European; socially estranged; and economically privileged. As witnessed with the Heaven's Gate cult, however, strict demographic delineations become blurred when dealing with the shifting matrices of sexuality, technology, capital, and desire.

One of the most seductive elements of dionysian discourse is the way in which it critiques the assumptions on which powerful "mainstream" institutions, such as the patriarchal family, are based. As Peter Stallybrass and Allon White have shown, the carnivalesque has traditionally (and somewhat ironically) been championed by the bourgeoisie, who romanticize the "power of the people" as a kind of vicarious transgressive outlet. Libidinal millenarianism is both a specific strain of the carnivalesque and a revulsion against it; as in the case of Huysmans or Heaven's Gate. It is also a form of decadent philosophy that appeals to a particularly jaded (and admittedly ethnocentric) aesthetic sensibility. While I believe that elements of this sensibility cut across gender, race, class, and sexual orientation, it would take another five years to demonstrate such a claim. We must, therefore, be mindful of the fact that whenever I say "we," I am indulging in a linguistic shortcut that both elides and conflates countless particularities, possibilities, and actualities.

As such, this book represents a sustained attempt to understand the recurring motifs of eroticized extinction and irresponsible heresy. Its concern is not to determine whether we are living *literally* or *figuratively* "after the orgy," but rather to show why that phrase resonates so powerfully in today's public sphere. The very notion of "libidinal millenarianism" is an attempt—almost literally, *virtually*—to "flesh out" themes and concerns of the technological sublime as it relates to the dionysian dynamic. If it were to truly mirror its subject matter, this book would be a chaotic and cyborgian intervention; a frenzied, sensual, incoherent, irrational, and rhetorical rubble. The constraints on form, however, testify to the stubborn and pervasive reign of Apollo, whom dionysians ignore at their peril.

1

Panic Merchants: Prophecy and the Satyr

> [T]here are strange Ferments in the Blood, which in many Bodys occasion an extraordinary Discharge; so in Reason too, there are heterogeneous Particles which must be thrown off by Fermentation.
>
> Anthony, Earl of Shaftesbury (14)

> For where panic is, there too is Pan.
>
> James Hillman (33)

The Greek god Pan is one of western culture's most enduring and ubiquitous trickster figures. Half-man, half-goat, Pan dwells in forests and glades trying to seduce nymphs, despite his grotesque demeanor. Born in Arcadia, he has thus become an icon for those who lament the Fall into civilization.

Pan's relationship to both Dionysus and Bacchus has become so confused that it is now difficult to distinguish one from the other. This is hardly surprising, considering their shared characteristics, and their inherently fusional-orgiastic function within classical philosophical and literary fables. As signifiers, "Dionysus" and "Pan" are free-floating archetypes, confused through various interpretations—Friedrich Nietzsche's being arguably the most influential. This is not necessarily a matter of historical blurring, but rather a sign of the almost Rorschachian ambiguity of his metaphysical presence (or absence) in modern times. As a trickster figure, Pan continues to elude us, and to enthrall the imagination for this very reason.

In her literary history of *Pan the Goat God* (published, significantly enough, in 1969), Patricia Merivale traces the evolution of this myth into the twentieth century. She concludes that his symbolic status as a sexual figure is "only a recent literary characteristic" (226), initiated by Robert Browning's vision of Pan as lurking within us, rather than roaming the landscape. This radical reassessment of Pan's "essential" character forever altered our perception of his mythical status. Consequently, the goat-god—rather like millenarianism itself—is "not exclusively sexual, but largely so" (90).

Beginning with Nietzsche's question—"what does the union of god and goat . . . really mean?" (226)—Merivale explores the general rekindling of interest in Pan during the previous fin de siècle, categorizing different species of literary Pans, and identifying genealogical overlaps between Pan and Dionysus. She reveals that Nietzsche's famous dialectic between Apollo and Dionysus had many precedents, many of which placed Pan in the antagonistic position. William Hazlitt, for instance, in his *Lectures on the Age of Elizabeth* (1820), saw the contest between Pan and Apollo as a critical metaphor, given the "repeated claim that Apollo is envious of his sweet pipings" (ibid.: 60). Lyly's *Midas* (1592) states that "Pan is a God, Apollo is no more!" (ibid.: 48), while Buchanan's 1885 poem, "The Earthquake" proclaims,

> Woe to the land wherein the Satyr reigns,
> And Pan usurps Apollo's throne!
> (ibid.: 110)

There was an enormous resurgence of interest in Pan as an ideological icon at the beginning of the twentieth century. According to E. M. Forster, the Pan-effect had not only continued but *accelerated* into the modern world, which is why in *Howards End* (1910) "panic and emptiness" accompany the life of "telegrams and anger" (ibid.: 190). Technology is thus identified as a compatible environment for the previously agrarian Pan.

Pan's sardonic laugh was heard across the battlefields of Europe by writers documenting that conflagration of Enlightenment ideals by horrific technologies, the First World War. Osbert Sitwell described the carnage allegorically: "Pan and Mars had broken loose together and had set out to conquer the man who wound and set the clocks that regulated civilized living" (ibid.: 221). Here Pan is presented as an inherited blood-lust in an age of mechanical production.

Indeed this guilt by association is directly connected to the literary motif of panic as a destructively sublime communion with the Infinite. The undefined "mystical fright" of sensitive nineteenth-century souls such as Fyodor Dostoevsky, prompted the emergence of the medical condition of "Panophobia," for which the popular term would soon become *panic attack* (Nordau 226). Moreover, one character in Arthur Machen's "Man Who Went Too Far" (1912) declares that "Pan means 'everything,' and to see everything would be clearly more than one could stand. And so to see Pan means death" (Merivale 168).

To feel the presence of Pan, therefore, means death and/or fulfillment. In fact this "and/or" provides the crucial pivot on which libidinal millenarianism rests, ever-suspended between orgasm and extinction. For if Gilles Deleuze and Felix Guattari are correct in claiming that "it is by headlong flight that things progress and signs proliferate," then we can also concede that "Panic is creation" (73). Moreover, such theoretical mobilizations serve to add an extra dimension to Pan's subtextual role in biblical accounts of the Last Judgment, and specifically Matthew's description of the division of sheep from goats (Matt. 25.31-46).

Pan's figural flexibility, therefore, is evidence of his catalytic force. For it is he, according to such narratives, who is responsible for the fire in the loins: the same loins that Norman O. Brown has identified as the site of the Last Judgment. Those who succumb to this libidinal fever are thus cast into the pit by the Christian God whose chief adversary is variously named Satan, Pan, or Dionysus.

Ever since Plutarch recorded the story of the death of Pan (*Moralia*, V 419), this deity has been invisible or "transparent," in Jean Baudrillard's terms. Yet like various charismatic figures—God, Nietzsche, and a steady stream of suicidal rock stars—Pan created a power-effect that increased after his death: "Pan is dead: long live Pan." Consistently, Pan has been situated outside of and *against* the Christian metaphysical tradition, yet parallel to it. If Nietzsche had ever thought that Pan/Dionysus was dead, he would certainly have believed that resuscitation was not only possible but imperative. In mythology, psychology, and philosophy, Pan lives on to haunt the invisible membrane between sexuality and textuality.

Pan can be understood accordingly as having metamorphosed into the flux and flow of language, and reincarnated in the notion of "Pan-ic." Indeed the very word *panic* expresses the contagious spread of fear through the herd. In his eighteenth-century polemic, "A Letter Concerning Enthusiasm," the Earl of Shaftesbury recounts an origin myth for this phenomenon:

> We read in History that PAN, when he accompany'd BACCHUS in an Expedition to the Indies, found means to strike a Terror thro' a Host of Enemys, by the help of a small Company, whose Clamors he manag'd to good advantage among the echoing Rocks and Caverns of a woody Vale. The hoarse bellowing of the Caves, join'd

> to the hideous aspect of such dark and desart Places, rais'd such a Horror in the Enemy, that in this state their Imagination help'd 'em to hear Voices, and doubtless to see Forms too, which were more than Human: whilst the Uncertainty of what they fear'd made their Fear yet greater, and spread it faster by implicit Looks than any Narration cou'd convey it. And this was what in after-times Men called a Panick. The story indeed gives a good Hint of the nature of this Passion, which can hardly be without some mixture of Enthusiasm, and Horrors of a superstitious kind. (14-5)

Shaftesbury goes on to emphasize the "social and communicative" aspect of panic, before linking it specifically to religious manias:

> One may with good reason call every Passion Panick which is rais'd in a Multitude, and convey'd by Aspect, or as it were by Contact or Sympathy. Thus popular Fury may be call'd Panick, when the Rage of the People, as we have sometimes known, has put them beyond themselves; especially where Religion has had to do. And in this state their very Looks are infectious. The Fury flies from Face to Face: and the Disease is no sooner seen than caught. (15)

Leaving aside the revolutionary potential of the "Rage of the People," we can acknowledge the viral rhetoric that depicts Pan's power. Shaftesbury's crucial move is to link the prophetic function of Pan with religion, and to remember that the pronouncement recorded by Plutarch—"Pan is dead"—was a reaction to the perceived failure of the oracles after the birth of Christ. "Enthusiasm," for Shaftesbury, is a commodity peddled by "Vendors of Prophecy." Consequently, panic is "easy to be carry'd away with every Wind of Doctrine, and addicted to every upstart Sect or Superstition" (28). It would be hard to think of a more relevant comment in the era of Waco, Heaven's Gate, and the Japanese Aum Shinrikyo cult.

After locating the germs of panic in the imagination, Shaftesbury goes on to describe the somatic signs of infection. In post-Freudian times, these are easily interpreted as manifestations of sexual eruptions. As with certain mystical experiences, the fine line between sacred and profane experience can be erased by the scorching fire of passion. "I learn from holy Scripture," Shaftesbury explains, "that there was the evil, as well as the good Spirit of Prophecy. And I find by present Experience, as well as by all History, Sacred and Profane, that the Operation of this Spirit is every where the same, as to the bodily Organs" (45). The spirit of Pan—described alternately as "the Blaze" or "the Extasy"—is described in sexual terms: its outward manifestations are "Quakings, Tremblings, Tossings of the Head and Limbs, [and] Agitation." When bodies are "labouring with Inspiration," "Eyes glow with the Passion" (45, 50) and breasts heave.

The Pan-effect thus continues in the form of the panic instinct. In his monograph on *Pan and the Nightmare*, James Hillman echoes Shaftesbury's belief that Pan thrives best in the imagination. "Pan is still alive," he writes, "although we experience him only through psychopathological disturbances, other modes having been lost in our culture" (1988;18). Since Pan never died (he was merely repressed) he has been savoring the potential power of his Return. This power leaks into culture via these psychopathologies, most notably "the nightmare and its associated erotic, demonic and panic qualities" (25).

By associating Pan with nightmares, Hillman evokes both an explicitly Jungian unconscious and the Freudian theory of repression. If we are to believe the founders of psychoanalysis, and the subsequent absorption of their ideas into popular knowledge (especially in the 1960s), then Pan shares this murky terrain with Eros. The nightmares that emanate monstrously from the fertile excrement of the unconscious are thus rooted in a suppressed sexuality and a primal sense of fear: "The poles of sexuality and panic, *which can instantly switch into each other or release each other,* exhibit the most crassly compulsive extremes of attraction and repulsion . . . . Pan, as ruler of nature 'in here,' dominates sexual and panic reactions, and is located in these extremes" (27—my emphasis).

In the 1960s, when the sexual revolution cannot be distinguished from the fear of nuclear Armageddon (as I shall argue in chapter 5), the iconic resurgence of Pan signaled uneasy anxiousness as well as hedonistic promiscuity. Because "anxiety and desire are twin nuclei of the Pan archetype" (31), it is impossible to determine which is cause and which is effect.

Symbolizing the paroxysm of erotic fear, Pan is the quintessential figure of libidinal millenarianism. Messianic figures from Zoroaster to David Koresh are all indebted to the proleptic powers of Pan. If it is true that "Apollo wheedled the art of prophecy" from Pan (Graves 1960;102), we can appreciate the complicated role played by Pan in apocalyptic discourses.

Because Pan is elusive as a symbolic figure or "metaphysical pattern," he represents different concepts to different schools of thought. All of them, however, connect his latent influence with the vengeful power of "Nature." In Tom Robbins's novel, *Jitterbug Perfume* (1990), Pan is portrayed as an almost transparent figure, disappearing into the ether due to his archaic status in a modern era. Nevertheless, this vanishing act does little to mask his musky stench, which is still powerful enough to coax the libido out of even the most prudish of souls. From Plutarch via Pascal to Robbins, Pan is depicted as a casualty of civilization. Nevertheless, he manages to harness a kind of amorphous sexual power that challenges the fragile laws of society.

In his weighty polemic against what he sees as the viruslike influence of Nietzsche's thought, Geoff Waite engages with the figure of Pan-Dionysus:

> In Greek mythology and in the German intellectual tradition, Dionysus is the proleptic god par excellence. He is "the coming god," not merely in the sense that his coming is anticipated in the future—for example, every destructive-creative springtime—but also in the strong sense that his primary attribute . . . is defined in terms of coming and recoming, not actual arrival. The true essence of the demigod consists in perpetually coming toward humanity from the future but not necessarily ever arriving. (134)

This offers a crucial insight into libidinal millenarianism, relating to both Jacques Derrida's concern with the sexual undertones of "coming" as an eschatological concept, and to the implicit identification of Pan with the apocalypse itself, as an end that never comes: the always deferred Terminal Orgasm. Since Pan is the phallic goat-god, it is no surprise that he can be appropriated by heterosexist narratives based on historical climax.

According to Hillman, Pan invented masturbation, which he describes as "a way of enacting Pan" (36). Autoerotic activities are also associated with the biblical figure of Onan, who was struck dead by God for his nonprocreative (i.e., proto-Sadean) behavior. Other than providing yet another fusion of sex and death, this moral fable illustrates the matrix of "panic phenomena" whereby the taboo is completed through transgression. By "enacting Pan" we thus dissolve the distinction between the natural and the (allegedly) unnatural.

The isolation of Des Esseintes in J.-K. Huysmans's *A Rebours* (1884), is a monastic-*cum*-onanistic response to the decadent orgy articulated through the main character's fondness for artifice. So too was Nietzsche's, whose falling out with high society is said to have begun with Richard Wagner's description of him as "an onanist." The solitary who surfs the Internet in search of porn is also responding (albeit "positively") to the orgiastic excess of a decadent society, expressed through technology. All these scenarios speak of a hypermediated form of alienation.

Pan thus straddles both the instinct to survive (the "lust for life"), and the "necro-porn" or "sacrificial sex" of certain romantic, decadent, and postmodern subcultures. According to those scandalized by such behavior, the Apocalypse will surely come when God decides to smite both the Onans and the libertines of our own decadent Western society. Hillman asks why we expect prophecy to "come with a long beard and a thunderous voice," when it could just as easily manifest itself as "a jet of desire" (53). Ejaculation both mimics and mocks the coming of the Lord. But if Terence McKenna is right, and "Western Civilization has shot its wad," then the apocalypse must have already happened.

The Goat in the Machine

> There is something inherently subversive about taking all this incredibly expensive technological equipment and putting a naked woman on it.
>
> Richard Kadrey in *Wired for Sex*

> I felt really sad for the panic buttons, because panic seems like such an outdated, corny reaction to all of the change in the world. I mean if you have to be negative, there's a reasonable enough menu of options available—disengagement—atomization—torpor—but panic? Corrrrrrrny.
>
> Douglas Coupland, *Microserfs*

Cybersex is a thriving industry in the *fin de millénium*. The user is able to interface with two-dimensional representations of his or her (although usually his) fantasy, stroking the screen while "enacting Pan." Mark Kingwell explains that because new technologies mobilize sexual imagery in sophisticated advertising strategies, we now "soothe ourselves with our candy substitutes. In erotica everything is promised and nothing delivered; consuming it, we subsist on a sugar diet of pure stimulated desire" (200).

This scenario was eagerly anticipated in the 1960s by Marshall McLuhan, who believed that the electronic media had a pan-sensual potential for transfiguring sexuality in such a way as to make "Henry Miller's style of randy rutting old-fashioned and obsolete" (Neville 70). While many would regard such obsolescence as wholly positive, it has become increasingly clear that the old phallocentric power structures have merely been encoded in the digital future. Kadrey's claim that there is something "inherently subversive" in digital representations of female nudity rests on a severely compromised definition of subversion, for it fails to take account of the adman's exploitation of libido.

Pixis Interactive is based in Silicon Valley, and is one of the biggest producers of digital pornography (or erotica, depending on how you see it). It releases computer games in which the lust-object stares out from the screen and addresses players in first-person mode. Such games are "interactive" because they offer players several options by clicking on a command linked to a particular operation (i.e., undress and turn around). One option, always available in an erotic emergency, is the Panic Button.

Arthur Kroker—who affixes the word "panic" to any buzzword of the day—has described the apocalyptic effects of this ultramodern technolorgy as *panic sex,* a term that maps the simulated terrain covered so thoroughly by Jean Baudrillard. Perhaps Hillman, however, describes the situation most clearly: "Let us say that the world of nature, Pan's world, is in a continual state of subliminal panic just as it is in a continual state of subliminal sexual excitation. As the world is made by Eros, held together by that cosmogonic force and charged with the libidinal desire that is Pan . . . so its other side, panic . . . belongs to the same constellation" (29-30).

As we have seen, this "continual state of subliminal excitation" also saturates the technological. In millenarian terms (and I explore this matter more thoroughly in chapter 3) the divine dwells inside or alongside technology, so that artifice creates a new "metaphorical pattern . . . incorporating anxiety and sexuality" (ibid.: 32).

According to Hillman, panic is not to be treated with Valium or suspicion, because it is a natural—even ethical—response to the technological sublime: "We must follow the path cleared by Nietzsche, whose investigation of kinds of consciousness and behaviour through Apollo and Dionysus can be extended to Pan. Then panic will no longer be regarded as a physiological defence mechanism . . . but will be seen as the right response to the numinous" (30).

In William Gibson's cyberpunk novel, *Mona Lisa Overdrive* (1988), there comes a point when technological acceleration is referred to as either the Rapture or "When it Changed." Like a vacuum sucking in oxygen, the new realm of cyberspace attracts new electronic deities, and the matrix finds itself populated by sentient, even sacred, creatures. Gibson refers to these gods as the Loa, from voodoo mythology. One could, however, propose Pan as the goat in the machine—a lustful ghost-god, overseeing virtual orgies with digital nymphs who are mere vapors of data.[6]

If Dionysus-Pan is indeed the proleptic god par excellence, then we must take the next step and acknowledge his presence in technological terms. "Prolepsis," Waite tells us, "has also to do with the mechanical reproducibility—fast-forward (anticipation) and fast-reverse (memory)" (132). Pan is no longer the god of nature, but of technology; or more accurately, the god of nature *in* technology. Indeed, as I write, there is a World Wide Website known as "Pan's Online Grove": dedicated to literary works inspired by the horny one, it also sells T-shirts imprinted with his image. Thus Pan has left the hidden spaces of both the forest and the psyche in order to inhabit the shadows of cyberspace.

Michel Maffesoli has thought long and hard about the legacy of Pan and its relation to both technology and sexuality. In *The Time of the Tribes* (1996), he continues to work self-consciously within "the Dionysian thematic," celebrating the "panvitalism" of the people. Maffesoli—who is "confident in the fact that certain 'outdated' considerations may be perfectly adequate to their time" (2)—identifies an "organic" explosion of microgroups that establish a creative and conflicting notion of the masses. His faith in the future depends on the atavistic power of Pan/Dionysus, which celebrates the "pagan fibre which . . . has never entirely disappeared from the masses" (41).[7] This tendency to seek a carnivalesque continuity relates to a familiar millenarian motif, namely, an imminent transcendence spawned by the orgiastic aura of "these closing days of the modern era" (1).

The lifeblood of Maffesoli's Dionysian sociolorgy concerns those mushrooming affinity groups that make up the social fabric of the *fin de millénium,* from populist subcultures to elitist secret societies. Stressing the kinship between proximity and promiscuity, he claims that such allegiances are at root erotic, and nurtured by a shared space or territory, whether real or symbolic. "We have dwelled so often on the dehumanization and the disenchantment with the modern world and the solitude it induces," he writes, "that we are no longer capable of seeing the networks of solidarity that exist within it" (72). Consequently, Maffesoli has no patience with those theories of hyperalienation that are promoted by Baudrillard and his disciples:

> A tendency to see life as alienation or to hope for a perfect or authentic existence makes us forget that daily routine is stubbornly founded on a series of interstitial and relative freedoms. As has been seen in economics, it is possible to demonstrate the existence of a *black-market sociality,* which is easily tracked through its diverse and minuscule manifestations. (21)

One such is the Minitel computer network in France, which, by anticipating the veritable plague of Internet fever, qualifies as one of Shaftesbury's contagious enthusiasms. The Minitel was an early electronic bulletin board, which allowed like-minded people to communicate across geographic frontiers. It was thus the latest technological evolution—after the printing press, the telegraph and the amplifier—capable of fostering a sense of community. By creating a network that eluded governmental regulation (for a time, at least) the Minitel anticipated Hakim Bey's notion of a Temporary Autonomous Zone: socialism with an interface. Both Pan and Dionysus dwell in such a symbolic space, because

> the growth in urban tribes has encouraged a "computerized palaver" that assumes the rituals of the ancient agora. We would no longer face the dangers, as was first believed, of the macroscopic computer disconnected from reality, but on the contrary, thanks to the personal computer and cable TV, we are confronted with the infinite diffraction of an orality disseminated by degrees. (25)

Technology is thus one of the key vectors of Maffesoli's orgy, encouraging new articulations of the "social divine."

Some of his claims are far-fetched: that we are moving from an "optical" period to a "tactile" one, for instance, or that alternative movements such as astrology and naturapathy are "in the process of overturning the social configuration." Nonetheless, the notion that postmodern society is in some sense reinventing archaic values is compelling. Tattooing, body-piercing, branding, scarification, and other rituals of the "new primitivism" are spectacular manifestations of such cyberatavism. Whether experienced on the street or in books like Adam Parfrey's *Apocalypse Culture* (1990), the subliminal Pan-ic of the "popular-secular apocalyptic" can hardly be denied. Indeed, only those who have not witnessed the ecstatic ritual of the "rave" could dismiss Maffesoli's prophecy that the "confusion of the dionysian myth has produced significant effects of civilization," and that perhaps "our megalopolises are the site of their rebirth" (129). Fleshing out this insight into our neo-decadent period, Maffesoli sees evidence of a spiritual renovation in

> beaches crammed with holiday-makers, department stores thronged with howling consumers, riotous sporting events and the anodyne crowds milling about with no apparent purpose. In many respects, it would seem that Dionysus has overwhelmed them all. The tribes he inspires demonstrate a troublesome ambiguity: although not disdaining the most sophisticated technology, they remain nonetheless somewhat barbaric. Perhaps this is a sign of postmodernity. Be that as it may, the principle of reality, on the one hand, forces us to accept these hordes, since they are there, and on the other, urges us to remember that time and again throughout history it was barbarity that brought many moribund civilizations back to life. (28)

Maffesoli's attraction/repulsion concerning "the masses" exhibits the patronizing nostalgia that marks this particular school of thought from Baudelaire to Baudrillard. And like the latter, Maffesoli preempts allegations of snobbery by stating that although "the founding being-together may never in fact have existed . . . it remains nevertheless the nostalgic basis" of his inquiry (128-129). That the aristocratic elitism of the nineteenth-century fin de siècle could mutate into the anarchic populism of the 1990s—*and still retain a direct lineage* – is one of the historical wonders of millenarian scholarship.

As a timely negotiation between the archaic and the futuristic, *The Time of the Tribes* almost succumbs to a sentimental form of utopianism. It believes that the mortal fragility of the orgy provides the key to social behavior, unlocking "a sign of the future in that which is ending" (78). This vision of the future as a "succession of 'presents'" not only preoccupied Friedrich Nietzsche's Zarathustra, but has also inspired popular culture's nihilistic energy from the Ranters to the punks. Moreover, Maffesoli's project consistently hinges on the "ambience of the moment" (145), prompting the question, "Does not each great caesura in human evolution—revolution, decadence, and the birth of empire—see the rise of an array of new lifestyles?" (96). The surfeit of new subcultures that emerged in the 1990s certainly suggests that culture is evolving according to some kind of dionysian directive. The question is, toward what?

2

The Rapture of Rupture

> [H]uman beings are aware that they will die. In that awareness, humans are always in the process of dying—whether denying or accepting—because they can imagine the end. A human death is an imagined death.
>
> David Chidester (ix)

> Transcendence is both real and impossible, as is the human race.
>
> Nick Land (143)

Before we contemplate life "after the orgy," however, we must look at the orgy itself, or at least those whose rhetoric was orgiastic. The Marquis de Sade, Georges Bataille, and Friedrich Nietzsche constitute a canon for any libidinal genealogy located within historical philosophy. Their works help to define many pivotal terms, while simultaneously tracing the discursive boundaries that encircle millenarianism. To review some of their core concepts is therefore to understand not only the ideological "pollution at the source," as it were, but also the many mutations their ideas have undergone during their crooked journey to the popular culture of today. As a consequence, we should familiarize ourselves with three distinct, yet interrelated concepts, in order to understand the isomorphic relationship between sexuality (Eros) and end-time scenarios (Thanatos): Sade's death of God, Bataille's eroticism, and Nietzsche's Dionysus. I shall go through each in turn.

Transgression and transcendence, are two common responses to a perceived threat of the End of the World. Western millenarianism is largely the history of interactions between these two philosophical strands. Each attempt to renegotiate and surpass limits, particularly the "ultimate limit" of death. Transgression aims to overcome the limit by crashing through it, perhaps perishing in the process, whereas transcendence seeks to rise above the limit while remaining intact. In his cross-cultural study of *Patterns of Transcendence*, Chidester notes that concepts of transcendence "always appear in relation to the human limit situation of death, but they approach that limit in remarkably different ways. Limit is an interesting word. From a Latin word *limen* meaning wall, door, or threshold, the limit of death may appear as a wall that blocks any progress, as a door to open, or as a threshold to cross into another world" (1990: xi).

Chidester goes on to identify one particular strategy as "experiential transcendence," which attempts to reconcile *being* and *not-being* by incorporating death into life: "Either through acceptance or ecstasy—that is, through profound and often intense experiences of rising above death while still alive—experiential transcendence may appear as a kind of rehearsal for death" (ibid.). If the metaphor of "rising above" is temporarily removed from this definition, then transcendence turns out to bear an uncanny resemblance to what is often portrayed as its opposite: transgression.

Georges Bataille's definition of eroticism—"assenting to life up to the point of death" (1986: 11)—could also serve as a general definition of transgression, for it provides a common thread that binds his own writings to those of Nietzsche and Sade. These three thinkers seek an ultimate affirmation in a universe perceived as indifferent, or even hostile, to human existence in general and personal identity in particular. Traditionally they have been framed as negative thinkers who write against God, against Nature, and against prevailing moral systems. According to Michael Foucault, however, transgression is an *affirmative* gesture that "must be liberated from the scandalous or subversive, that is, from anything aroused by negative associations" (1977: 35).[8] The individual projects of Sade, Nietzsche, and Bataille transcend this negativity by spilling over into an ecstatic embrace of both life and death, which Nietzsche calls "No-doing and Yes-saying."

By transgressing the laws of nature and society, Bataille, Nietzsche, and Sade seek to create a philosophy that transcends the fate that condemns individuality to a life-sentence of sentience. This is a more complex maneuver than at first appears, for there is no smooth progression from transgression to transcendence. These two impulses do not run parallel like Eros and Thanatos, snaking together at multiple moments like a DNA coil. Rather they run perpendicularly, intersecting only at one crucial point, namely, that end point where rupture spills over into rapture.

On the face of it, transgression and transcendence are diametrically opposed. For if the transgressive engages actively with the physical world (through symbolic inversion), the transcendent is comparatively passive in relating to the physical world only through symbolic aversion. Quintessential examples would contrast Sade's libertine in blood-drenched ecstasy with the evangelist's rapturous believer ascending to heaven. Both, however, are ecstatic moments, incorporating a sense of vertigo experienced as psychic hemorrhage. Both are thus forms of Chidester's "experiential transcendence."

The mystical writings of Saint Theresa of Avila provide an excellent example of the point at which transcendence and transgression not only display certain similarities but actually exchange fundamental properties: "In his hands I saw a long golden spear and at the end of the iron tip I seemed to see a point of fire. With this he seemed to pierce my heart several times so that it penetrated to my entrails. When he drew it out I thought he was drawing them out with it and he left me completely afire with a great love for God" (Bataille, 1986: 224).

These two impulses bubble to the surface most visibly and violently in the radically unstable space of the erotic. As Freud hypothesizes in relation to civilization's discontent (1962), an eroticized death is the shadow that mocks our more noble efforts, and indeed may even spell the end of all of our endeavors.

The three authors I focus on in this chapter—Sade, Nietzsche and Bataille—all exemplify "heterotopic" or transgressive writing. Simon During argues that such a discursive mode rejects traditionally "stable" or "realistic" textual codes in order to "clear an ideological space: a space for action, experimentation, chance, freedom, mobility" (7). By celebrating the base materialism of the body against the spirituality of the soul or mind, transgressive writing seeks to explode those orthodox notions of coherence and consistency that run in tandem with humanist narratives. Fragmentation and rupture are privileged above unity and rapture. Contradictions are reconciled, but not through the patient route of logic or dialects. Instead they either undergo a dionysian unification through violent fusion, or else remain unreconciled like pieces of broken glass to slash curious but unprepared readers.

This is why Sade's writings can tolerate glaring inconsistencies. At one moment, in his book *Philosophy in the Bedroom*, Dolmance tells Eugenie, "your body is yours and yours alone, and only you have the right to use it as you see fit" (1995: 53); later he will tell her, "your sex can never serve Nature better than when it prostitutes itself to ours" (116). In the space between such inconsistencies are forged the possibilities of the heterotopic text, including the possibility of its own imminent collapse.

Nietzsche, Sade, and Bataille share a hatred of Christianity and "the gnostic desire to escape the loathed body" (Weiss, 130). They also share an urgent interest in the "libidinal economy"—the symbolic and political "science of drives" (Land 30) which they hoped would soon break Christianity's choke-hold over the Western mind. They not only perceived, but consciously and actively fueled, the sense of an ending.

They differed, of course, on details of the impending collapse. Nietzsche and Sade believed in a spiritual caste system for men who were marked for greatness and superiority, whereas Bataille remained relatively faithful to his more democratic Marxist leanings. Nietzsche never wrote pornography, whereas Sade and Bataille did so tirelessly. Sade tried to say everything in an encyclopedic compulsion, whereas Nietzsche and Bataille believed the essential to be ultimately unsayable. And Bataille, at times, strayed toward the mystical, whereas Sade and Nietzsche saw such tendencies as symptomatic of a weak mind. Nevertheless, to compare the transgressive strain in their writings provides an opportunity to unbandage that festering area where the scatological resides within the eschatological.

Sade and the Death of God

> There is no better way to know death than to link it with some licentious image.
>
> Marquis de Sade (Bataille, 1986: 11)

In "A Preface to Transgression" (1977), Foucault traces a direct link between the writings of Sade, the "death of God" and the formation of "sexuality" in the official languages of modernity. He explains that the excesses of the Divine Marquis were designed to provoke a God who was either nonexistent or too pathetic to respond. When Newtonian models of scientific inquiry began to erode the moral panopticon of an all-seeing, vengeful deity, Sade took it upon himself to explain that human behavior was now "liberated." As Foucault notes, "the death of God does not restore us to a limited and positivistic world, but to a world exposed by the experience of its limits" (32-33). Through excess we discover "that sexuality and the death of God are bound to the same experience." Eroticism, for Foucault at least, is this "experience of sexuality which links, for its own ends, an overcoming of limits to the death of God" (ibid.). The loss of subjectivity in ecstasy and sexual rapture thus becomes confused with the philosophical loss of sovereignty in the death of God.

Civilization rests on a rigorous separation of the human from the natural domain. The incest taboo is often cited as the universal constitutional organization of culture (see especially Claude Lévi-Strauss's *Elementary Structures of Kinship*). We must therefore remind ourselves of the oxymoronic nature of the term *human nature,* since it is "precisely the unnatural which is particularly human" (Weiss, 1989: 43). To consolidate human community and communication we rely on the *super*natural: a sacred communion. By removing the theological crutch of religion, Sade's creed first exposes the complicity between immortality and morality, and then replaces it with mortality and immorality.

As a consequence of Sade's deicide, and the resulting psychosocial revolution, transgression becomes a game of not only crossing limits but of constituting new ones. After God's funeral we are in virgin epistemological territory, having buried transcendental guarantees of individual sovereignty in the same coffin (along with the "limit-condition" that he represented). Hence, any discussion of transgression necessarily revolves around the twin-pin of Nature and the Sacred.

Sexuality is our most obvious substitute for the spiritual loss that flows from what Salman Rushdie once referred to as our "god-shaped hole." In addition to psychoanalytic notions of primal lack we must now suffer another, perhaps even more unbearable absence, for which we have only ourselves to blame (or thank, depending on your perspective). By killing God we also murder that divine part of ourselves that hitherto identified us as uniquely human. Thus, sexuality—or at least the language of sexuality—rushes into this new abysmal space like air into a vacuum. In this sense, Sade's horrific compositions trace the outline of God's absence like chalk scrawled on the pavement at the scene of the crime.

Transgression consists of "profanation in a world which no longer recognizes any positive meaning in the sacred" (ibid.: 30). Sade can delight in such expletives as "Black Christ Vomit!" at the moment of orgasm, even though only a few pages earlier he had claimed that blasphemy holds no intrinsic value, "since there is little use defiling the name of a God who now has ceased to exist" (94). The Supreme Being, however, retains the power to be reevoked and defiled in the interests of the pleasure of transgression, because he represents "those *ultimate boundaries* of religion, propriety, humaneness and virtue" (ibid.: 71—my emphasis). Sade's virulent nihilism is thus an active negation of the moral manipulation of the sacred, and is thereby implicated with (organized) religion by association. Such complicity leads Land to conclude that "Sade's writings are baked to charcoal in the sacred" (145).

Transgression is parasitic in nature. It needs limits in order to exist, for to exceed them is its raison d'être. Like a shooting star, it burns intensely for a moment and then extinguishes itself. Such a concept is obviously open to romantic interpretation—an allegation to which Nietzsche and Bataille are vulnerable. However, there is no time or place for transgression *on the other side* of the limit, since it is born and dies in that moment of rupture-rapture. In Foucault's words, the unbearable finitude of transgression "consumes and consummates us" (1977: 49). As a consequence, transgression defines itself against traditional metaphysical or Christian notions of transcendence that seek serenity inside infinity. Put simply, the transgressive philosopher has no faith in any "afterlife."

Foucault explains that "the limit and transgression depend on each other for whatever density of being they possess: a limit could not exist if it were absolutely uncrossable and, reciprocally, transgression would be pointless if it merely crossed a limit composed of illusions and shadows" (ibid.: 34). Sade understood this relationship when he stated that "there is nothing that can set bounds to licentiousness . . . [for] the best way of enlarging and multiplying one's desires is to try to limit them" (Bataille, 1986: 48). Freedom thus becomes the liberty to impose one's own limits and to enjoy their provocative charge. The libertine is like the writer, for both thrive on restrictions. The libidinal landscape inhabited by desire could not function as such if it were horizonless. Freedom in a vacuum is impossible, whereas freedom in a void is merely meaningless.

Avoiding the Void

> Nature has endowed each of us with a capacity for kind feelings: we should not squander them on others.
>
> Dolmance (Sade 48)

> If you want to use all created beings, you have the right to do so; for every creature that you use, you drive up into its Origin.
>
> Heresy of the Free Spirit (Cohn, 1993: 179)

It is difficult to reconcile the concept of virulent nihilism with the religious anticipation of a Last Judgment or Kingdom of God. Indeed, Linda Grant's study, *Sexing the Millennium,* rests on the premise that "libertinage is the antithesis of millenarianism" (1993: 39). For Grant libertines realize that "only through the body's pleasure can we feel, experience and be," and consequently they are prepared "to cross every known sexual frontier out of a kind of existentialism, an egotism that makes them believe they are separate from the rest of humanity" (ibid.). This distinction, however, fails to account for the multivalent properties of "end-pleasure," and its proven capacity to attach itself to a variety of different ideological positions. Libertinage, and specifically Sade himself, represents the point at which millenarianism adapts itself to modernity by turning itself inside out while retaining its basic shape—all under the guise of a secular rationality.

In *Philosophy in the Bedroom* (one of his most "accessible" texts), Sade juxtaposes theory and practice, pleasure and pain, sex and death, and transgression and transcendence in a narrative that is at once didactic and subversive. The innocent and malleable Eugenie is initiated into libertine ethics and aesthetics by the experienced Dolmance, who teaches her the violent consequences of a nonexistent God. Dolmance explains that "virtue is just an illusion whose worship causes perpetual suffering in countless transgressions of true desire. I ask you: can such denials be natural? Would Nature truly advocate that which offends her?" (38).

Nature is a complex code word in Sade's semiotic system. In its most obvious and superficial sense, "nature" functions as a replacement for the deceased Christian God, and is equally wrathful in demanding human obedience. Conversely, "nature" functions as yet another norm or law to pervert. This is the paradoxical dynamic of Sade's philosophy, and its unresolved energy powers the libidinal piston of his excess. As Allen S. Weiss points out, "Nature is that which must be transgressed in order to affirm one's humanity, one's sovereignty; yet that nature can never be transgressed, since we are part of it—an impossible dialectic" (1989: 45).

The most common libertine argument against existing social mores is that they transgress the Law of Nature. Sexual excess can thus be justified as the transgression of a transgression (which, according to the laws of a double negative, cancels itself out). Sade's concept of Nature, however, functions as a philosophical Trojan Horse in which to conceal his own missives *against* Nature; for as a consistently transgressive thinker, he abhors *all* external laws, including Nature's. Sade would certainly have appreciated Nietzsche's rhetorical question: "for how should man force nature to yield up her secrets but by successfully resisting her, that is to say, by unnatural acts?" (1956: 61).

However, Sade's valorization of Nature has little in common with the philanthropic romanticism of a Jean Jacques Rousseau or Wilhelm Reich.[9] On the contrary, since he emphasizes the *malevolent* agenda of Nature's seemingly insatiable appetite for destruction. "Her" hidden agenda is thus revealed to Eugenie during Dolmance's enthusiastic defence of sodomy:

> How absurd to say that this mania offends Nature, when she originates it! Would she ordain an action that offends her? Never! . . . Propagation persists due to her tolerance. Would she make law an act that threatens her omnipotence, given that propagation is just a consequence of her primary aims, and that if our race met with annihilation she would cast new creations of primordial intent, whose perfection would be so much more flattering to her pride and power? (66)

Madame De Saint-Ange replies; "Can you know, Dolmance, that by this system you could prove that the total destruction of the human race is nothing more than a service to Nature?" (ibid.).

By interpreting Nature's "primary aim" as destruction rather than creation, Sade calls the bluff of a tradition based firmly on anthrocentric optimism. Hence, in a passage that anticipates the more radical views of today's environmentalists, Dolmance says;

> Esteeming ourselves the highest creatures in the universe we stupidly assume that every hurt endured by so sublime a being must thus be cataclysmic; we have believed that Nature would perish if our magnificent species happened to cease to exist; in fact, total annihilation of that race would, by returning from our trust the creative power lent to us by Nature, reinvigorate her . . . what does she care if the human race is wiped from the Earth? (76, 128)

Such opinions help us to gauge the extent of Sade's antihumanism. Far from contributing to the Enlightenment project, Sade is determined to diminish our species' status as the apex of evolution and as Nature's most noble creation. In his book, *Juliette,* Sade introduces a fictional Pope who dispenses this advice: "So rend away, hack and hew, torment, break, wreck, massacre, burn, grind to dust, melt . . . . Unable to please her [Mother Nature] by the atrocity of a global destruction, at least provide her the pleasure of local atrocity" (Airaksinen 63).

Although Sade is commonly portrayed as an isolated or unprecedented monstrosity, his inverted ethical system can be detected in the teachings of the medieval Free Spirit, which emerged in Europe half a millennium before the marquis. The central doctrine of this heresy was the sovereignty of the self. Allowing one to behave like a god, it led to proto-Sadean maxims such as this: "It would be better that the whole world should be destroyed and perish utterly that a 'free man' should refrain from one act to which his nature moves him" (Cohn, 1993: 178). Cohn describes this seminal form of nihilism as "an entirely convincing picture of an eroticism which, far from springing from a carefree sensuality, possessed above all a symbolic value as a sign of spiritual emancipation" (ibid.: 150-151). Sade experienced that emancipation only through his writings.

In provocative contrast to the most basic of civilized ideals, Sade thus asks; "Who could deem our race so important that anyone failing to seek its continuance is a common criminal?" (128). It is not surprising that disciples of the Free Spirit were executed as heretics, and that Sade was incarcerated by both sides of the political spectrum, for no philosophy of the social can tolerate the recommendation to "form or destroy as thou wilt at thy ease," because "tomorrow's sun shall rise just the same" (65). Sade's utopia is society's dystopia, a hellish no-place that contests both nature and culture.

Sade thus unmasks human hubris, whether directed toward God (metaphysics) or Nature (physics). Both forces are vengeful, and ultimately destroy their own creations. In a chilling precursor to the personal apocalyptic agenda of today's extreme millenarians, Dolmance insists that "we are but the blind instruments of her impulses; were she to bid us set fire to the very universe, our only possible crime would be in not obeying" (181).

Sade realized (long before Charles Darwin, Nietzsche, and Jean Paul Sartre) the consequences for human freedom if God turned out to be an illusion. For if so, we would be liberated from the abstract but vengeful justice of the Last Judgment. After the death of God, our experience of the world becomes profoundly finite and mortal. And yet our sovereign mandate is to "appropriate the organic flow" (Nuttall 72). A fleeting transcendence is therefore possible, according to Sade, but only through playing god ourselves, in a solipsistic process of objectification, violation and transgression.

In his study *Of Glamor, Sex and De Sade*, Timo Airaksinen reminds us of Sade's influence on so-called decadent literature, in that his "ethics and utopian speculations can be understood as a rebellion against nature from within, by means of artificial constructions" (1991: 56):

> Pleasure, which is nature's vengeance, is transformed into reaction towards nature: the intolerably uncontrollable sensual irritation is directed against innocent victims via pain and mental anguish. But this presupposes mastery over what is natural. The result is a skillfully built artificial world . . . . The human devel-

> opment is from scavenger to avenger to predator. It leads from shit, through murder and torture, towards orgasms. Coprophilia, necrophilia, and nothingness illustrate the three stages of man's cosmic fate. (50)

Pleasure is thus "a cycle of sensual, cerebral and orgasmic stages, where the middle point is artificial and thus independent of nature" (47). Sade is dependent on morality (and ultimately "the natural") because he *needs* such constraints in order to transgress them. His orgies are not chaotic explosions of Eros, but highly stylized and organized arrangements that often end in death. Desire becomes a mechanical product. "If sexual activity mirrors the chaos of true nature," observes John Walker, "Sade's libertines proceed to render the act distinctly un-natural, each Dionysian transgression generating more Apollonian verbalizing." Or as Bataille succinctly puts it, Sade "starts from an attitude of utter irresponsibility and ends with one of stringent self-control" (1986: 174-175).

Sade's pleasure is thus circular and temporary, for "after its consummation nothing remains" (Airaksinen 90). The transcendence achieved by the marquis's monstrous characters occurs *inside,* and not *beyond,* the shattered limits (ibid.: x). In stark contrast to the Bible, Sade's writings do not teach us how to avoid the void, but rather how to revel in it: "shower my smoking heart with wilder perversions; then witness how I hurl myself headlong into the abyss!" (123).

Sade's most fundamental premise rests on humanity's ambiguous relationship to Nature, as both its "blind instrument" and conscious perverter. As his Juliette says, "Man is in no wise Nature's dependent . . . [but] her froth, her precipitated residue" (Walker). Herein lies our alienation, that is, our consciously mediated relationship with its unconscious rhythms. Anticipating Bataille's definition of eroticism, Dolmance asks, "are we not born solitary, isolated?" (138). In Sade's writings, however, the gulf that separates one person from an other effectively breaks any emotive or moral conductivity between human beings. Pity, compassion, and empathy are illusions imposed in the interests of social unity and Christian hegemony. From this Sade derives his basic ethical tenet: "why then should we go easy on an individual who feels one thing while we feel another?" (96).

This solipsistic philosophy is capable of absorbing even the shock waves of homicide by interpreting such an act as merely fulfilling the wishes of Nature. Imagine a defense lawyer trying to convince a jury that "murder does not destroy; he who commits it merely alters forms, giving back to Nature those elements from which that skilled artisan instantly sculpts other beings" (76). Again we see the nexus between mortality and morality. Since there is no God to condemn and punish, there is no reason to refrain.

In contrast to the homogenizing or (ultimately) democratizing tendencies of Nature, however, Sade's textual universe sustains a hierarchy headed by the libertine. For while Sade suggests that we should mimic the destructive forces of nature, he offers an escape route for those who believe that such an ethic should not be turned against themselves: "if a person understands the meaning of the principle correctly, he can destroy without being destroyed. In this way the principle offers a justificatory argument for the wicked person, and shows him a way out of the maelstrom of meaningless suffering and death" (Airaksinen 53).

This "way out" (which, incidentally, is the motive behind *all* millenarianism, whether or not it is explicitly libidinal) is the point where transgression spills into transcendence, and—just as importantly with Sade—vice versa. "Perhaps the most important lesson to learn," writes Airaksinen,

> is that pleasure must be understood as transcendence, as the crossing of limits so that one enters the void where all is permissible, nothing matters, and nothing can be achieved. Only through crime is *transcendence transformed into transgression,* the feeling of the total void . . . . Ethics is not concerned with such a void; on the contrary, it is concerned with a careful redefinition of things, and their social control . . . . Good aims are well-defined, and therefore [to Sade] they are not worthwhile. Evil things, on the other hand, are incomprehensible, and thus are pleasant like orgasm, or the jump into the void. (67—my emphasis)

Libertinage is accordingly for Grant, "an erotic politics for the end of a millennium when you believe that there will not be another thousand years . . . . It leads to death; why not? Everything else does" (39). This explains why, in our age of AIDS, terrorism and nuclear weapons, the writings and (usually diluted) practices of the "divine marquis" are enjoying a renaissance in the Western metropolis. Absence of faith in the existence and durability of a person's soul is all that distinguishes Sade from traditional millenarians. Airaksinen agrees that "the Christian flagellant . . . is not far from the Sadean libertine. Both reach for personal transcendence through pain and blood. Both also deny the necessity of the mediating role of the church between themselves and their God" (176).

Sade thus seeks a deeper truth in the orgasm, which—when combined with murder—inflates the *petite mort* into a *grande mort.* Witness Eugenie's oft-echoed climactic cry, "I can bear it no longer! Ah, I'm dying!" or Dolmance's less decorous, "Christ's shit, I perish! I expire! The graveworms chitter through" (34, 111). By the end of the narrative, Eugenie shows that she has been indoctrinated completely into libertinism by announcing her orgasm with the words, "that's it, I'm annihilated" (151). Land insists that "the little death is not merely a simulacrum or sublimation of a big one," but rather "a corruption that leaves the bilateral architecture of life and death in tatters" (191). Within such libidinal blueprints we discern the "particular scaling of death that is close to Sade, a numerical hypertrophy that tips orgy into massacre" (ibid.: 194).

Sade's elitism also sanctions his basic distinction between libertine-master and innocent victim. Death is experienced only vicariously by the former, through the murder of the Other. If, as Land believes, the only possibility of redemption is through *self*-annihilation (15), then the libertine privileges survival above ultimate transcendence. In Bataille's language, the Sadean subject clings to his discontinuity. The libertine's orgasm—despite Land's lyrical assertion to the contrary—is only a *simulation* of death, and thus conforms to the trajectory of the "thanatic asymptote."

Eroticism and the Thanatic Asymptote

> Eroticism is in time what the tiger is in space.
>
> Bataille (1988: 11–12)

The works of Bataille take their cue from the work of the Marquis de Sade, often reading like sustained footnotes to the libertine challenge. Pornographic literature (or "pornology" as Deleuze prefers) was favored by these compatriots as the most appropriate medium in which to express the horrors of existence, especially those that modernity consistently attempts to either obscure or exorcise. A significant portion of their work explores and strengthens links between the "little death" of orgasm and the "big death" of the organism, for both agree that "we can only reach a state of ecstasy when we are conscious of death or annihilation, even if remotely" (Bataille, 1986: 267).

Although the philosophical meridian-shadow of Freud separates their respective writings, they share an obsession with the death-drive and its expression in erotic encounters. Sade would certainly support Bataille's claim that "the feeling of elemental violence . . . kindles every manifestation of eroticism. In essence, the domain of eroticism is the domain of violence, of violation" (ibid.: 16).

Bataille's philosophical study, *Erotism* (1986), subscribes to Sade's vision of the world as a primordial vortex from which Nature sculpts creations earmarked for destruction. However, his depiction of human behavior within this secular framework departs from the marquis's philosophy at certain significant moments. For while Bataille seeks a nihilistic sovereignty, he does not propose a solipsistic model of behavior in God's absence. Instead he emphasizes the quasi-mystical urge for fusion and continuity—or, in psychoanalytic terms—the unconscious desire to return to dead matter.

Unlike Sade, Bataille believes that "man achieves his inner experience at the instant when bursting out of the chrysalis he feels that he is tearing *himself,* not tearing something outside that resists him" (ibid.: 39—my emphasis). Thus, while Bataille considers violence to be an inherent aspect of the erotic, he sees it as focused on the self (through subjective perception) rather than projected outward onto a victim.[10] This is not to say that the erotic object is never sacrificed for pleasure, or that power is distributed equally between the partners. What it means, is that erotic interaction is not inherently hierarchical. Nor is it orchestrated by a sovereign subject determined to survive the experience (as is the case in Sadean narrative). For Bataille, the erotic is equally dangerous territory for all involved.

"What does physical eroticism signify," he asks, "if not a violation of the very being of its practitioners?—a violation bordering on death, bordering on murder?" (ibid.: 17). This "border" is crucial in Bataille's philosophy, kinetically charged with the potential of its crossing. In Sade's textual universe, the border of murder is crossed only by the Other: the orgasm of the libertine functions as a spasm of evil empathy, a souvenir recovered from a fatal journey. Bataille seems to concur when stating that "If you die, it is not my death" (ibid.: 12). The libertine, however, dies only the metaphoric death of orgasm, verbalizing and externalizing it. Bataille's system permits more room for hesitation, resistance, and ambivalence—more foreplay between Eros and Thanatos.

Eroticism is the field in which "discontinuous beings" play out their nostalgia for continuity. According to this tradition, from the moment we are born our conscious individuality wrenches us out of the "continuity" of the universe. We become discontinuous beings who yearn for our former state. As the decadent writer Marcel Schwob puts it,

> The soul of the female lover wishes to dwell in the beautiful body of the one which she loves, and the soul of the male lover ardently desires to dissolve itself in the substance of his mistress. Alas, that exchange is never attained. The souls climb up to the lover's

> lips; they meet one another; they mingle with one another . . . but they cannot migrate. (Stableford, 1992: 284)

Between one human being and another there exists "a gulf, a discontinuity" that can never be crossed; "nevertheless we can experience its dizziness together" (Bataille, 1986: 12-13). This dizziness is the erotic experience. Thus, "erotic activity, by dissolving the separate beings that participate in it, reveals their fundamental continuity, like the waves of a stormy sea" (ibid.: 22).

In a different metaphor, Bataille describes sexual union as a "half-way house between life and death" (ibid.: 168). So while sex is the biological urge to procreate, eroticism is the venting of metaphysical frustration that accompanies the same act. This should not be confused, however, with nineteenth-century romantic notions such as the Siren song or Valkyrie, for death is certainly no passive and serene return to Mother Nature's womb. Death is the most violent thing of all, for it "jerks us out of a tenacious obsession with the lastingness of our discontinuous being" (ibid.: 16). Erotic activity thus initiates a partial dissolution of the subject.

Although Bataille defines eroticism as assenting to life up to the point of death, this does not imply, "up to, *and including,* death." (Sade's particular sacrilege was his attempt to turn the "aura of death," which constitutes the erotic, into actuality.) Instead of tracing the outline of an absent God, Bataillean eroticism follows the movement of what I call the "thanatic asymptote": the seemingly endless approach of the death-drive. The pull of our (unconscious) obsession with this primal continuity is accompanied by the "tormenting desire that this evanescent thing should last" (ibid.: 15). Part of us seeks self-destruction, while the other advocates self-preservation in the hope that this "evanescent thing"—the flickering flame of our individual existence and experience—will continue in its isolation. If we can't have life-after-death we seek death-within-life. Eroticism then becomes simply our flirtation with death.

Paul Virilio provides us with a useful metaphor of eroticism when he describes the sensation of bungee-jumping into the void: "the ultimate getting off, anticipating a *near death experience*" (1995: 93). During such an experience, we do not want a safety net, for this would diminish the rush of our adrenaline-inducing vertigo; yet we do not want to remain there, either, for we soon feel sick. We want to experience "It" momentarily and then be yanked back to safety. This is the thanatic asymptote. In lovemaking, as our bodies cleave together in a grotesque and pathetic attempt at fusion, we actively court oblivion, only to panic and cling to the life buoy of our individuality. Like a mathematical asymptote, we attempt to get closer to the line, yet never actually cross it. In Saint Theresa's words, "I die because I cannot die" (Bataille, 1986: 240).

Of course people frequently *do* cross this line, and not only in the writings of Sade. However, when this particular transgression occurs, the tension that produces eroticism snaps, leaving only sex crimes or accidental suicides from onanistic experiments. In terms of our *flirtation* with death, however, we end up teasing only ourselves, for the Reaper is as patient as he is indifferent.

Eroticism thus consists in the violent juxtaposition of the "rupture of discontinuity" with the "rapture of continuity" (ibid.: 104). This is a metapsychological process that incorporates—perhaps even defines—the religious. For if eroticism simulates that dynamic disharmony that lies at the heart of religious experience, then "the Christian religion is possibly the least religious of them all" in its rejection of the sensual body (ibid.: 32). (Not to mention its individualistic and discontinuous vision of heaven.) However—in a neat twist—the Christian notion of sin increases the sense of shame, which Bataille believes gives birth to eroticism. This enables Christianity to be actively anti-erotic while creating the conditions under which eroticism flourishes; as any fan of the pop-star Madonna could tell you. Transgression thus reveals what Christianity attempts to conceal, namely that "the sacred and the forbidden are one, [and] that the sacred can be reached through the violence of a broken taboo" (ibid.: 126).

The experience of transgressing religious and social taboos provokes a crisis in the subject that is incapable of distinguishing between pleasure and anguish. Since the commonest taboos relate to sex and death, both have become sacred matters through religion. Indeed Bataille tells us that *"transgression does not deny the taboo but transcends it and completes it"* (ibid.: 63):

> If we view the primary taboos as the refusal laid down by the individual to co-operate with nature regarded as a squandering of living energy and an orgy of annihilation we can no longer differentiate between death and sexuality. Sexuality and death are simply the culminating points of the holiday nature celebrates with the inexhaustible multitude of living beings, both of them signifying the boundless wastage of nature's resources as opposed to the urge to live on characteristic of every living creature. (ibid.: 61)

According to this logic, wastage and loss are thus something to celebrate. The self is experienced *as* loss, in a squandering of its own values. In symbolic opposition to the Christian and capitalistic fetish of accumulation, Bataille offers a potlatch of the spirit (not to be confused with the soul). Bataille's writings attempt to transcend the blind will of nature, while shedding the illusion that such transcendence will last any longer than an instant. Transgression is thus an incarnation of the impulse to make order out of chaos: "By introducing transcendence into an organized world, transgression becomes a principle of an organized disorder" (ibid.: 119). As a transgression indistinguishable from Chidester's "experiential transcendence," Bataille's orgasm seeks to incorporate death within life in order to surpass it.

Bataille, like Sade, is at pains to ensure that transgression is not interpreted as either a "back-to-nature" instinct or the return of our latent or repressed animality. This would be to mistake intangible experience for anatomy, because physical sexuality relates to eroticism in the same way that the brain relates to the mind:

> In the human sphere sexual activity has broken away from animal simplicity. It is in essence a transgression, not, after the taboo, a return to primitive freedom. Transgression belongs to humanity given shape by the business of work. Transgression itself is organized. Eroticism as a whole is an organized activity, and this is why it changes over the years. (ibid.: 108)

Bataille's definition of eroticism thus develops historically, anticipating Herbert Marcuse's belief in placing the sexual act at the basis of the social edifice. However, Bataille resists liberal-humanist applications by insisting that "if transgression is impossible, then profanation takes its place. Degradation, which turns eroticism into something foul and horrible, is better than the neutrality of reasonable and nondestructive behaviour" (ibid.: 140). This view is championed today by "libidinal materialists" (Land xxi) such as Michel Mafessoli, Norman O. Brown, and Land.

Bataille's nature, like Sade's, is a vortex of destruction. It demands that we crash headlong into our ruin. For Bataille, "humanity became possible at the instant when, seized by an insurmountable dizziness, man tried to answer 'No'" (1986: 62). 'No,' however, is the hallmark of death (Brown, 1990: 252), and so the more we say it, the less we escape from it. In such a logical labyrinth, our only alternative is to adopt Nietzsche's strategy in saying "Yes" to whatever the universe hurls at us. As a result, feeble mortal negation gives way to a powerful Dionysian affirmation.

Nietzsche's Dionysus

> I assess the value of people, of races, according to how nec-

essarily they are unable to separate the god from the satyr.

Nietzsche (1979: 58)

Reality is never anything but a sector of the imaginary field in which we have accepted the renunciation . . . of our fantasms of desire.

Jean-François Lyotard (1964: 284)

In one of his earliest published works, *The Birth of Tragedy* (1872), Nietzsche employs the Dionysian/Apollonian distinction to analyze the tragic and noble cultural climate of the Hellenic golden age. He does so while simultaneously berating the present state of his German contemporaries. In his final complete work, *Ecce Homo* (1888), Nietzsche continued to champion the Dionysian spirit—calling himself the last disciple of the philosopher Dionysus.[11] Nietzsche's career is thus bookended by excursions into the Dionysian. While a great deal of philosophical terrain had been covered in the sixteen years separating these two works (in which Nietzsche's notion of Dionysus went through some subtle changes), his working definition of this deity remained remarkably consistent.

Dionysus and Apollo represent two antagonistic life forces or artistic principles: one rational, moral, and idealistic; the other irrational, amoral, and realistic. Dionysus is a musical god who exults in the flux of dissolution, whereas Apollo represents the plastic arts, imposing form and order on the chaotic realm of Nature. Above all, Dionysus symbolizes "the extreme limit of affirmation" (Nietzsche, 1979: 79).

The Christian God for Nietzsche represents "the low-water mark in the descending development of divine types. God degenerated into the contradiction of life, instead of being its transfiguration and eternal Yes! God as the declaration of war against life, against nature, against the will to live! . . . deification of nothingness, the will to nothingness pronounced holy!" (1982: 585-586).

Nietzsche offers Dionysus as the alternative to Christianity—the anti-Christ. The intoxicating laughter of Dionysus in fact prefigures Bataille's "practice of joy before death," (Pefanis 46), a project of self-overcoming rather than self-preservation. The philosophical embodiment of Dionysus in the late nineteenth century is thus an eruption of the pagan life force, the return of the libido, which for two millennia had been suffocated by the body-hating teachings of "monotonotheism" (1982: 586). For Nietzsche, as for James Joyce's Molly Bloom, "pagans are all those who say Yes to life, for whom god is the word for the great Yes to all things" (ibid.: 641).

Nietzsche thus anticipates Foucault's point that the soul has been the prison of the body, and not the other way around, as traditional asceticism would have us believe: "The preaching of chastity is a public incitement to anti-nature. Every expression of contempt for the sexual life, every befouling of it through the concept "impure," is *the* crime against life—is the intrinsic sin against the holy spirit of life" (1979: 77).

This sits easily with Sade's views on how Christianity stifles sexuality. And like Bataille, Nietzsche is not content simply to do away with the sacred. Instead he aims to show that the Christian version of sacrality is debased and impoverished. These "protonihilists" are thus not antireligious, for their writings form part of a search for the pantheistic legacy of the pagans. Nietzsche refused to reduce the sacred to such shopworn concepts as "the sublime," "the metaphysical," "the ideal," and "the infinite" (Weiss, 133). Transcendence is considered a valid goal, so long as its ephemeral qualities are understood and appreciated.

Dionysus is born from the "superfluity of life" (Nietzsche, 1979: 81). He is a symbol of that entropy or erosion that the Apollonian impulse of self-preservation must constantly, not to mention vainly, counteract. Assuming that a form of ressentiment accompanies the subject's entry into temporal consciousness (i.e., the knowledge that we have to die sooner or later), then a Dionysian consciousness renounces such a vendetta against the ravenous appetite of time. Since we have no way of persuading Saturn to refrain from eating his children, we may as well turn his meal into a feast of Caligulan proportions.

Nietzsche speaks of the Dionysian rapture, "whose closest analogy is furnished by physical intoxication" (1956: 22). However, Dionysian excess (in contrast to 1960s' interpretations of it) is not the motive for drunken hedonism, but instead represents the impulse to "tear aside the veil that conceals the abyss at the heart of reality" (Gillespie 208). (This is the same impulse, let us not forget, behind *The Revelation* of St. John, and affirms the libidinal thrust of apocalyptic rhetoric.)

Dionysian rapture is a form of transcendence in stark contrast to the mode of escape envisaged by the saints. It serves as the basis of an unflinching attempt to surpass the trivialities of the self: "A spirit thus emancipated stands in the midst of the universe with a joyful and trusting fatalism, in the faith that only what is separate and individual may be rejected, that in the totality everything is redeemed and affirmed—he no longer denies" (Nietzsche, 1979: 13).

In an insight that obviously influenced Bataille, Nietzsche writes; "It is as though in these Greek festivals a sentimental trait of nature were coming to the fore, as though nature were bemoaning the fact of her fragmentation, her decomposition into separate individuals" (1956: 27). This drive toward unification functions throughout Nietzsche's writings, wearing different masks as the Overman, Zarathustra, the Antichrist, the will to power or Dionysus himself.

Nietzsche believed that the Greeks were capable of comprehending the unbearable nature of Dionysian reality only if it was tempered by an Apollonian frame or focus, which created the illusion that for a moment we control—or at least can distil for our pleasure—the abysmal core of existence. In *The Birth of Tragedy,* Nietzsche explains how Hellenic drama was a sublime "neurosis arising from health, from the youthful condition of the race" (1872: 8). Tragedy is thus "a concrete manifestation of Dionysiac conditions, music made visible, an ecstatic dreamworld" (89). Through this unlikely (if not impossible) partnership between Apollo and Dionysus, the Greeks experienced tragic emotion momentarily, and felt they had solved the enigma of existence.

Dionysian wisdom is thus equivalent to Bataille's erotic epiphany, which also fails to end discontinuity, although it allows "this fractured unity to shine forth out of the individual" (Gillespie 209):

> For a brief moment we become, ourselves, the primal Being, and we experience its insatiable hunger for existence. Now we see the struggle, the pain, the destruction of appearances, as necessary, because of the constant proliferation of forms pushing into life, because of the extravagant fecundity of the world will. We feel the furious prodding of this travail in the very moment in which we become one with the immense lust for life and are made aware of the eternity and indestructibility of that lust. Pity and terror notwithstanding, we realize our great good fortune in having life – not as individuals, but as part of the life force with whose procreative lust we have become one. (Neitzsche: 102-103)

For Nietzsche, this rendering of the "world will" is a supreme aesthetic achievement, which two millennia of Christian degeneracy and enforced amnesia have made us no longer capable of. In Hellenic tragedy the "great Dionysian question mark" (ibid.: 13) was bent into an exclamation mark for a fleeting moment by the power of the playwright, only to spring back into its natural shape at the end of the performance. (Nietzsche, however, would soon lose interest in Apollo, along with the romantic humanism he represents. He came to see Apollo as not only a reactive force that tries to deny the power of Dionysus, but as part of the great Germanic-Christian conspiracy against life.)

Already, in *The Birth of Tragedy,* Nietzsche singles out Christian morality as the "will to deny life, a secret instinct of destruction, a principle of calumny, a reductive agent – the beginning of the end?" (11). As he explains, his "vital instincts turned against ethics and founded a radical counter-doctrine, slanted aesthetically, to oppose the Christian libel on life. But it still wanted a name . . . I christened it rather arbitrarily – for who can tell the real name of the Antichrist?—the name of a Greek god, Dionysos" (ibid.).

In "christening" his philosophy thus, Nietzsche created his own eschatology, appropriating the historical figure of the Antichrist for his own Armageddon, which awaits the final *demise* of Christ rather than his return. Nietzsche speculated that nihilism would blossom during the next 200 years (1888-2088): "This period will be characterized by three great affects, disgust, pity, and a lust for destruction, which will produce the catastrophe that will usher in a thousand-year Dionysian *Reich*" (Gillespie 181). Here we see Nietzsche in his millenarian prophet mode, which influenced Adolf Hitler more in tone than in content.

Nietzsche, however, is notorious for those inconsistencies and incoherences that are now identified as distinctive features of transgressive writing. However, one contradiction in particular resists reconciliation: although Nietzsche hated "every kind of temporal expectation and promise" (1982: 604), he personally anticipated a cultural turning point of millennial proportions. Consequently, at one moment he laments the life-strangling notion of a Last Judgment, and at another triumphantly claims that "all that is now called culture, education, civilization will one day have to appear before the incorruptible judge, Dionysos" (1956: 120). It seems that the sticking point is not judgment itself, but *who* is doing the judging.

Despite his fear that one day he would be pronounced holy, Nietzsche aimed his emotive rhetoric at the familiar rhetorical terrain of apocalyptic end-time scenarios:

> This plenitude and sequence of breakdown, destruction, ruin, and cataclysm that is now impending—who could guess enough of it today to be compelled to play the teacher and advance proclaimer of this monstrous logic of terror, the prophet of a gloom and eclipse of the sun whose like has probably never yet occurred on earth? (Gillespie xi-xii)

Indeed Nietzsche—usually more original than this—subscribes to the millenarian motif of anticipating a thousand-year period of truth that would herald the consummation of a Dionysian empire. The young Nietzsche believed that this imminent kingdom was presaged in the tragic and turgid strains of Wagner's music:

> And yet there have been indications that the German spirit is still alive, and marvelously alive, like a knight who sleeps his enchanted sleep and dreams far underground. From out of these depths a Dionysian song rises, letting us know that this German knight in his austere enchantment is still dreaming of the age-old Dionysian myth . . . . One day the knight will awaken, in all the morning freshness of his long sleep. He will slay dragons, destroy the cunning dwarfs, rouse Brünnhilde, and not even Wotan's spear will be able to bar his way. (1956: 144)

Such prophecies are often the rallying cries of those wishing to excite and organize people in the interests of a nationalistic agenda. Indeed, Norman Cohn's classic study of millenarianism (1993) exhaustively demonstrates that eschatological speculations are never free from political content or consequences. Nietzsche clearly saw it as his responsibility—as Dionysus' last disciple—to announce and usher in this age. Thus, against John's *Revelation* he posited his own revaluation (*Umwertung aller Werte*)—a sweeping de- and reconstruction of values that was to have apocalyptic consequences: "I swear to you that in two years we shall have the whole earth in convulsions" (1979: 11).

While Nietzsche's apocalypse may not have been biblically spectacular, its tremors continue to be felt on the seismograph of political entropy, cultural nihilism and, other maladies covered by the diagnosis "postmodernity" (see Geoff Waite's *Nietzsche's Corps/e* (1996) for a reading of Nietzsche's plaguelike influence over the present). Indeed, toward the end of *Ecce Homo* (1888), Nietzsche's identification with the Dionysian Antichrist is almost complete: "For when truth steps into battle with the lie of millennia we shall have convulsions, an earthquake spasm, a transposition of valley and mountain such as has never been dreamed of" (127).

Nihilism and the Thirst for Annihilation

> What? You search? You would multiply yourself by ten, by a hundred? You seek followers? Seek zeros!
>
> Nietzsche (1982a: 468)

> When we speak it rattles like a jagged stone in our throats. A little over two millennia ago we began to cough up strange new words with our blood and bile, and in certain quarters

> the excruciation of libido began to be called "philosophy."
>
> Land (152)

The word *nihilism* has had many different and sometimes contradictory meanings. Modern history, as interpreted by Nietzsche, is the story of how a dominant nihilism—identified variously as Christianity, capitalism, or humanism—becomes globalized. The fact that nihilism treats all transcendence as inherently transitory results in a massive renegotiation concerning notions such as "freedom" and "meaning."

Nihilism can be either active or passive, and Land explains the difference succinctly: "passive nihilism is the zero of religion, whilst active nihilism is the religion of zero" (145). While Sade, Bataille, and Nietzsche exemplify the latter, Arthur Schopenhauer and the media caricature of "Generation X" afford us a glimpse of the former.

Land evokes the nihilistic worldview as it pertains to the subject:

> Life is ejected from the energy-blank and smeared as a crust upon chaotic zero, a mould upon death. This crust is also a maze—a complex exit back to the energy base-line—and the complexity of the maze is life trying to escape from out of itself, being nothing but escape from itself, from which it tries to escape: maze-wanderer. That is to say, life is itself the maze of its route to death; a tangle of mazings which trace a unilateral deviation from blank. (47)

It is no surprise that such a perspective has been silenced, persecuted, ignored, and derided by all sides of the political spectrum. Nihilism does not encourage the mental foundation needed to support such social utilities as elections, telethons, or cake-stalls. Although passive nihilism is less confrontational and antagonistic, it carries a similar socially corrosive effect (as illustrated by the young Woody Allen in *Annie Hall,* who refused to do his homework "because the universe is breaking up"). Nietzsche, however, had no time for its accompanying apathy.

For centuries the notion of immortality has been used as a deterrant to those who would stray from the flock, serving as a backdrop to the corrective corridors of hell. As Nietzsche reminds us, "the concepts *beyond, Last Judgement, immortality of the soul* and *soul* itself are instruments of torture, systems of cruelties by virtue of which the priest became master" (1982: 612). Eternity is a loaded concept, for its value depends wholly on either the promise of eternal bliss or the threat of eternal punishment. Instead of the heavenly "forever," Nietzsche posits the ethical hypothesis of an "eternal return" on earth.

If we remind ourselves that Dionysus is the prophetic god of *coming*, then we can see the libidinal subtext of Nietzsche's concept, whereby the Eternal Return (*Ewige Wiederkunft des Gleichen*) translates more accurately as the Eternal Recoming (*Kunft* deriving from the word *kommen*, "to come") (Waite 323). This extremely complex philosophical metaphor is open to many conflicting interpretations. Yet the eternal return is akin to what Land calls "the abortion of transcendence" (143), since it actively denies the presumption of an Afterlife. If people are confronted with infinite repetition (as in Harold Ramis's Hollywood-Nietzschean fable *Groundhog's Day*) then the emotional luxury of regret becomes superfluous. It is thus up to the individual to turn such existential restrictions into their own heaven or hell.

Consequently, Nietzsche believes that Christianity is best understood as that which worships "the inverse values to those which alone could guarantee it prosperity [and] the exalted *right* to a future" (ibid.: 34). We must become strong enough to bestow this right on ourselves, for it is not simply given us by divine authority. The future is that realm in which the liberated mind is free to enjoy "further experimentation, a continuation of the fluid state of values, testing, choosing, criticizing values *in infinitum*" (1982: 644). Christianity cannot tolerate such indeterminacy, which is why it erects two ideological walls against it:

> one, *revelation,* the claim that the reason in these laws is not of human origin, not sought and found slowly and after many errors, but of divine origin and hence whole, perfect, without history, a gift, a miracle, merely communicated. Then, *tradition,* the claim that the law has existed since time immemorial and that it would be irreverent, a crime against one's forefathers, to raise any doubt against it. The authority of the law is founded on the theses: God *gave* it, the forefathers lived it. (ibid.)

"What did God give man revelation for?"(ibid.: 641), asks Nietzsche—meaning why did we give it to ourselves, and why did we decided to narrate history as a story foretold? While a fatalistic conclusion is essential in Nietzsche's beloved Greek tragedy, its aesthetic mandate does not translate to the historical realm. As Land points out, "it is precisely because history has made no sense that we have learned from it, and the lesson remains a brutal one" (155).

Nietzsche loathed the limitations associated with telic discourses, which is why he placed Socialists in the same despicable category as Christians. (As Nietzsche would say, revelation and revolution: that rhymes, that does not only rhyme.) The "revaluation" of *Ecce Homo* thus counterbalances the combined weight of revelation and revolution: "The purpose of history, guided by genealogy, is not to discover the roots of our identity but to commit itself to its dissipation" (Weiss, 63). Only the Dionysian disciple possesses the kind of subjectivity strong enough to rejoice in such dissipation, and to revel in nihilistic freedom: "The problem I thus pose is not what shall succeed mankind in the sequence of living beings (man is an *end*), but what type of man shall be *bred,* shall be *willed,* for being higher in value, worthier of life, more certain of a future" (1982: 570).

The magnification of man is thus offered as a way of transcending the emasculating effects of the nihilistic. Hence Nietzsche's urgent quest for the Overman, the equivalent of Brahmanic consciousness in his heavily gendered spiritual caste-system. Such an elitist quest—whether initiated by Nietzsche or Hitler—is a final and desperate bid to halt the corrosive march of modernity. That antiapocalyptic historical consciousness that nurtured the quest for the Overman prompts Land to announce that only since Nietzsche has our history come to seem (imminently) terminal (134).

In summary, Sade, Nietzsche, and Bataille figure the *limen* of death as a wall rather than as a door or bridge. Death stands as a provocation. But instead of waiting for the assistance of divine ascension to see over it, they crash headlong through it. Against the humanism of secular modernity, Sade valorized artifice over Nature, and chronicled an apocalyptic form of sexual nihilism. Bataille then adapted Sade's libidinal language to a more fusional and *self*-destructive model, so that eroticism came to signify humanity's sense of discontinuity, and its flirtation with death. Given that the "thanatic asymptote" follows the same historical and ideological arc as libidinal millenarianism itself—always approaching but never actually arriving—we can see how these writers contributed to the apocalyptic climate of the twentieth century.

The philosophies of Sade, Bataille, and Nietzsche were all fabricated in times of perceived crisis or ending: the Terror, the Holocaust, the fin de siècle. Whereas Sade and Bataille wished to push the orgy to its apocalyptic conclusion, Nietzsche used it more as a symbolic springboard for his own brand of libidinal millenarianism, namely, that reevaluation of all values which saturates twentieth-century discourses of the self and society.

Bataille, Nietzsche, and Sade all cut through the Grand Narratives of modernity in order to expose its collusion with Christian moral systems. Contemporary theorists such as Weiss, Land and Lyotard classify their works as symptomatic of "libidinal aesthetics," and group them variously with Pierre Klossowski,

Maurice Blanchot, Raymond Roussel, Louis Ferdinand Céline, Antonin Artaud and others. Their writing is not the legitimate model of a reflective author sculpting "his" life into a coherent narrative, but rather the site of a visceral outpouring of the repressed, denied, profane, and unclean.

Transgression does not seek merely to reverse or balance the dissymmetry of an enforced order, but also to dissolve the authority of "progress" in a gesture of joy, despair, and defiance. That such a project is reminiscent of both deconstruction and some versions of poststructuralism should not surprise us, for Sade, Nietzsche, and Bataille have had a major influence on the intellectual development of more contemporary prophets such as Lacan, Derrida, Deleuze, Blanchot, and Foucault.

Foucault's later writings, however, attempt to rectify the failure of Bataille, Nietzsche, and Sade to complete the spiral back into the Apollonian, "a movement crucial for the critique of our present episteme" (Walker). These writers

> remain semi-immersed in deadly Dionysian nature, the "society of blood" characteristic of the pre-enlightenment age. As a result, though "subversive," they provide no definitive answers for the problem of an ultra-Apollonian, post-Enlightenment power which seeks to produce subjects so to "normalize" and control them. (ibid.)

Foucault acknowledges that "incursions into the Dionysian are always quickly bound in again by order" (ibid.), and that this boundary-policing is becoming increasingly insidious in the market-driven millennium. As a consequence, libidinal economists must not merely affirm the Dionysian, but learn to manipulate Apollonian normalizations of the Dionysian in turn.

3

The Virtual Apocalypse

> These [technological] discoveries bend our senses and our organs in a way that causes us to believe that our physical and moral constitution is no longer in rapport with them. Science, as it were, proposes that we should enter a new world that has not been made for us. We would like to venture into it; but it does not take us long to recognize that it requires a constitution we lack and organs we do not have.
>
> G. Claudin, 1858 (Schivelbusch 152)

As we prepared for our transition into the twenty-first century, an emergent discussion of digital communication technologies warned of the possible "annihilation of space and time." We must remind ourselves, however, that the invention of the steam engine and the railroad inspired similar declarations in mid-nineteenth-century Europe. In 1839 an article in the *Quarterly Review* discussed "the gradual annihilation, approaching almost to the final extinction, of that space and of those distances which have hitherto been supposed unalterably to separate the various nations of the globe" (41). [12] Here we can detect the initial movements of a new geographic consciousness that has steadily moved toward a utopian Pangea. This universal ideal is now realized in the globalist rhetoric of Internet-interested parties such as the Microsoft Corporation, whose slogan is, Where Do You Want to Go Today?

In his classic history of *The Railway Journey*, Wolfgang Schivelbusch discusses the "disorientation experienced by the traditional space-time continuum when confronted by . . . new technology" (1980: 44). His study reveals that planetary shrinkage was prophesied long before McLuhan imaged the world as a "global village." In 1843 for instance, Heinrich Heine observed how "[s]pace is being killed by the railways, and we are left with time alone . . . .

I feel as if the mountains and forests of all countries were advancing on Paris. Even now, I can smell the German linden trees; the North Sea's breakers are rolling against my door" (ibid.).

As was to be the case with both atomic power and the modem, the train encouraged a belief in new opportunities for understanding our fellow men and women. "To thus foreshorten for everyone the distances that separate localities from each other," Constantine Pecqueur noted, "is to equally diminish the distances that separate men from one another" (ibid. 74). Schivelbusch emphasizes this confusion of the spatial with the social by early nineteenth-century progressive thinkers, who believed that the railroad would be a "technical guarantor of democracy, harmony between nations, peace and progress" (73).

Yet what happens when two points, previously buffered by distance, are brought together by new technologies? According to Schivelbusch, an accident occurs "As the space between the points—the traditional travelling space—is destroyed, those points move into each other's immediate vicinity: one might say that they collide" (45). Such a collision necessarily involves some kind of initial psychic shock. The earliest recorded reactions to train travel, however, tend to dwell on the threat of *physical* danger before contemplating the philosophical "shock" of this newfound velocity.

The accident is one of the four modes of Being in Aristotle's *Metaphysics*. However, not until the industrial revolution—when measurable accidents increased—did the word lose its association with coincidence or fate. The accident thus became a by-product of industry in the modern era, a technological phenomenon that brings death on a scale previously unheard-of outside the spheres of natural disaster or war.[13]

In our own time, the accident has become intimately connected to the government's management of resources. Because it is factored into every economic equation, we have developed—at least according to Ernst Jünger—a "second and colder consciousness" (Buck-Morss 138-139). As Jean Baudrillard observes, "The blood on the roads is a desperate form of compensation for the State's tarmac gifts . . . . The accident thus takes its place in the space that institutes a symbolic debt towards the State" (1993: 43). Nevertheless, as inheritors of Jünger's "second consciousness" we do not, on the whole, think of accidents as being so perilously near as they were to early commuters on the first trains. Take, for instance, the first major railway disaster, on May 8, 1842 on the Paris-Versailles line, which killed or wounded over one hundred and fifty people. This accident immediately threw much of Europe into panic, accounting for the sense of fear and helplessness that permeates many historical accounts of this new technology and its passive mode of transport.

To Thomas Creevy, writing in 1829, traveling by train "is really flying, and it is impossible to divest yourself of the notion of instant death to all upon the least accident happening" (Schivelbusch 131). Sixteen years later a German traveller describes a "certain dampening of the spirits that never quite goes away despite all the pleasant aspects of train journeys," which he attributes to the ever-present "close possibility of an accident, and the inability to exercise any influence on the running of the cars" (ibid.). Those who survived accidents physically unscathed seemed unable to absorb psychologically the shock of experiencing the unprecedented destructive power of technology. "There is something in the crash," wrote William Camps in 1886,

> the shock, and the violence of a railway collision, which would seem to produce effects upon the nervous system quite beyond those of any ordinary injury . . . [and these] . . . to such an extent, that the unfortunate sufferer may not altogether recover throughout the remainder of his life, which I apprehend, may, in some instances at least, be reasonably expected to be curtailed in its duration. (139)

One nineteenth-century physician, Max Nordau—who I discuss in more detail in chapter 4—regarded the increasing cases of "railway spine" and "railway brain" (ill-defined nineteeth century afflictions) as evidence of human fragility in the face of accelerating technologies (41). Schivelbusch also attributed the profound impact of railroad trauma to the relative sophistication of the technology, for "the more efficient the technology, the more catastrophic its destruction when it collapses" (133). Consequently,

> [t]here is an exact ratio between the level of the technology with which nature is controlled, and the degree of severity of its accidents. The preindustrial era does not know any technological accidents in that sense . . . . The preindustrial catastrophes are natural events, natural accidents. They attack the objects they destroy from the outside, as storms, floods, thunderbolts, hailstones, etc. After the industrial revolution, destruction by technological accident comes from the inside. (ibid.)

What are the implications of such an argument in the post- (or at least "late") industrial era, as mechanical production in the west gives way to electronic maintenance? The Union Carbide disaster in Bhopal, Chernobyl, and daily transit accidents vividly illustrate the continuing relevance of such a theory. At first glance, at least, new technological vectors suggest a cushioning of potential impacts. Yet the lessons of railroad trauma should continue to be heeded, for as we have seen, people may survive a crash physically untouched but mentally devastated. Why should things be any different in virtual reality?

Psychoanalysts sometimes posit a causal link between the imminence of accidents and the eroticization of trains. Noting the "connection between mechanical agitation and sexual arousal" (Schivelbsch 197), Sigmund Freud identified the railroad as the most powerful agent of such stimulation. (Indeed, it is no "accident" that one of the most enduring phallic symbols is the train.) Freud believed that "a compulsive link of this kind between railway-travel and sexuality is clearly derived from the pleasurable character of the sensations of movement" (ibid.). Early train travelers experienced the fearful independence of their own sexuality as somehow corresponding to derailment: "Their fear is related to the danger of finding themselves in a kind of unstoppable motion that they can no longer control. The same patients generally exhibit fear of locomotion in any vehicle they cannot bring to a halt themselves at any time" (83). Freud even goes so far as to attribute the nausea of motion sickness to the repression of sexual desires awakened by train travel (197). While open to dispute, such theories point to the constellation, which exists between sexuality, neurosis, and a technological apocalypse. The nineteeth-century condition of "libidinal neurosis" (Schivelbusch 143) thus speaks of an erogenous component within the acceleration of Western culture, and specifically in the endeavor to treat the "erotic as a regulated machine" (Lyotard).

J.-K. Huysmans's mouth-piece, Des Esseintes, eroticizes the train itself, by feminizing two locomotives "lately adopted for service on the Northern Railroad of France":

> One, the Cramspton, an adorable blonde, shrill-voiced, slender-waisted, with her glittering corset of polished brass, her supple catlike grace, a fair and fascinating blonde, the perfection of whose charms is almost terrifying when, stiffening her muscles of steel, pouring the sweat of steam down her hot flanks . . . . The other, the Engerth, a massively built, dark-browed brunette, of harsh, hoarse-toned utterance, with thick-set loins. (22-23)

Vague sexual arousal is intensified here into that fetishistic gaze which was to be exercised in the Futurist writings of F. T. Marinetti and reach its apotheosis in J. G. Ballard's novel, *Crash* (1975). According to an 1855 article in the *Journal of Public Health and Sanitary Review,* "[t]he causes of the evil are not to be found in the noise, vibration and speed of the railway carriage . . . but in the excitement, anxiety, and the nervous shock consequent on the frequent efforts to catch the last express; to be in time for the fearfully punctual train" (Schivelbusch 203).

A contemporary example of "fearfully punctual" technology is the home computer, and the escalating industry that generates its built-in obsolescence. Those who cannot afford to purchase a computer are denied access to the social and economic mobility that such technology—potentially, at least—produces. That tiny percentage of the world population that *can* afford computers is then obliged to upgrade continuously in order to keep pace with one of capitalism's purest forms. In 1868 such a phenomenon was described by Haviland as being "hurried to death" (Schivelbusch 203), and in 1970 by Alvin Toffler as "future shock." Both testify to a temporal version of the everyday collisions documented by historians, statisticians, photographers, artists, and coroners.

Virilio's Accident

> If I were asked to condense the whole of the present century into one mental picture I would pick a familiar everyday sight: a man in a motor car, driving along a concrete highway to some unknown destination. Almost every aspect of modern life is there, both for good and for ill—our sense of speed, drama and aggression, the worlds of advertising and consumer goods, engineering and mass manufacture, and the shared experience of moving together through an elaborately signalled landscape.
>
> Ballard (1996: 262)

> There are no accidents, only nature throwing her weight around.
>
> Camille Paglia (38)

There is a scene in Huysmans's *A Rebours* (1884) where Des Esseintes attempts to break free from his stagnant lifestyle by taking a trip across the Channel to England. He only makes it as far as a tavern on the rue d'Amsterdam near the train station. As he eats his dinner while waiting for his train to depart, he overhears some Englishmen talking nearby, who inspire him to imagine the journey that lies ahead. He soon finds himself so overcome by an "enervating lassitude" that he decides it would be "a nuisance" to make his connection. "After all," he says, "I have felt and seen what

I wanted to feel and see. I have been steeped in English life ever since I left home; it would have been a fool's trick to go and lose these imperishable impressions by a clumsy change of locality" (130).

Because the trip has occurred already in his mind, Des Esseintes needs no corresponding journey in reality to legitimize his "memories." His voyage has been conducted entirely in that imaginative realm we now call "virtual", "and this merely by a trifling subterfuge, by a more or less close simulation of the object aimed at by these desires" (20). This is the perfect arrangement for a connoisseur of sensation who is nevertheless too apathetic to venture outside his domicile.

Des Esseintes thus anticipates the quintessential attitude of twenty-first-century couch potatoes when he asks; "What was the good of moving, when a man can travel so gloriously sitting in a chair?" (130). This chair then becomes a significant site of early virtual movement, allowing the world to revolve around the self like stars around a prodigal sun. Over a century later, Ballard was quoted as saying, "I keep meaning to go [to the United States], but it's just *inertia*. Also, I think one doesn't really need to travel—TV travels for you" (Juno 35). He goes on to remark that "[i]f one had to categorize the future in one word, it would be 'home.' Just as the 20th century has been the age of mobility, largely through the motor car, so the next era will be one in which instead of having to seek out one's adventures through travel, one creates them, in whatever form one chooses, in one's home" (159). The combination of accelerated communication technologies with increased global mobility has produced a paradoxical tendency toward stasis. From reality's gridlock to the Internet's "net-lag," things are grinding to a halt. As Mark Kingwell notes, "We are always speeding up to a standstill" (159).

We are thus living on the threshold of an era in which fiber-optic cables carry vicarious experiences to and for us. After all, we live in an age where we can dine with our family via real-time technologies, even when scattered to the four corners of the globe. As Paul Virilio notes (perhaps recalling Des Esseintes); "When cosmic imagery is completely digitalized in the next century by computer processes, cybernauts will be able *to travel in their armchairs* as simple televiewers, discovering a surrogate world that will have emerged from information energy" (1995: 154).

As we have seen, however, acceleration comes at a price: namely, the psychic coordinates of the Victorian worldview. Virilio revives the doom-mongering of the first half of the nineteenth century when he writes that "with acceleration there is no more here and there, only the mental confusion of near and far, present and future, real and unreal—a mix of history, stories and the hallucinatory utopia of communication technologies" (ibid.: 35).

This digital disorientation leads us into Baudrillard territory, whereby the copy is indistinguishable from the original, the simulation from "the real." Virilio, however, takes this a step further than Baudrillard, by arguing that such a distinction is already dated. Instead, "reality has become symmetrical," splitting into two distinct parts: the virtual and the actual. "This," Virilio argues, "is a considerable event which goes far beyond simulation" (Wilson).

Virilio thinks that this split is an effect of "the digital or computer bomb, which destroys the principle of reality itself" (ibid.). Acknowledging that the nuclear bomb and the computer were invented simultaneously, he sees them now locked into an apocalyptic "race for ubiquity and instantaneity" (1995: 7): "These new technologies try to make virtual reality more powerful than actual reality, which is the true accident," he continues. "The day when virtual reality becomes more powerful than reality will be the day of the big accident. Mankind never experienced such an extraordinary accident" (Wilson).

Many engines have helped propel human history, but two in particular drove the final century of the last millennium: the automobile and the computer. The information engine and the combustion engine combined to colonize our perception of the world, and our place in it. "The communications industry would never have got where it is today," Virilio tells us, "had it not started out as an *art of the motor*" (1995: 23). Television thus becomes a "museum of accidents," and even a term like *impact study* exposes the way in which progress has been metaphorically motorized.

In discussing the *reality-engine* (a Virtual Reality term), Virilio concludes that "[t]o navigate space, cyberspace, as one formerly steered a motor vehicle . . . is indeed the great aesthetic mutation of information technologies" (ibid.: 145). For this reason, the Internet is also referred to as the "information super-highway." Such a metaphor, however, speaks volumes about the way in which we view our passage through time. Our emphasis on speed has meant that we do not consider the Internet as a "sea" of data, despite ample opportunities to do so. We *surf* the net, as well as *trawl* through it for information; we have software *piracy,* and the registered logo of the new defunct *Netscape Navigator* featured both a ship's wheel and a lighthouse.

In *Fast Cars, Clean Bodies* (1995), Kristin Ross identifies the car as the central vehicle of all twentieth-century modernization. Personal mobility resulted in a newfound freedom, and produced a new subjectivity whose circumference (unlike domestic space) was simultaneously nowhere and everywhere. If we map this new decentred subjectivity onto the information superhighway, we get what

Scott Bukatman calls "terminal identity": a pun on the apocalyptic technology of the cybernaut. In popular-romantic accounts, hackers are like James Dean: young male rebels, tearing along the fiber-optic autobahns at breakneck speed, and seeking the self-transcendence of "escape velocity." Like Dean, however, they are also heading for a crash. Ballard's *Crash* and Neal Stephenson's *Snow Crash* (1993) give us two perspectives of this (always) impending impact.

The crash is seen by the media, the government, and the medical profession—and therefore by most of us—as an aberration. We have car *accidents*, the name itself eliding any notion of purpose or responsibility. But what if, as Baudrillard suggests, the crash could be separated from the notion of an accident and considered as something more deliberate than just a fatal by-product. Something more than simply "the part conceded to fate by the system itself and calculated into its general reckoning" (1991: 315). In this case the accident is "no longer on the margins; it is at the heart. It is no longer the exception to a triumphant rationality; it has become the Rule, it has devoured the Rule" (ibid.).

Indeed, a comprehensive North American study published in the same year as Ballard's *Crash* begins with "a specific theory of the etiology of accident—namely, that in many, perhaps even most accidents, suicide or suicidelike factors are in evidence" (Tabachnick et al. ix). A similar hypothesis inspired Ballard to ask if we are "merely victims in a meaningless tragedy," or whether "these appalling accidents take place with some kind of unconscious collaboration on our part?" (1996: 263).

The counterdestructive potential of the car crash was a key motif in the writings of the Italian Futurist, Marinetti. As "probably the most aggressive and naïve attempt to establish an aesthetic on the preaching of de Sade and Nietzsche" (Nuttall 75), Futurism reacted to the political climate leading up to the First World War by embracing technology and rejecting the Luddite legacy of romanticism. Reversing the hierarchy of man-over-machine, Marinetti composed homages to the tightly coiled power of machinery, which enabled humans to transcend their condition by fusing with pure velocity: "We stand on the last promontory of the centuries! . . . . Why should we look back, when what we want is to break down the mysterious doors of the Impossible? Time and Space died yesterday. We already live in the absolute, because we have created eternal, omnipresent speed" (48-49).

Prefiguring the "road rage" mentality of busy commuters, the Futurists proclaimed the need to "persecute, lash, torture all those who sin against speed" (103). They also anticipated various cyborg philosophies regarding an enhanced posthumanity, linking Nietzsche and Nordau to William Gibson and Stelarc. The techno-*Übermensch* will be "endowed with surprising organs . . . adapted to the needs of a world of ceaseless shocks" (99). Alternatively, he may confirm Marshall McLuhan's suspicion that man himself has become merely "the sex organs of the machine world" (1974: 46).

Marinetti's *Founding and Manifesto of Futurism* (1909) was itself (in Ballard's phrase) a "death-born Aphrodite," heavy with the Freudian symbolism of the Accident. The narrative describes a group of like-minded people who, driving through the countryside and fervently discusing the future of Europe, crash into the "maternal ditch" of a factory drain. This accident jolts them into a new sense of awareness which—prefiguring Ballard's characters—enables a deeper appreciation of the relationship between humanity and technology. Emerging from the slimy wreckage of his car, a reborn Marinetti proclaims the "immanent, inevitable identification of man with motor" (1991: 99). The accident—injected with personal and global significance—thus becomes the catalyst for both subjective revelation and apocalyptic Revelation: 'Look there, on the earth, the very first dawn! There's nothing to match the splendor of the sun's red sword, slashing for the first time through our millennial gloom!' . . . . I stretched out on my car like a corpse on its bier, but revived at once under the steering wheel, a guillotine blade that threatened my stomach" (48).

In public life, however, the accident remains a glitch, a bug or blockage in a system designed for "figures of incessant circulation" (Baudrillard, 1991: 315).

Bacchanical Man and Ballard's *Crash*

> No more riots, no need for much repression; to empty the streets, it's enough to promise everyone the highway.
>
> Paul Virilio (1986: 25).

In a 1984 interview with *REsearch* magazine, Ballard describes a serene pattern of circulation that transcends basic notions of law and order:

> It seems to me that we're moving into an area where the moral structures of society, the whole social basis of the lives we lead are provided for us externally without any sort of contribution by our-

> selves—they're provided to a large extent by the nature of modern science and technology. We don't think of say the modern traffic system as being a moral structure, but in a sense the green and red lights that move traffic around safely are making a whole set of moral decisions for us, which allow us to get on with the business of, say, having a row with the girlfriend as we go around the cloverleaf in complete safety . . . . This leaves our imagination free and untrammeled by moral considerations. (Revell 46)

In 1996 it was estimated that America were six years away from the prototype of an automated highway system for "smart vehicles," which would move passengers around like "oversized slot-cars" (Wiesenfelder 128). Recently the U.S. Department of Transportation awarded $161 million to the National Automated Highway System Consortium, a General Motors-led alliance to "provide fully automatic vehicle operation in dedicated lanes." The objective is "to streamline traffic and *virtually* eliminate highway accidents" (ibid.—my emphasis).

What would Ballard make of such a smooth mode of circulation, whose express purpose is to reduce accidents to "if not zero—then close to it?" (ibid.). Is this the point at which a moral structure becomes totalitarian? Baudrillard protests such a system when he writes that "we support the concept of road signs when it comes to sexual distinctions, or to fashion, or to the corruption and disarray of our values, but we don't support it when it comes to the realm of order" (1983: 46).

While busy with *Crash,* Ballard wrote a journalistic piece called "The Car, The Future" (1971), which uncannily predicts the Automated Highway System. By the closing years of the century, he says, "[i]t seems inevitable that we will gradually surrender our present freedom to step into our cars and drive where and when we wish." This is because "[t]raffic movements and densities will be increasingly watched and controlled by electronic devices, automatic signals and barriers" (265). Ballard foresees that one of the first casualties of the twenty-first century will be that symbol of personal agency, the steering wheel: "the private car will remain, but one by one its brake pedal, accelerator and control systems, like the atrophying organs of our own bodies, will be removed" (ibid.).

At the threshold of the digital age, Ballard understood the deeply symbiotic relationship between mechanical and electronic technologies. For when considering what will take the place of the steering wheel, he imagines it is likely to be

> a wheel of a different kind—a telephone dial. When our great-grandchildren sit down in their cars in the year 2050, they will see in front of them two objects—one that resembles a telephone, the

> other a telephone directory. The directory will contain a list of all possible destinations, each with a number that may be dialled. Having selected his destination, our driver will look up the number and then dial it on the telephone. His signal will be transmitted to the transport exchange . . . [also known as] Central Traffic Control. (265-266)

This hybrid vision of the future blurs the boundary between highway and superhighway. For even when we fight inertia, and decide to change location, we still do so through electronic mediation.

Viewed from above, our highways have hitherto resembled the movement of bits of data around the infobahn. In Ballard's automated highway, however, the fractal model of the Internet is replaced by a centripetal processing-station. Obviously, such a rigorously defined system would rob the car of its very essence: the illusion of freedom. But as Ballard reminds us, the automobile provides other kinds of freedom than mobility, including the "perverse" freedom to kill ourselves—or others—by terminal velocity. After all, the crash is "almost the only way in which one can now legally take another person's life" (Ballard, 1975: 37).

One person who relishes such a freedom is the protagonist of Ballard's abject text, *Crash*. Vaughan is a self-styled "modern martyr of the superhighways" (1975: 162). Formerly a computer specialist who worked on the "application of computerized techniques to the control of all international traffic systems" (ibid.: 53-54), he became a morbidly fetishistic MD with the desire to literalize his Freudian death-"drive." In doing so, Vaughan abandons a corporate-sponsored quest for order to embrace the necrophiliac-nightmare logic of the car crash.

The Canadian filmmaker David Cronenberg (who filmed *Crash* in 1996) has often explored the dynamic between a dionysian attraction to chaos and the social drive toward order.[14] As both "our foremost theoretician of viral sex" (Dery, 235), and "*the* filmmaker of terminal identity" (Bukatman 80), Cronenberg was really the only candidate for the job. Asked about one of his earlier movies, *Shivers* (1975), Cronenberg replied: "I had read Norman O. Brown's *Life against Death* . . . in which he . . . discuss[es] the Freudian theory of polymorphous perversity. . . . Even old Norm had some trouble when he tried to figure out how that kind of Dionysian consciousness would function in a society where you had to cross the street and not get hit by a car" (ibid.: 277). *Crash* is an explicit treatment of this very conundrum. The only truly dionysian response, it concludes, is to let yourself get hit.

An entire discipline has mushroomed around Ballard's excremental book, which is essentially about a group of people who see the highway system as an amoral structure, and certainly have no interest in negotiating it "in complete safety." In Jünger's terms, the inhabitants of Ballard's story are the alienated subjects of this "second" and "colder" consciousness, which evolved simultaneously (and in order to cope with) the dehumanizing conditions of the industrial age.

Described by its author as "the first pornographic book based on technology" (Juno 98), *Crash* exhibits the "clear equation . . . between sex and the kinaesthetics of the highway" (Ballard, 1975: 147). The characters are in search of "a new sexuality born from a perverse technology" (10), manifested in the violent conjunction of flesh, celluloid, and chrome. Ballard's fetishistic text is obsessed with the juxtaposition of body and machine, especially when mediated through the lens. The Bataillean notion of an unconscious yearning for fusion—a nostalgia for a lost continuity—is taken to its late twentieth-century conclusion in *Crash*, where people press their genitals into dashboards in a humourless parody of the urge to mate with machinery:

> [Vaughan] moved around the car, marking the profile of his penis on the doors and fractured windows, on the trunk lid and rear fender. Carrying his penis in his hand to shield it from sharp metal, Vaughan climbed into the front seat and began to draw the outline of his penis against the instrument panel and centre arm-rest, marking out the erotic focus of a crash or sex-act, celebrating the marriage of his own genitalia and the skull shattered dashboard binnacle against which the middle-aged woman dentist had died. (13)

The interchangeable properties of "car crash or sex-act" highlight the historical flirtation between Eros and Thanatos. Unlike Sade, however, Vaughan is willing to push the thanatic asymptote over the line into his own literal death.

Bukatman believes that Ballard's major accomplishment is to have created a character who "seeks joyful synthesis with precisely those objects that . . . reinforce the discontinuous experience of being" (293). Bodily fluids thus comingle with engine oil to create an explosive and transcendent cocktail, which takes alienation into previously unexplored "posthumanist" territory.

In 1976, Baudrillard published a piece praising *Crash*. It has since been smothered in an avalanche of criticism accusing him of being both "dangerously partial and naïvely celebratory" (Sobchack, 1991: 327). Yet it remains illuminating, if only as a cracked mirror reflecting a distorted image of Ballard's text.

Perhaps Baudrillard's most contentious claim is his assertion that

> [t]here is no affectivity behind all this: no psychology, no ambivalence or desire, no libido or death-drive. Death is a natural implication in this limitless exploration of the possible forms of violence done to the body, but this is never (as in sadism or masochism) what the violence purposely and perversely aims at, never a distortion of sense and sex . . . . There is no repressed unconscious. (314)

Such an interpretation leapfrogs the familiar psychoanalytic models that seek to explain extreme behavior. The book evacuates all motive and emotion, reflecting the author's belief that we must transfigure Freud's internal libido by projecting it onto the external world of objects. This is why Baudrillard believes that traditional descriptions such as "perverted" and "voyeuristic" should not be applied to the behavior of *Crash*'s characters, since these concepts belong to an obsolete order: "There is no possibility of dysfunction in the universe of the accident; thus no perversion either. The Accident, like death, is no longer of the order of the neurotic, of the repressed, of the residual, or of the transgressive; it is the initiator of a new manner of *non-perverted* pleasure" (315). The libido is not projected *onto* the outside world, but leaks into the mind from outside, via technology. The carnage in *Crash* is thus offered as something other than a return of the repressed.

Graeme Revell implicitly recognizes the novel's debt to Sade, noting that "this abandonment of sentiment and emotion is no cause for regret; rather it has cleared a space for the free play of our perversions and especially our apparently unlimited capacity for abstraction" (145). The question of desire in this text is indeed perplexing, since it is both omnipresent and strangely absent, as in the Sadean universe. Living up to his name, Pan is present everywhere in Vaughan's "panicky universe." He is located, however, not within a pagan or biological impulse, but in the sterile and traditionally unerotic mise-en-scène of the postindustrial Western metropolis: "This obsession with the sexual possibilities of everything around me had been jerked loose from my mind by the crash. I imagined the ward filled with convalescing air-disaster victims, each of their minds a brothel of images. The crash between our two cars was a model of some ultimate and yet undreamt sexual union" (23). The narrator soon becomes overwhelmed with the polymorphous eroticism of his hospital, whose "elegant aluminized air-vents in the walls of the x-ray department beckoned as invitingly as the warmest orifice" (34).

Baudrillard believes *Crash* heralds the arrival of "an unprecedented sort of sexuality . . . a kind of potential dizziness linked to the pure inscription of the body's non-existent signs" (1991: 314). Yet this contrasts sharply with Ballard's relentless emphasis on the organic as well as on the technological. Although Ballard appreciates the seductive power of the sign—he talks of crashes releasing codes lying dormant within us—his keen materialism, based in his love of the dionysian, refuses to embrace such an intellectual conceit.

Yet Ballard's novel certainly rethinks the relationship between technology and transgression in order to update the dionysian imperative. Discontinuity is no longer something to be negotiated solely between people, for machinery is now (as McLuhan insisted) an equal part of the erotic equation. It is even endowed with its own "machine libido" (Juno et al. 156). Echoing Huysmans's literary diagnoses (discussed in chapter 4), Ballard observes that "the social novel is reaching fewer and fewer readers," because "social relationships are no longer as important as the individual's relationship with the technological landscape of the twentieth century" (ibid.: 99). Indeed, the narrator of *Crash* explicitly states that he "realized that the human inhabitants of this technological landscape no longer provided its sharpest pointers, its keys to the border-zones of identity" (40). Where Baudrillard and Ballard diverge, however, is on whether this meta-alienation is a desirable state of affairs—that is, whether it results in "a sexuality that is without referentiality and without limits" (Baudrillard, 1991: 313), or whether it leads to an extremely messy death.

Baudrillard's alleged "body-loathing" represents the desire—shared by both the Australian performance artist Stelarc and the techno-Darwinian Extropian cult—to transcend the body while simultaneously (and miraculously) leaving consciousness intact. (This desire to transcend the flesh did not, of course, originate in the cyberage. In *The Temptation of St. Anthony* (1874), Gustave Flaubert writes; "Aren't you tired of this body that weighs on your soul and cramps it like a narrow cell would? Demolish the flesh, then . . . we shun the flesh, we execrate it" [in Virilio, 1995: 80].) In contrast, Ballard, who often writes about human resilience, wants to dismember the present in order to remember the future—to narrate "a transcendence which is also always a surrender" (Bukatman 329). He thus seeks to interrogate the apocalyptic undercurrent of certain techno-tendencies.

The outraged reactions that greeted Baudrillard's piece suggest that it struck a nerve. His cerebral celebration of the soon-to-be obsolete body provoked his numerous critics to cry, *Enough cyberbole!* (Dery, 247). They argued that in celebrating the *jouissance* of collision, Baudrillard ignores Ballard's explicit references to the book's (albeit elusive) morality. In the introduction to the French translation of *Crash,* Ballard writes; "Will modern technology provide us with hitherto undreamed-of means for tapping our own psychopathologies? Is this harnessing of our innate perversity conceivably of benefit to us? Is there some deviant logic unfolding more powerful than that provided by reason?" (Juno et al. 98).

Here we can see that Ballard's book is still firmly rooted in Freudian territory: for although there may be no emotional depth behind the actions of Vaughan and his cohorts, there still exist the contaminated residues of psychology, ambivalence, desire, libido, and death (categories that Baudrillard rejects). As N. Katherine Hayles maintains, "desire is not absent. Rather it is reconfigured and intensified" (322). Desire in *Crash* is like a spark in the void, present only when flesh and technology collide.

Considering the terms of this debate, it seems that Ballard may have underestimated the powers of persuasion wielded by postmodernists on late-modernist texts. It is certainly naive of him to state in the same introduction that "the ultimate role of *Crash* is cautionary, a warning against the brutal, erotic and overlit realm that beckons more and more persuasively to us from the margins of the technological landscape" (Juno et al. 98). Elsewhere Ballard claims that his "fiction really is investigative, exploratory, and comes to no moral conclusions whatever" (Revell 43), somewhat vindicating Baudrillard's perspective.

Yet we need to beware of "the scandal of metaphor," as Vivian Sobchack attests in her famous response to Baudrillard. With reference to her own experience of thigh cancer, she remembers "the cold touch of technology" on her flesh as "distractions from [her] erotic possibilities, and not, as Baudrillard would have it, erotically distracting" (1991: 328). Mobilizing her own experience against Baudrillard's exponential powers of abstraction, Sobchack warns against the "self-exterminating impulses" of those cyborg discourses that talk of *the* body as thought, rather than of *my* body as lived (and thus miss the irony and politics of Donna Haraway's manifesto). Hence her attack on those who seek to transcend the flesh through a masculinist and masturbatory urge to "beat the meat" (1995: 209). Sobchack insists a jolt of pain relocates us firmly in our mortal subjectivity and isolation, countering the sci-fi strategy of reducing the human to an assemblage of "organs without bodies." Despite what Baudrillard (and, to a certain extent, Ballard) would have us believe, she argues, the crash does not provide an ejective epiphany *outside of* our banal alienation.

Since having her leg amputated, Sobchack has produced an addendum to her essay. "What many surgeries and my prosthetic experience have really taught me," she writes, "is that, if we are to survive into the next century, we must counter the millennial discourses that would decontextualize our flesh into insensate sign or digitize it into cyberspace" (ibid.: 209). She warns that "if we don't keep this subjective kind of bodily sense in mind as we negotiate our techno-culture, then we, like Vaughan, like Baudrillard, will objectify ourselves to death" (1991: 329). Her impassioned point is well taken. Yet to conflate Baudrillard with Vaughan is to misread the pulse of the issue, since to attack Baudrillard is to assault a decoy. To criticize an *acknowledgment* that such a tendency exists—no matter how cynical or complicit it may be—is something akin to moral censorship, because it condemns the source of such urges instead of seeking its meaning. Ballard's book continues to fascinate precisely because it both condemns *and* romanticizes a cyborgian sexuality. Ethical politics do not thrive in ambivalent spaces, of which *Crash* is a prime example. Does this mean we should vilify it?

Brooks Landon admits that Ballard's text is something of an endurance test for more than the intellect: "Reading *Crash* makes my knees hurt, my teeth ache, my skin crawl, my stomach churn, my balls shrivel because—God help me—the book is so perfectly, so threateningly *right*, even (gulp) *normal*" (327). Such bodily reactions say a great deal about its dionysian affiliations. So long as a body is connected to the brain that reads it, *Crash* will have a visceral impact. Baudrillard's "obscenity" was to take the text's terms too far: by overemphasizing the technological over the organic, he thereby scatters the seeds of a "transgressive conservatism." The mistake made by his critics, on the other hand, is to overemphasize a lingering morality in Ballard's text, and thereby to neglect the nihilistic power of its amoral world. Hopefully a nascent politics of exhaustion can be forged between these antagonistic perspectives on technophilic millenarianism.

Who could deny, however, that by faithfully following the trajectory of western culture to its technological (near) conclusion, *Crash* continues the libertine and decadent legacy? By updating its themes within a familiar dionysian constellation, *Crash* perpetuates the cult of the artificial, the eroticism of the machine, and the libidinal tang of apocalypse.

Technol-orgy: From Autogeddon to Infocalypse

> Our atrocity, the one that distinguishes us from all others, is the act of gathering the pieces and running them through a computer to establish the identity of the dead.
>
> Baudrillard (1983: 43)

> It's all kind of paranoid and audio-visual.

Cherry 2000

Crash introduces us to Ballard's vision of *Autogeddon:* a vast, orgasmic car-crash:

> The passengers in the airliners lifting away from the airport were fleeing the disaster area, escaping from this coming Autogeddon. These premonitions of disaster remained with me. During my first days at home I spent all my time on the veranda, watching the traffic move along the motorway, determined to spot the first signs of this end of the world by automobile, for which the accident had been my own private rehearsal. (41)

Autogeddon is Ballard's millenarian vision of the urban landscape in the twentieth century, which increasingly was "being created by and for the car" (1996: 262). In case his readers miss the apocalyptic flavor of this concept, Ballard refers to "another cargo of eager victims—one almost expects to see Breughel and Hieronymus Bosch cruising the freeways in their rental company cars" (42). In cosmological terms, it is the *big prang:* the collective extension of that drive-in *rite de passage* that turns the backseat of cars into "upholstered altars on which virginity is ritually sacrificed" (Dery, 190). Yet for those characters who inhabit the universe of *Crash,* Autogeddon is a spectacular cyborgy, which is to be encouraged rather than avoided.

Vaughan fantasizes with libidinal fervor about the arrival of Autogeddon: "In his mind Vaughan saw the whole world dying in a simultaneous automobile disaster, millions of vehicles hurled together in a terminal congress of spurting loins and engine coolant" (13). He is not the only one to experience orgiastic anticipation, for everybody contaminated by the collision is aroused in some sense. Baudrillard—never one to pass up the possibility of an orgy—quotes the passage in which a large group of people witness an accident. Responsive to the "pervasive sexuality [which] filled the air," they feel like "members of a congregation leaving after a sermon urging us to celebrate our sexualities with friends and strangers, and were driving into the night to imitate the bloody eucharist we had observed with the most unlikely partners" (1991: 319). The gore-stained wreckage becomes a catalyst for a heightened dionysian awareness. Vaughan is thus both a martyr *and* a satyr of the super-highways; a "Maldoror of the motorways" (Juno 140).

All of this serves to remind us that—like previous millenarian prophecies—Autogeddon has failed to arrive on schedule, and thus we must look elsewhere for the end. Ballard deplores the passing of the car and the "old-fashioned" idea of freedom it enshrined. "In terms of pollution, noise and human life the price of that freedom may be high," he concedes. "But perhaps the car, by the very muddle and congestion it causes, may be holding back the remorseless spread of the regimented, electronic society" (1996: 266). In identifying this encroaching evil, he anticipates the next panic site of apocalyptic rhetoric.

Knowing enough about history to assume that his vision of Autogeddon will be superseded, Ballard begins to map the way in which the age of the automobile gives way to the "mysterious scenarios of computer circuitry" (1975: 154): "The wounds on my knees and chest were beacons tuned to a series of beckoning transmitters, carrying the signals, unknown to myself, which would unlock this immense stasis and free these drivers for the real destinations set for their vehicles, the paradises of the electric highway" (ibid.: 44).

Both the car and the film-projector have collaborated to colonize Western minds in the post-war period. Today, this process is replicated in the domestic space of the computer workstation. The premating ritual of sitting shoulder to shoulder and staring straight ahead at some "reel time" spectacle—whether on the movie screen or through a windscreen—confers on speed itself a libidinal inevitability. As Linda Grant notes, "we're so frightened of sex that the only way we can involve ourselves with it is separated by a sheet of glass" (266). The unfolding complicity between the car and the projector, as witnessed in cybersex, conceals the (profoundly phallocentric) desire either to crash through the hymenlike impenetrability of the screen, or—as Benjamin would put it—to witness the car careen out of the screen and into "reality."

In *Crash,* slow-motion replays of crash-tests first soothe and then arouse the narrator. Television cables carry dystopian images that act as aphrodisiacs to the jaded palates of James Ballard and his wife, who distractedly consume

> [a]ll those scenes of pain and violence that illuminated the margins of our lives—television newsreels of wars and student riots, natural disasters and police brutality which we vaguely watched on the colour TV set in our bedroom as we masturbated each other. This violence experienced at *so many removes* had become intimately associated with our sex acts. The beatings and burnings married in our minds with the delicious tremors of our erectile tissues, the spilt blood of students with the genital fluids that irrigated our fingers and mouths. (30—my emphasis)

Traditional warnings against the evils of mediation reach an ironic zenith in this portrait of "the most terrifying casualty of the century: the death of affect" (Juno et al. 96).

The Pan-opticon becomes inverted by the citizen of the society of the spectacle. ("The spectacle is the ultimate commodity in that it makes all others possible"—Bukatman 37.) Where the subject once experienced itself as the object of surveillance, now, through the penetrating presence of technology, the subject is the all-seeing center in a scopophilic organization of the senses. The possibility of libidinal burnout is thus heightened through information overload, the "deadening effect of the mass media" (Guattari 5).

The inherently Apollonian process of vision ensures that such scopophilic investments are "not libidinal tropisms like any other, but compromises; coaxing drives into the domesticated state associated with representation," ultimately funneled into the market (Land 70). Yet in our image-saturated society, this "compromise" has usurped all other libidinal possibilities. As a consequence, the schism between vision and "experience" becomes the locus of erotic pleasure in an alienating spiral that coils increasingly, and frustratingly, around the self.

Virilio's "museum of accidents" (also known as "television") thus coincides with Ballard's "atrocity exhibition" (also known as "the crash"). Hence, due to our "second and colder consciousness," shock—like panic—appears anachronistic, for we are too seduced and tranquillized by mediated stimuli to react in such nineteenth-century modes. "Nothing's shocking," insists Perry Farrell, a musician described by *Spin* magazine as "Dionysian."

Susan Buck-Morss comments on Jünger's belief that this "second" consciousness is intimately connected to photography, because the camera lens is an

> "artificial eye" which "arrests the bullet in flight just as it does the human being at the instant of being torn to pieces by an explosion." The powerfully prosthetic sense organs of technology are the new "ego" of a transformed synaesthetic system. Now they provide the porous surface between inner and outer, both perceptual organ and mechanism of defense. Technology as a tool and a weapon extends human power—at the same time intensifying the vulnerability of what Benjamin called "the tiny, fragile human body"—and thereby produces a counter-need, to use technology as a protective shield against the "colder order" that it creates. (138-139)

Vaughan fastidiously enacts Walter Benjamin's observation that humanity's "self-alienation has reached such a degree that it can experience its own destruction as an aesthetic pleasure of the first order" (1992: 235). In *Crash* the ultimate conclusion of this alienated "colder order" is mass suicide by automobile. Autogeddon is thus not only the tragic unfolding of this claustrophobic and profane world, but also its exit. When his car launches off the freeway, Vaughan's extinction is just another site where a transgressive act spills over into the more general desire for "experiential transcendence" (Chidester xi).

Vaughan thus seeks to get up enough speed to reach escape velocity. In the context of Ballard's persistent literary efforts to bring the world to an end (*The Drowned World, The Drought, The Crystal World,* etc.), the redemptive agenda of *Crash* detaches itself from the colorless horizon of the Shepparton highways. As Ballard reminds us, "we're all looking for some sort of vertical route out of the particular concrete jungle that we live in" (Juno et al. 164).

Yet the crash-site enshrines a sobering reminder of mortality's painful relationship to transcendence:

> I stared down at this dusty necklace, the debris of a thousand automobile accidents. Within fifty years, as more and more cars collided here, the glass fragments would form a sizable bar, within thirty years a beach of sharp crystal. A new race of beachcombers might appear, squatting on these heaps of fractured windshields, sifting them for cigarette butts, spent condoms and loose coins. Buried beneath this new geological layer laid down by the age of the automobile accident would be my own small death, as anonymous as a vitrified scar in a fossil tree. (Ballard, 1975: 47)

Crash's pornographic depiction of disaster-footage thus points to television (and to its multimedia heirs) as that vector of violence that ultimately—or should that be *soon*?—replace the asphalt roads as the biggest killer in industrialized nations. Fully aware of the possibilities facing the next generation, Ballard ensures that "Vaughan's transgressive car crashes have been superseded by the kinetic appropriation of cyberspace" (Bukatman 294).

What does this mean for someone in front of a computer screen rather than behind a windscreen? What happens when we are so fused with the machine that it does not so much shatter around us, but inside us, as part of us? Just as Ballard's vision of Autogeddon anticipates its own updating in Neal Stephenson's concept of the Infocalypse, the macro-spectacle of *Crash* becomes the micromillennial meltdown of *Snow Crash*.

Snow Crash and Scopophilia

> Hiro's father, who was stationed in Japan for many years, was obsessed with cameras. He kept bringing them back from his stints in the Far East, encased in many protective layers, so that when he

> took them out to show Hiro, it was like watching an exquisite striptease as they emerged from all that black leather and nylon, zippers and straps. And once the lens was finally exposed, pure geometric equation made real, so powerful and vulnerable at once, Hiro could only think it was like nuzzling through skirts and lingerie and outer labia and inner labia . . . . It made him feel naked and weak and brave.
>
> Neal Stephenson, *Snow Crash* (23)

Vaughan is rarely seen without a camera. It is the conductive medium through which all his abject obsessions flow. In our society of the spectacle, the camera is *the* essential scopophilic tool. The narrator of *Crash* remembers Vaughan at night with "nervous young women in the crushed rear compartments of abandoned cars in breakers' yards, and their photographs in the postures of uneasy sex acts. Their tight faces and strained thighs were lit by his polaroid flash, like startled survivors of a submarine disaster" (7).[15]

Vaughan's fetishistic universe produces, "magnified sections of lip and eyebrow, elbow and cleavage [that] formed a broken mosaic" (ibid.). He uses celluloid to cut women up in the sinister simulation of car accidents. Discussing the crucial role of the camera in *Crash*, Baudrillard notes that "the added depth and the raising of the visual medium to the second order can, by itself, suffice to fuse together technology, sex and death" (1991: 317).

In the epigraph to this section, the protagonist of Stephenson's *Snow Crash* (appropriately named Hiro Protagonist) not only fetishizes the camera, but deflects the gaze back onto the site of its own production. This maneuver is the same as that made by Des Esseintes in *A Rebours* when he eroticizes the train instead of the journey. As a child of the spectacular society, Hiro discovers the metapleasures of lens-lust. His world is the twenty-first century, and thus Hiro takes for granted both the flattening of emotion and the two-dimensional bodies of the photographed. In the urban metropolis, the sign itself is paramount, so that the sexy billboard-body is experienced as more real than the model's "actual" flesh-and-blood body. "The generation by [super]models of a real without origin or reality" (Baudrillard in Ruddick 360) thus enables the hyperreal to erase the real.

Here we see the conditions that culminate in "death fashion" (as discussed in chapter 6). This convergence between nihilism and capitalism recalls Virilio's assertion that "to link beauty and murder is to create an impasse, a no-way-out situation; it is to stimulate the desire to destroy the world, to 'finish it off'" (1995: 19). An example of this millenarian trend in the marketplace is a 1995 advertisement for Diesel Clothing, which depicts a four-car pileup. All the victims are young, attractive, impeccably dressed, and strewn over the road in various states of death or injury.

Kathleen Woodward has noted the "beguiling, almost mesmerizing relationship between the progressive vanishing of the body . . . and the hypervisuality of both the society of the spectacle and . . . the psychic world of cyberspace" (Sobchack, 1995: 211). *Snow Crash* acknowledges this relationship by introducing the simulated bodies of "avatars" in virtual space before dragging the narrative back into the real world of the flesh. Stephenson thus replaces Gibson's Cyberspace with the Metaverse. In this more pragmatic and prosaic rendering of tomorrow's Internet, hackers are no longer merely disembodied digital flows. Instead, they strut around as avatars—software simulations of their own bodies in varying degrees of likeness, depending on how much they can afford and how good they are at programming.

In a time when human roadkill litter the privatized streets, the Metaverse is a virtual space with relative freedom of movement. When it was first designed, computer-literate people treated the Metaverse as a cyberplayground or electronic Eden, and continued to do so until the general public began to infiltrate their final frontier:

> [O]nce the Metaverse began to fill up with obstacles that you could run into, the job of traveling across it at high speed suddenly became more interesting. Maneuverability became an issue. Size became an issue. Hiro and Da5id and the rest of them began to switch away from the enormous, bizarre vehicles they had favored at first—Victorian houses on tank treads, rolling ocean liners, mile-wide crystalline spheres, flaming chariots drawn by dragons —in favor of small maneuverable vehicles. Motorcycles basically. (354)

At first the Metaverse is likened to Paradise before the Fall. What destroys it is not an apple but a hypercard, a contaminated piece of software which, once "opened" by the avatar of a hacker, infects the binary "bio-ware" of the brain, and spectacularly "snow-crashes" their system. The snow-crash virus is a bit-map, "a series of white and black pixels, where white represents zero and black represents one" (351). Consequently, computer programmers are particularly vulnerable, since years of binary coding have formed deeply dichotomous structures in their neocortexes. As one character notes, "The corporate assembly line hackers are suckers for infection. They're going to go down by the thousands, just like Sennacherib's army before the walls of Jerusalem" (126).

(The concept of "language as a virus," on which William

Bourroughs based his oeuvre, is as old as *The Iliad,* which describes Proteus as sending Bellerophon to Lycia with "signs of disastrous meaning, many lethal marks that he wrote in a folded tablet, and told him to show them to his father-in-law, to ensure his death" (Virilio, 1995: 27). Gibson's Black Ice security software—a "kind of neural-feedback weapon"—also kills those who come into contact with it like "some hideous Word that eats the mind from the inside out" (1995: 210).

The disastrous effects of this snow-crash virus confirms Schivelbusch's observation that the more efficient the technology, the more catastrophic its destruction when it collapses (133). Hiro meditates on the implications of an impending digital plague:

> It serves them right, he realizes now. They made the place too vulnerable. They figured that the worst thing that could happen was that a virus might get transferred into your computer and force you to ungoggle and reboot your system. Maybe destroy a little data if you were stupid enough not to install any medicine. Therefore, the Metaverse is wide open and undefended, like airports in the days before bombs and metal detectors, like elementary schools in the days before maniacs with assault rifles. (351)

Before the advent of snow-crash, victims of a (virtual) fatal situation would be kicked off the system and then have to cope with the bother of logging on again. This was the closest simulation of death in the Metaverse. But once the snow-crash virus has been introduced, the phrase "my system crashed" acquires more sinister implications. For when your computer crashes, so does your brain. The logical outcome of such a symbiotic relationship is what Bukatman calls a "terminal identity":

> If Hiro reaches out and takes the hypercard, then the data it represents will be transferred from this guy's system into Hiro's computer. Hiro, naturally, wouldn't touch it under any circumstances, any more than you would take a free syringe from a stranger in Times Square and jab it into your neck . . .
> "Does it fuck up your brain?" Hiro says. "Or your computer?"
> "Both. Neither. What's the difference?" (44)

In realizing the catastrophic potential of software, Stephenson not only complements Virilio's vision of the computer as a bomb, but also continues the genealogy that links steam to electricity. "At the beginning," says a systems and software engineer, "anyone who could weld metal was putting steam engines together and they were exploding and killing people all over the place. There was no science of metallurgy. Software is in that phase now" (Robotham

12). Stephenson depicts the next step, at which software becomes dangerous not because of accidents, but because it can be used by terrorists, thereby viewing the Internet as a potential parasite preying on the human nervous system. *Snow Crash* thus fulfills *Crash*'s urge to meld with the machine, and shows how this leaves us vulnerable to our own perverted infections.

So what exactly is "snow crash," and where does it come from? In constructing a complex and layered genealogy throughout his book, Stephenson traces the history of European civilization and language back to a Sumerian "metavirus." Transmitted through language and culture, it also resides physically inside the brain like the herpes virus. On account of its Darwinian resilience, the metavirus comes in many forms, including its newest incarnation in digital binary code: the snow crash. It is thus the "the atomic bomb of informational warfare—a virus that causes any system to infect itself with new viruses" (200). Stephenson reconciles the biological with the semiotic by routing transmission through the eyes and into the brain. In doing so, he opposes Descartes's cyborg cheerleaders, reminding us that the consequences of technology are always suffered by human bodies, no matter how neglected, despised, and denied.

Scientists often wonder where virulent strains go when they are not wreaking havoc on the general populace. A case in point is the Ebola virus, which emerges every few years only to "disappear" again completely. Stephenson's metavirus lies dormant in that reservoir of ur-language, the universal biological communication code. This ur-language can be accessed or unleashed through "glossolalia," or speaking in tongues: "The twentieth century's mass media, high literacy rates, and high-speed transportation all served as superb vectors for the infection. In a packed revival hall or a Third World refugee encampment, glossolalia spread from one person to the next as fast as panic" (403).[16]

Such virulence questions the plausibility of our own survival. If this metavirus has been with us since the Sumerians, why haven't we been wiped out already? What has spared us from "Infocalypse"? Stephenson's theory resembles Baudrillard's paradoxical belief that a plague cannot survive by "totaling" a system—if a virus is 100 percent virulent it will become extinct for lack of a host. Humanity's natural immunity to the metavirus is provided by "the Babel factor":

> Like mass hysteria. Or a tune that gets into your head that you keep on humming all day until you spread it to someone else. Jokes. Urban legends. Crackpot religions. Marxism. No matter how smart we get, there is always this deep irrational part that makes us potential hosts for self-replicating information . . . .

> The only thing that keeps these things from taking over the world is the Babel factor – the walls of mutual incomprehension that compartmentalize the human race and stop the spread of viruses. (400)

Both the metavirus, and language itself, thus spread through society by means of glossolalia, blood transfusions, and fiber-optic cables. The snow-crash strain, transmitted electronically through the twenty-first-century Internet, is therefore susceptible to "accidents" as defined by Norman Tabachnick, M.D. and his colleagues in the case of car-crashes: "An accident involves a transfer of physical (or chemical, or thermal, or electrical) energy between two separate reservoirs of energy," they write. "People . . . can be damaged or destroyed when something without much resilience hits them with great force or when something very hot or highly charged with electrical energy comes into contact with them" (xii).

Snow crash falls within the bounds of such a definition: "Snow crash is computer lingo. It means a system crash—a bug—at such a fundamental level that it frags the part of the computer that controls the electron beam in the monitor, making it spray wildly across the screen, turning the perfect gridwork of pixels into a gyrating blizzard" (42). This recalls Ballard's description of Vaughan's "semen emptying across the luminescent dials that registered forever the last temperature and fuel levels of the engine" (1975: 6). Both writers portray digital disfunction and biological excess in ejaculatory terms; Ballard literally, and Stephenson metaphorically (a particularly significant point if we recall Derrida's libidinal reading of Revelation).

Within the logic of the narrative, the Babel factor thus plays the same role in *Snow Crash* as the accident does in *Crash*. It impedes "incessant circulation" by functioning like a spermicide to prevent the *dissemination* of information. Yet since hackers of all nations speak the same language (if in different dialects), the Babel factor cannot protect the Metaverse. As Baudrillard warns, "virtual languages" are ways of reinventing "anti-Babel, the universal language, the true Babylon, where all languages are confounded and prostituted one to another" (1996: 90-91). The possibility of highway Autogeddon is thus mirrored by the immanence of superhighway Infocalypse.

Cyborgies in the Dionysian Landscape

> [T]he virtual camera is in our heads. No need of a medium to reflect our problems in real time: every existence is telepresent to itself.
>
> Baudrillard (1996: 26)

> Now, not everyone has the good fortune to be a machine.
>
> Baudrillard (1996: 84)

One advantage of cybersex—acknowledged by critics and supporters alike—is its apparent immunity to Sexually Transmitted Diseases. Yet the existence of computer viruses suggests that this may be just another conceptual Eden waiting for its Fall. If a snow-crash-like virus were to become a reality, then cybersex would carry all the risks of bodily contacts. Such a possibility plugs into those tales of mass contagion that have inspired millennial fever from the Earl of Shaftesbury to Stephenson.

Consider Ng, another *Snow Crash* character. He was severely injured in a helicopter crash during the Vietnam war, and now spends his whole life inside an enormous truck that roams the highways and byways of the post-Ballardian landscape. Whereas Vaughan experienced psycho-symbiosis with his vehicle, Ng has actually merged with his truck in a cyborg relationship of interdependency: "Where the driver's seat ought to be, there is a sort of neoprene pouch about the size of a garbage can suspended from the ceiling by a web of straps, shock cords, tubes, wires, fiber-optic cables, and hydraulic lines" (225). Living inside this pouch like some kind of cyber-marsupial, Ng terrorizes the roads in the tradition of *Convoy* (1978) and *Mad Max: Road Warrior* (1979). "America is wonderful because you can get anything on a drive-thru basis," he remarks. "So this vehicle is much better than a tiny pathetic wheelchair. It is an extension of my body" (226).

To recall Des Esseintes's "virtual chair" is to clarify the links between imagination and artifice, scopophilia and technology. According to Rodolphe Gasché, Des Esseintes occupies a world in which he "can withdraw from all aggressions and solidly sensual acts, a world where sensuous desires are satisfied by illusions and ingenious trickery, which *alter in turn the nature of these desires themselves*" (194—my emphasis). Prosthetically enhanced, Ng is heir to Des Esseintes's armchair, while his pouch allows him access to the Metaverse, where he frequents a Japanese harem.

His crippled torso floats in some kind of "pleasure gel," which simulates the movements of his virtual concubines. Luckily for him, Ng was never a hacker, and so is not susceptible to the snow-crash virus. For now at least, he can indulge in his cybersexual fantasies without fear of contagion.

The prospect of human beings in different parts of the world dressed in teledildonic data-suits and thrusting into empty air strikes many people as both pathetic and surreal. Nevertheless, it has inflamed the erotic imaginations of such diverse groups as corporate designers, filmmakers, postmodern theorists, compulsive onanists, and cyber-Dionysians (plus combinations thereof). Gerard Van Der Leun calls sex "a virus that almost always infects new technology first" (Dery, 218). This view is confirmed by Mike Saenz, who designs X-rated and interactive CD-ROMS. "Lust motivates technology," he says. "The first personal robots, let's face it, are not going to be bought to bring people drinks" (ibid.).

The 1987 science-fiction movie, *Cherry 2000,* takes its title from a technologically sophisticated pleasure-cyborg, whose lack of conversational skills is compensated for by the best sexual technique that Silicon Valley has to offer. According to one particularly sleazy character, her behavior in the bedroom is "like slammin' an octopus." Not being waterproof, she unfortunately short-circuits during a particularly amorous encounter with her "husband," Sam Treadwell, on the sud-soaked kitchen floor: "sorry kid, total internal meltdown." Although he could buy any replacement model he chooses—the Bambi 14 ("brand new, never been used") or the Cindy 990 ("strictly domestic actually . . . below the waist, no-man's land") —Sam romanticizes about the Cherry 2000, believing himself to be in love with her "intangible" qualities. Unfortunately he must go into the Lawless Zone in order to retrieve another compatible synthetic body before he can install her microchip—that tiny disc on which her (albeit limited) personality is digitally encoded.

Cherry 2000 thus extends James Ballard's description of his wife's (presumably nonsilicon) breasts as prime examples of "soft technology" (27).[17] Twenty-first-century urban mating-rituals are portrayed as highly mediated: every sexual encounter between actual humans is computer-simulated beforehand, and then agreed to on a contractual basis. Needless to say, spontaneity is one of the first casualties of this artificial, alienating, and legally binding system. Real women are presented as alternatively confrontational, shrill, or demanding, which is why Sam Treadwell believes in the relative authenticity, not to mention the 1950s' compliance, of his Cherry 2000.

The link between women and technology in the masculinist imaginary, discussed by McLuhan in his chapter, "Motorcar: The

Mechanical Bride," from *Understanding Media* (1974), is thematized as the film unfolds. The sex-bot's body is referred to as "the chassis," while one particular model – praised for its "craftsmanship, diskdrive and pelvic-roll" evokes nostalgia for the days "when Detroit still cared." To mention the car capital of America in the context of computer hardware is to emphasize not only the symbolic affiliation between these two technologies but also the libidinal investments that sustain and articulate their more mundane applications. Although the Cherry 2000 is an "advanced" fantasy in the 1980s, in the year 2017 she has become "a thing of the past . . . . They don't make 'em like this anymore." The temporal slippage effected by this futuristic anachronism is to remind us that, with the right tools and technology, the mode of reproduction can create works of art which—contra Benjamin—actually *do* have the aura of originals.

Although present technology is not yet advanced enough to produce a Cherry-like cyborg, that goal is already on the agenda of today's marketeers. The "RealDoll" web site offers glorified blow-up dolls, made out of silicon and articulated steel skeletons, for around $4,500. They have names like *Stacy* and *Julie*, and according to the company's feedback-section perform miracles in the bedroom. After allegedly having sex on air with his RealDoll, the radio personality Howard Stern echoed Sam Treadwell's feelings on this matter: "Best sex I ever had! I swear to god! This RealDoll feels better than a real woman! She's fantastic! I love her!" (http://www.realdoll.com).

René Descartes himself allegedly owned a female automaton called "Francine", however we'll never know the feelings he had for his proto-Cherry. It is possible, however, that Sam is negotiating the same philosophical problems concerning sexuality, identity, knowledge, and truth. To his detractors, Sam insists that "there was romance" in his sexual encounters with his cybernetic companion, who had "a dreamlike quality about her." The film's ultimate message, however—conveyed through Sam's protracted seduction by E. Johnson, the "real" female tracker—is that "there's a lot more to love than hotwiring."

Such new configurations of libidinal technology provoke many questions concerning authenticity, morality, and mediation. For instance, what would Vaughan have made of virtual reality and cybersex? Would he have used it to exploit his autoerotic fantasies, crashing again and again into an avatar of Elizabeth Taylor in order to experience it from every possible angle without actually dying? His love of car-porn suggests that he would.

Long before the term *cybersex* was coined, Ballard (with customary prescience) expressed his belief

> that organic sex, body against body, skin area against skin area, is becoming no longer possible, simply because if anything is to have any meaning for us it must take place in terms of the values and experiences of the media landscape, the violent landscape—this sort of Dionysiac landscape of the 1970s . . . . We've got to recognize that what one sees through the window of the TV screen is as important as what one sees through a window on the street (Juno et al. 157).

This Dionysiac landscape has only intensified from the 1970s to the present, so that people are still obsessed with Ballard's famous equation, "sex times technology equals the future" (ibid.: 164).

Ballard thus saw the car-crash as a "liberation of human and machine libido," completing the cathartic function of the media. The sterile bloodletting that is screened (in both senses) daily in our lounge-rooms then swivels between Sadean and Bataillean versions of simulated sacrifice. Ballard goes on to raise "the possibility of Vietnam having some good effects, or of car crashes serving a useful purpose within the societal organism, or of a purgative aspect to the assassination of public figures, just as there used to be in ancient ritual murders, and always has been in the death of charismatic figures" (ibid.: 154).

The most famous car crash of the century killed Princess Diana. When news broke—in the pre-millennial year of 1997—that the princess had died in a Mercedes Benz speeding at 196 kilometres per hour, shockwaves extended through the fiber-optic tentacles of the mass media. The first news reports were an unconscious herald that Autogeddon had finally arrived. Blame focused initially on the paparazzi, who chased her and billionaire boyfriend, Dodi Al Fayed, into the treacherous Parisian tunnel; and this anger was maintained despite the revelation that the chauffeur had been both criminally drunk and unlicensed at the time. Public anger soon fused with guilt as the realization dawned on the people that their insatiable appetite for pictures of the princess had fed the supply-and-demand spiral that eventually hounded the princess to death.

In the first few days after the accident, self-flagellation by both the media and the public became part of the mourning process. What Haraway has called "the deeply predatory nature of a photographic consciousness" (1985: 89) rebounded back on to the global readership: the sacrifice had left blood on the hands of everyone but the "innocent" princess. Seeing that Diana was the most photographed person on the planet, the Chinese maxim, "to have your picture taken shortens your life" seemed to have come to its logical conclusion.

Any notion that the princess's death was cathartic, had "some good effects," or was the source of "*collective* satisfaction"

(Baudrillard, 1993: 165), would be reviled by the millions of mourners at her state funeral in London. There is little doubt, however, that the scopophilic logic that helped cause the accident in the first place reverberated on a symbolic level throughout the following months during media autopsies of the event. Rolls of film snapped seconds after the moment of impact were said to capture a "beautiful" princess, trapped like a dying swan in the shell of twisted metal and shattered glass. In fact, Ballard's novel prefigures this cyber-Ophelia in depicting a female crash victim around whom "the entire car had deformed itself . . . in a gesture of homage" (93). Although, these photos were boycotted by magazines and newspapers fearful of an inevitable backlash, some of them were to surface in tabloids published outside England. They instantly acquired a mythical status and abject power over the nation: the masses were going to pay for their murderous curiosity by resisting the perverse pleasure of seeing their princess's terminal portrait.

Vaughan would no doubt have eroticized Diana's demise even more passionately than Jayne Mansfield's, for all the elements of his obsession were present in a heightened and hyperreal form. Unlike the crashes of James Dean, Albert Camus, or Princess Grace, the camera-eye was on the scene immediately—and not only as a witness, but as a major contributing factor. Its probing lens was pressed up to what little glass remained, finally snapping the trapped princess—perfectly still, perfectly compliant—in close-up: in death, the perfect model.

The speed of information, the speed of capital, and the speed of libidinal projection coalesced in the princess's sacrifice to her scopophilic subjects. In Ballard's terms, this crash was effectively willed into being by the unconscious groundswell of thanatic desire and erotic anxiety. For although the pornographic subtext of Diana's death was not acknowledged by either staunch royalists or by the chastised tabloids, it was taken for granted by the explosion of Internet sex-sites that first claimed to have the grisly paparazzi pictures (only to admit that they were just trying to attract attention to their banal wares). And those photographs continue to circulate, invisible or obscured, like Bataille's accursed share within Baudrillard's symbolic economy.

Virilio discusses the psychic crisis provided by Virtual Reality technologies, which create the impression that one could throw away one's eyes "and still be able to see." Because "we haven't adjusted yet, we are forgetting our body, we are losing it. This is the accident of the body" (Wilson). Nowadays, "the creation of a virtual image is a form of accident. This explains why virtual reality is a cosmic accident. It's the accident of the real" (ibid.). Hence, in our search for continuity we have thus gone beyond simulation, and split the real into "actual" and "virtual" dimensions: a profound existential break. Not content with splitting the atom—the very building blocks of matter—we also bisect real time, the fabric of consciousness. Can it be a coincidence that both occur at the end of the millennium?

The information age therefore operates with two dominant scopic models or metaphors for Western culture. One can be represented by the climactic scene of *2001: A Space Odyssey* (1968), the other by the United States' "smart bombs" of the Gulf War. The first shows a close-up of the astronaut Dave Bowman's eye as he is bombarded by images and information. (The vehicle he is traveling in is also ocular in shape.) He emerges through this experience, like Marinetti, an evolved being, having climbed up the next rung of humanity through a transcendent velocity. The second model is a camera-eye, which processes information right up to the moment it crashes and explodes. As Judith Butler notes, these weapons are

> a bomb with a camera attached in front, a kind of optical phallus; it relays that film back to a command control and that film is refilmed on television, effectively constituting the television screen and its viewer as the extended apparatus of the bomb itself. In this sense, by viewing we are bombing, identified with both bomber and bomb, flying through space, transported from the North American continent to Iraq, and yet securely wedged in the couch in one's own living room. (11)

As our fragile mammal brains try to decode signals beamed at us with increasing speed and accuracy, we find ourselves subject increasingly to Nordau's "organic wear and tear." Every generation believes that it stands at the apex of a culture that is accelerating exponentially. In the early eighteenth century, The Earl of Shaftesbury observed the negative pressure exerted "when the Ideas or Images received are too big for the narrow human vessel to contain" (53).

Like us, information wants to be free—free to crash in a thanatic, ecstatic and orgiastic confusion. "When everything rushes at man," writes Virilio,

> man-the-target is assailed on all sides, and our only salvation now is to be found in illusion, in flight from the reality of the moment, from the loss of free will whose advent Pascal evoked when he wrote, "Our senses cannot perceive extremes. Too much noise deafens us, too much light dazzles . . . . Extreme qualities are our enemies. We no longer feel anything; we suffer." (1995: 132)

Take, for instance, Kathryn Bigelow's movie, *Strange Days*

(1995). The harrowing rape scene—in which a woman is forced to experience the subjectivity of her murderer through VR technology —relates to the "smart bomb" or Princess Diana model of culture. Needless to say, it is the more nihilistic perspective. In this scene—which is essentially a reprise of Michael Powell's *Peeping Tom* (1960)—we witness the apocalyptic convergence of Ballard and Bataille.

The latter, whose most famous work followed a disembodied eye, did not address the violence of technologically mediated eroticism, whereas Ballard (who put the *car* into carnage and carnality) has prepared us for this terminal point in our "civilization." In Bigelow's metavoyeuristic rape scene, suicide and homicide, narcissism and onanism, converge in a libidinal feedback-loop that ultimately leads to the fragging of identity and the brain-fry of snow crash.

Virilio emphasizes the fact that although "people make fun of cybersex . . . it's really something to take into account: it is a drama, a split of the human being!" (Wilson). *Strange Days* is one of the first popular films to explore the implications of such a split. It follows one day in the life of Lenny, a dealer in SQID (Superconducting Quantum Interference Devices), who peddles real-life experiences recorded with highly sophisticated Pan-sensory equipment. These enable the (usually male) customer to virtually rob a store or become an eighteen-year-old girl taking a shower. His sales pitch insists that "[t]his is not like TV only better. This is life, it's a piece of somebody's life. It's pure and uncut, straight from the cerebral cortex. I mean you're there, you're doing it, you're seeing it . . . hearing it . . . feeling it. I'm the magic-man, the Santa Claus of the subconscious." Or as sceptics tell him, "You sell porno to wire-heads."

Bukatman has discussed the phenomenon of image addiction, which he believes "might be regarded as a primary symptom of terminal identity" (26). Indeed, he believes such intense dependence has become "the very condition of existence in postmodern culture" (69). The desperate behavior of Lenny's clients in *Strange Days* supports Burroughs's claim that the "[i]mage is a form of junk, an addictive substance that controls its user" (Bukatman 75). The consequences of "scoring," however, simultaneously display the millennial fear of penetration and infection: the image as both drug and virus. This "cybrid" seems to mutate in the public unconscious as fast as those postantibiotic superbugs in our oversterilized hospitals.

The events in *Strange Days* occur not on an ordinary day but on New Year's Eve, 1999—an appropriate time for Virilio's "big accident." Most of Lenny's customers (and indeed Lenny himself) forego the adrenaline rush of law-breaking for the dionysian rewards of orgiastic "experiences." The anchors of traditional morality begin to break loose with the advent of such disorienting technology. The popularity of these secondhand sexual transgressions, and the irrational violence they unleash, suggests that hi-tech progress has no trouble in outstripping ethics or "civilized" behavior. Once again, Pan is the goat in the machine (or so Bigelow would lead us to believe).

Strange Days supports Ballard's theory that if "violence, like pornography, is some kind of evolutionary standby system, a last-resort device for throwing a wild joker into the game," then a "widespread taste for pornography means that nature is alerting us to some threat of extinction" (Juno et al. 156). If so, we have the key coordinates of libidinal millenarianism, whereby a resurgent nature—traditionally represented by Pan (or Pan-like tricksters)—will escape from technological repression. As we shall soon see, *A Rebours'* Des Esseintes demonstrates his antagonism to nature by retreating into the virtual world of vicarious sensory experience. His fantasies are not explicitly libidinal because he is already tired of the libertine lifestyle. He lives after the orgy. The characters of *Strange Days*, on the other hand, are determined to recreate, rewind, and replay the elusive orgy, looking for answers to the future within its sadistic choreography.

Ballard again documents the implications of technological transgression:

> For the first time it will become truly possible to explore extensively and in depth the psychopathology of one's own life without fear of moral condemnation . . . . Many, perhaps most of these, need to be expressed in concrete forms, and their expression at present gets people into trouble. One can think of a million examples, but if your deviant impulses push you in the direction of molesting old ladies, or cutting girls' pigtails off in bus queues, then, quite rightly, you find yourself in the local magistrates court if you succumb to them . . . . But with the new multi-media potential of your own computerized TV studio, where limitless simulations can be played out in totally convincing style, one will be able to explore, in a wholly benign and harmless way, every type of impulse. (ibid.: 159)

The moral of *Strange Days*, however, is that such technology—far from being "wholly benign and harmless"—encourages violence against women in both realms. Ballard does not anticipate a blurring of the boundaries between actual and virtual realities: he assumes not only that they will remain discrete, but that we will be able to experience them as such. Consequently, Virilio's digital accident has enormous implications for our understanding of transgression and how it relates to the artificial. For when virtual reality becomes more powerful than actual reality, every transgression will have to be reassessed—legally, ethically, and metaphysically.

In a transgressive act, whether real or simulated, the subject experiences a tearing of the self, and briefly inhabits a liminal and unstable psychic space. Although the murder-rape scene in *Strange Days* causes nausea and panic in those who view it through the SQID, they nevertheless watch it to the end. Like the viewer of "smart bomb" technology, they are captivated by their "own" destruction. This is the ultimate thanatic asymptote.

In one of his *Doom Patrols* (1997), Steven Shaviro states that the Apocalypse

> may be called *virtual* (as when we speak of "virtual images") rather than *actual,* since it affects not the immediate experiential world but "the soul of the world, the world's dream of itself." But such a virtual event is perfectly real, as Deleuze repeatedly says, even if it isn't actual; the psychic apocalypse, like a neutron bomb, may leave physical structures untouched, but it turns human society into a collection of "dead shells, zombie cultures, shambling aimlessly towards oblivion."

Ballard's *Crash* anticipates its adaptation to the digital landscapes of the information revolution in the sense that virtual perception—whether through drugs or SQID trodes—are depicted as Trojan Horses that we willingly admit into our minds. A different drug, LSD, is taken by James Ballard to heighten his perception of impending impact: "This hyper-irritation reminded me of my own long recovery from a bad acid trip some years earlier, when I had felt for months afterwards as if a vent of hell had opened momentarily in my mind, as if the membranes of my brain had been exposed in some appalling crash" (165).

Many characters in *Strange Days* have a snow-crash-like ending to their image addiction, with their brains frying like eggs. The utopian promises of virtual reality are hijacked and warped into dystopian forms in the backstreets of Los Angeles, as an urge to transcend the limits of the self gives way to the violation of others. The implicit moral of *Strange Days* has the same heavily gendered liberal-humanistic agenda as *Cherry 2000*'s ultimatum: choose between the robobabe and the "real" woman. Both films thus romanticize unmediated sexual congress, displaying a nostalgia for skin against skin. As Baudrillard says, "contact (as in lenses)" (1990: 56). As if recalling Franz Kafka's apocalyptic vision of "souls who no longer have eyes but only eye sockets" (Virilio, 1995: 157), or the effects of the meteor-shower in John Wyndham's *Day of the Triffids*, these morality tales for the society of the spectacle dispense the traditional Victorian warning: "stop it, or you'll go blind."

Carmageddon

> The Pope will, of course, not have a hip like God made, but one that a bio-engineer made.
>
> Gianfranco Fineschi: orthopedic surgeon
> (*Big Issue,* London, May 1994: 4)

> Premises of the Machine Age.—The press, the machine, the railway, the telegraph are premises whose thousand-year conclusion no one yet has dared draw.
>
> Nietzsche's diary, 1880 (Waite 153)

I began this chapter by documenting some early reactions to train travel and to its perceived physical and mental stresses on the human organism. Nordau, for instance, attributed the "degeneration" of European stock partly to the unprecedented speed and potential violence of traveling by train. I have traced this thanatic asymptote to the primal scene of the accident, where the apocalyptic orgy lurks within the telos of *techné.*

Techné—Martin Heidegger's "danger that saves"—seems both *more* dangerous and *closer* to salvation in the symbolic space of our information age. As framed by Don DeLillo's *White Noise* (1985), "This is the whole point of technology. It creates an appetite for immortality on the one hand. It threatens universal extinction on the other. Technology is lust removed from nature" (285). As we reinternalize technology, we find that the natural and the artificial fuse once again—this time in the dionysian flux of (snow) crash. In this context, each new generation of the apocalyptic code is constricted by the flaws and bugs of the one before.

As I write there is a computer-game on the market called "Carmageddon", in which the object is to kill as many people as possible. Extra points are awarded for spectacular multiple homicides, and for sideswiping aged pedestrians. It is an antisocial example of Hakim Bey's Temporary Autonomous Zone, a virtual place in which people can enact ethically unsound urges without fear of the law. As an adrenaline-fueled footnote to Ballard's novel, it is the latest in a long line of decadent texts that "satyrize" the innuendo locked within technology's "standing reserve." The trick is to know when to save, before the game crashes itself and erases any evidence of progress.

If Pan is the goat in the machine, as I have repeatedly claimed, then he represents a digital refiguration of the Sadean perspective of nature—nature as mandate *and* prohibition, Eros *and* Thanatos, liberator *and* oppressor, master *and* servant. This premise does more than merely reconcile apparent opposites. It recognizes the impossibility of being "against nature." One can only be against *human* nature, that is to say, culture.

Each of the texts I have examined might be considered as a trace of DNA found on the corpse of God. From this molecular Dionysian-Nietzschean ambience, we can reconstruct a crime that rages against history, and yet constitutes the compost for its renewal. Ironically, the fearful anticipation of an apocalyptic end is thus the engine of history itself, which continues on its way like the battered participants in a crash derby.

The amnesiacal journalist, Steve Erickson, has written that "technology is the only faith remaining after politics and religion have betrayed us." Technology and sex will continue to converge "until a vague new sexual gestalt infiltrates the labyrinth of all our libidos, including those of us who stay the fuck away from the Internet" (53). The redemptive potential of technology, however, is less important than the epiphany created by its spectacular crash. This is why the blockbuster movie, *Speed* (1994), struck such a chord with audiences: it was a metaphor for their lives in a Kamikaze Culture, in which to dip below fifty miles an hour is to explode (see also Joseph Natoli's *Speeding to the Millennium* on this point). The task of the average young urbanite is to steer the deadly projectile of existence into "the highways of the mind" (McLuhan, 1974: 113). Yet even though we remain glued to our ergonomic chairs and seventeen-inch computer screens, physically not going anywhere at all, we nevertheless demand speed. We pay large sums of money to upgrade our processing *speed,* to buy more *time* so we don't have to stare at Microsoft's hourglass-cursor, which reminds us of our mortality by keeping us in digital limbo. As Baudrillard has said, "[a]t more than a hundred miles an hour, there's a presumption of eternity" (Ross 21).

4

Decaying Forward: Satiety and Society

Thunder against it. Complain that it is not poetic. Call it a period of transition and decadence.

Gustave Flaubert's entry for "Epoch (our)"
in his *Dictionary of Received Ideas*

In history as in nature, the rotten is the laboratory of life.

Karl Marx (Weiss, 90)

One of the most valuable documents about the nineteenth-century fin de siècle is Max Nordau's wide-ranging polemic, *Degeneration*. Published in German in 1892 as *Entartung,* and translated into English three years later, this book champions the progressivist liberal-humanism of its author against such classic decadent texts as J.-K. Huysmans's *A Rebours*. Offering a basic taxonomy of "degenerates," it classifies these "aberrant" people as either "mystics" or "egomaniacs," and identifies them as enemies of the Enlightenment project. The degenerate is treated with a clinical eye for dissection and diagnosis (indeed, Nordau was a physician). If we consider the Victorian context of his observations, it should come as no surprise that his prescriptions focus on symptoms rooted in various sexual pathologies. Nordau's importance stems from the fact that he argues against his age's libidinal millenarianism, while simultaneously perpetuating its terms and concerns.

Nordau compares the fin de siècle mood to "the impotent despair of a sick man, who feels himself dying by inches in the midst of an eternally living nature blooming insolently forever" (3). Sex and death are further intertwined when he describes this cultural pathology as equivalent to

> [t]he envy of a rich, hoary voluptuary, who sees a pair of young lovers making for a sequestered forest nook; it is the mortification of the exhausted and impotent refugee from a Florentine plague, seeking in an enchanted garden the experiences of a Decamerone, but striving in vain to snatch one more pleasure of sense from the uncertain hour. (ibid.)

Nordau's definitions of "healthy" and "sick" circle around a shared territory ("the uncertain hour"), which is both liminal and libidinal. All further diagnostic distinctions emerge from this highly charged and ambiguous rhetorical space.

Believing that eroticism "includes precisely the most characteristic and conspicuous phenomena of degeneration," Nordau cites Richard Wagner and other "higher degenerates" as exemplary victims of "erotic madness" (182). His Darwinian argument then traces this madness to two historical forces, which merge in the middle of the nineteenth century to create a degenerative effect in those who are too weak to assimilate change. The first force is time itself, which healthy men acknowledge as a force indifferent to human measuring systems, such as the calendar. The marking of time, however, nevertheless suggests to impressionable and mystically inclined minds the supernatural patterns of divine plans, pointing toward some kind of conclusion. Nordau argues that just because we have to know what day it is in order to conduct our daily business, we shouldn't instill the years with numerological significance. For him, the approaching twentieth century thus becomes burdened with the "childish" projections of fatalistic fantasies. This delusional tendency is further aggravated by the second historical force, namely, the rapid industrialization of Western Europe. Nordau argues that this unprecedented historical leap reinforces a sense of cultural acceleration, whether this is interpreted as directed toward a brighter future or a dark abyss.

The cultural effect of these combined forces is thus an overwhelming fatigue. The late nineteenth century inherited stress fractures caused by the exhaustion of the previous generation, which had to cope with "this enormous increase in organic expenditure" (39):

> Humanity can point to no century in which the inventions which penetrate so deeply, so tyrannically, into the life of every individual are crowded so thick as in ours . . . . The humblest village inhabitant has to-day a wider geographical horizon, more numerous and complex intellectual interests, than the prime minister of a petty, or even a second-rate state a century ago. If he do but read his paper, let it be the most innocent provincial rag, he takes part, certainly not by active interference and influence, but by a continuous receptive curiosity, in the thousand events which take place

> in all parts of the globe, and he interests himself simultaneously in the issue of a revolution in Chili, in a bush-war in East Africa, a massacre in North China, a famine in Russia, a street-row in Spain, an international exhibition in North America. A cook receives and sends more letters than a university professor did formerly, and a petty tradesman travels more and sees more countries and people than did the reigning prince of other times. (ibid.)

This extract provides a wealth of material on nascent forms of democratization, globalization and "future shock," all of which continue to inform public debates on cultural health at the beginning of the twenty-first century. Moreover, it points to an earlier "information revolution"—which ran parallel to the industrial revolution—anticipating today's "screen fatigue," "empathy burnout," Chronic Fatigue Syndrome, and other fin de siècle analogues.

Nordau preempts subsequent diagnoses on the social body:

> All these activities, however, even the simplest, involve an effort of the nervous system and a wearing of tissue. Every line we read or write, every human face we see, every conversation we carry on, every scene we perceive through the window of the flying express, sets in activity our sensory nerves and our brain centres. Even the little shocks of railway travelling, not perceived by consciousness, the perpetual noises, and the various sights in the streets of a large town, our suspense pending the sequel of progressing events, the constant expectation of the newspaper, of the postman, of visitors, cost our brains wear and tear. (ibid.)

According to Nordau's depiction of modernity, culture races ahead of its subjects in a macro-political version of jet lag, described as the process whereby "our stomachs cannot keep pace with the brain and nervous system" (ibid.). The decadent "aesthetic schools" of thought are represented as hysterical symptoms resulting from "the excessive organic wear and tear suffered by the nations through the immense demands on their activity, and through the rank growth of large towns" (43).

But this should not be mistaken for a sympathetic diagnosis, clearing the ground for some kind of social welfare program or policy change. Instead it merely confirms those processes of natural selection that necessitate the survival of the fittest.[18] Since Nordau believes that the bodies of the "less vigorous" fill the "ditches on the road of progress" (40), the targets of his contempt are degenerates who lie in those ditches, singing drunkenly to the stars.

Definitions of "decadence" are notoriously ambiguous. Decadence can be alternately Apollonian, Dionysian, Christian, pagan, masculine, feminine, chaotic, controlled, refined and/or debauched, depending on whom you choose to believe at the time. In his own definition, Mario Praz (1960) signals the inherently millenarian character of decadence as an attraction to disaster:

> The very ideas of Decadence, of immanent Divine punishment like the fire of Sodom, of the "cupio dissolvi," [the desire to dissolve], are perhaps no more than the extreme sadistic refinements of a *milieu* which was saturated to excess with complications of perversion.
>
> In process of time it has become possible to see that it was a question of mental attitude, of a momentary dizziness on the brink of a precipice, which, epidemic as it was, soon wore itself out . . . the year 1900 no more marked the date of a cataclysm than the year 1000. (1960: 416)

In his book on *Decadence and the Making of Modernism* (1995), David Weir cites the compelling definition, "decline at its peak" (174), after quoting the Russian poet Vyacheslav Ivanov on how decadence is "the feeling, at once oppressive and exalting, of being the last in a series" (5). The convergence of these two definitions—a kind of negative climax alongside a conflicting sense of finality—is where I begin my analysis of the nineteenth-century fin de siècle, particularly as it relates to Huysmans's *A Rebours.*

Much has been written about this book, often on account of its status as the singular artifact of "a one-man movement" and as what Brian Stableford calls "the Bible of would-be Decadents of all kinds" (1992: 1). The novel's slim narrative tells the story of a fatigued degenerate (in Nordau's terms) called Duc Jean des Esseintes, who isolates himself in a domestic version of Charles Baudelaire's "artificial paradise" in order to perversely enjoy the stagnation of self, outside and "against the grain" of Parisian social life and the planet's natural rhythms. (The decadent notion of "self" is complex, and revolves around the Baudelairean project of aestheticizing the self into an objet d'art through techniques of artifice. The "manufactured self" was to become less subversive, particularly after F. T. Marinetti, once its links with capitalistic subjectivity—the "self-made man"—were clarified. In other words, the artificial dandy is easily absorbed into the corporate cyborg.)

Like Sade's protagonists, Des Esseintes attempts to create his own "Temporary Autonomous Zone" (a notion I explore further in chapter 6) in order to act out his disgust with the tyranny of natural processes. Having found no satisfaction in the debaucheries of a decadent lifestyle, the duke withdraws into the neurotic sphere of his own libidinal solipsism, magnifying and distilling the ennui of the 1880s into an extremely idiosyncratic text. This decision could be seen as a particularly acute case of the more general "repetitious, masturbatory response to chronic, low-grade anxiety which leads in turn to boredom and guilty withdrawal" (Levin, 1996: 200). Des Esseintes cultivates black plants, which grow into ugly, tumorous shapes; he takes his meals by enema in order to thwart the natural design of the body; he thrives on illusion, courting ventriloquists and filling his aquarium with mechanical fish. If there was ever a character to represent a life "after the orgy" it is Des Esseintes.

David Weir notes that "the backward glance seems implicit in the concept of decadence: all is before, nothing is after" (5). Indeed, Des Esseintes seems to be merely killing time before he dies, since he doesn't have the courage to kill himself. But Weir goes on to refute such an interpretation, focusing instead on those dynamic properties which lurk in decadent works like dormant seeds. Indeed, he quotes Matei Calinescu, who reminds us that "[a] high degree of technological development appears perfectly compatible with an acute sense of decadence. The fact of progress is not denied, but increasingly large numbers of people experience the results of progress with an anguished sense of loss and alienation. Once again, progress *is* decadence and decadence *is* progress" (11). This seemingly paradoxical process enables Weir to claim that Huysmans influenced James Joyce and other modernists who radicalized literature in the first half of the twentieth century, and to reaffirm Herbert Marcuse's point that "the term 'decadent' far more denounces the genuinely progressive traits of a dying culture than the real factors of decay" (1986: 60).

Controversial in content, the form of *A Rebours* was equally troubling to readers who were disturbed by its flagrantly antinaturalist approach to representing time and the unfolding of events. Where Stendhal thought of the novel in general "as a mirror dragged along a highway" (Virilio, 1995: 44), Huysmans saw it as an inverted telescope connecting the navel to the vast, mouldy canvas of history. The story in *A Rebours* is less a sequence of episodes than a series of set pieces, which could be rearranged with no damage to the ensuing "plot." Some critics have been perceptive enough to see the book's lack of direction as an integral part of its thematic concerns, rather than as evidence of flawed technique. Indeed Weir draws on established scholarship to conclude that a sense of "overness at the outset" (94)—a kind of historical Doppler effect—is embedded into the very structure of *A Rebours*.

In identifying a *psychology of belatedness* (155) as an essentially decadent characteristic, Weir not only invokes Nordau's organic lag, but also echoes the claim that decadence "means no more than a morbid complacency in feeling oneself *passé*" (Weir 6).

"When the period at which a man of talent is condemned to live is dull and stupid," Des Esseintes confesses, "the artist is, unconsciously to himself, haunted by a sensation of morbid yearning for another century" (Huysmans 168). The duke's "postorgy" predicament thus testifies to the fact that the only thing worse than feeling that you missed the party is having actually *been* there and found that it wasn't so great. Unlike the Proustian principle, which would dominate Western literary models of time in the twentieth century, there is no nostalgia here for one's own past; instead, Des Esseintes yearns for another era, or so it would seem.

When *A Rebours* was first published, Barbey d'Aurevilly wrote that "for a decadent of that force to have been produced, and for something like M. Huysmans' book to have sprouted in the head of a human being, it would have to be necessary for us to have become what we are—a race in its final hour" (Weir 85). And yet, according to d'Aurevilly, this final hour had been stripped of its traditional significance before the Second Coming, because the fin de siècle was nothing more than "the dress rehearsal of the Last Judgement without king or god" (Shaffer 139).

In the late nineteenth century, the second law of thermodynamics seemed to have a cultural counterpart, signaled by an outbreak of malaise—the entropic heat-death of sociality. It prefigured Albert Einstein's theory of relativity, whereby time decreases in inverse proportion to velocity. As Nordau noted with genuine concern, "[w]e stand now in the midst of a severe mental epidemic; of a sort of black death of degeneration and hysteria, and it is natural that we should ask anxiously on all sides: 'What is to come next?'" (537).

Such anxieties about the end of history—coupled with a nostalgia for more poetic times—are familiar in the millennial discourses of our own times. The decadents were a species of apocalyptic harbinger, repeating the familiar "end is nigh" mantra, but with a new tone influenced by the Marquis de Sade, Arthur Schopenhauer and other nihilistic (i.e., more secular) philosophies of declining civilizations. Initially attracted to its anti-Christian rhetoric, Friedrich Nietzsche would renounce such intellectual posturing in his last published work, *Ecce Homo* (1888), as simply "the will to the end" (96).

While there are obvious parallels between then and now, Weir distinguishes between the laments of late-nineteenth-century aesthetes from the historical predicament of postmodernists:

> [S]omehow the cultural millennium never arrives, and the age that succeeds a decadent period is always decadent itself in turn. The postmodernist, multiculturalist condition expresses, I believe, the same paradoxical nostalgia for the millennium that Flaubert felt, except that now the old hope for a new cultural world seems

perpetually forestalled by the apocalypse of the past.

> Flaubert and Baudelaire both thought of decadence as transition; to them, their age was in decay, but at least it was decaying forward. (202)

Weir goes on to note that postmodernism is "engaged in an active pursuit of a prior condition in order to apprehend the present" (198). Indeed, he asks, "what is progress *now* but a desire to go backward to a time when it was possible to go forward? Progression à *rebours* illustrates that even those with the best intentions are destined for decadence" (203).

According to Weir, then, contemporary decadents pine for those days when the avant-garde was a distinct cultural force, and exhibited fertile regenerative powers precisely *through* its decadence, by decaying *forward*, in a kind of compost-effect. Des Esseintes, an important precursor to this dynamic energy, longed for a degenerative momentum located—for him—in late Roman times. (Indeed, à *rebours* can also be translated as "countdown," further complicating the relationship between anticipation and exhaustion.) In tracing the roots of modernism to the decadents, Weir presents degeneration and regeneration as the two poles in a cultural feedback loop that initially fosters progress, and then creates the *illusion* of progress. This relates to Marx's belief that "time is everything, man is nothing; he is no more than the carcase of time" (Brown, 1970: 272). Of course it also evokes his famous view that history repeats itself, the first time as tragedy, and the second time as farce. But what of the third, fourth, and fifth times? And what if it really began as a farce in the first place?

A particularly insightful essay by Rodolphe Gasché (1988) reconciles the differences between these two poles, and problematizes the notion that the last fin de siècle believed itself to be decaying forward. According to Gasché, the stagnation of history first occurred neither in Berlin in 1989, nor in Paris in the 1920s, but in Fontenay in 1881; the year in which Huysmans began work on *A Rebours*. (This book was not translated into English until 1922, although it is referred to in Oscar Wilde's *Picture of Dorian Gray* [1891] as a text with viral properties.)

By interpreting *A Rebours* as primarily a "wake over the essence of time" (189), Gasché fully exposes the latent *lateness* of Huysmans's text. Des Esseintes's self-isolation, coupled with his fetish for historical artifacts, is interpreted as the desire to experience change in its purest form, rather than as nostalgia for one "ideal" moment of history. This is in stark contrast to Nordau's argument that the world was changing too fast for its human population to keep pace. For Des

Esseintes, the emerging technologies do not represent cultural progress, but instead the ironic Sadean legacy of human obsolescence.

Gasché insists that Des Esseintes does not mourn past ages, and indeed Huysmans himself leaves the question open in a letter to a friend: "I do not care for the period in which I live, and . . . from time to time I seek an escape route into the 'beyond'" (Beaumont 60). This "beyond" is not constituted by the zeitgeist that produced his favourite authors or painters. Instead it relates to a "nostalgia for the present" (Jameson). Gasché characterizes it thus:

> Des Esseintes does not mourn past ages. Nor does he dream of a future that would resemble a past characterized by fullness and harmony. He is nostalgic of epochs that serve as a transition between other epochs. As they have no other substance than that of their fleeting time itself, they thus represent time and history in their purest form, as the very essence of change. (188)

Literally, Des Esseintes' emblematic historical consciousness "amounts to an end of time itself," so that the object of his nostalgia is "historical formation in general as a thing past" (189). To use a simplistic metaphor, Des Esseintes didn't so much miss the boat, as the stream that carried it. Looked at in this way, the theoretical lens of libidinal millenarianism can help us to avoid barnacled interpretations of decadence and degeneration as merely the excreta of progress. Linear and fatalistic histories, such as the Christian narrative of Revelation, are thus complicated by the decadent agenda. What does it mean to be "after" in an age of profound temporal confusion? By placing Des Esseintes's homage to the artificial in the context of an attempted "redemption from matter" (199), Gasché sees such a project as unfolding in the uncanny silence before the storm of twentieth-century politics. All of which prompts us to ask the question, If Huysmans did not see the world as decaying forward, where did he think it was heading?

De-fragging the Self

> Mystics, but especially ego-maniacs and filthy pseudo-realists, are enemies to society of the direst kind. Society must unconditionally defend itself against them . . . . There is no place among us for the lusting beast of prey; and if you dare return to us, we will pitilessly beat you to death with clubs.
>
> Nordau (557)

In separate letters to friends, Huysmans paints a couple of telling self-portraits. The first, composed during a break from writing *A Rebours*, reports, "[s]omething strange! Since we have been suffocating in this heat, the bit of old rag I have had in my pants these months has picked itself up, and here I am, fornicating away furiously. It must be the beginning of general paralysis, what else can it mean?" (Beaumont 49). Read on its own, this salacious confession conveys that nervous energy preceding total collapse that is a millenarian motif. When combined with the second portrait, however, it provides a conducting rod between decadence and the technological core of my topic: "Ah, such fine news: on the one hand I have a stomach upset and on the other, neuralgia. How inferior this human machine is, compared to man-made machines. They can be de-coked, unscrewed, oiled and parts replaced. Decidedly, nature is not a very wonderful thing" (Beaumont 76). Because Des Esseintes is practically impotent, the narrative of *A Rebours* is thoroughly post-coital. The only thing that excites his loins is hard artifice (technology) or soft artifice (illusion and simulacra). Anticipating the disorienting logic that would preoccupy much of Jean Baudrillard's work, Des Esseintes delights in the fact that any waterfall "can be imitated by the proper application of hydraulics, till there is no distinguishing the copy from the original" (22). This continuum between hard and soft artifice—united in the concept of *techné*—informs all libidinal millenarian practice.[19]

The logic of Nordau's "organic wear and tear" leads Des Esseintes to take his food via an enema: "his predilection for the artificial had now, and that without any initiative on his part, attained its supreme fulfillment! A man could hardly go farther; nourishment thus absorbed was surely the last aberration from the natural that could be committed" (9). The exhaustion of the body, combined with the exhaustion of all perverse possibilities, heralds a twofold apocalypse experienced as a personal crisis.

This Cartesian crisis—whereby the subject's mind rebels against the degeneration of his own body—climaxes in the teachings and behavior of the Heaven's Gate cult. Whereas many religions attribute bodily urges to the "foreign influence" of the flesh (as a kind of enemy within), Marshall Applewhite portrayed the body as a vehicle, a biological computer. Because this "container" had to be flushed out regularly in order to keep the mechanisms working, every week he administered Des Esseintes-like enemas to his followers: a combination of lemonade, cayenne pepper, and low-grade maple syrup.

This practice was portrayed by the media as a barbaric and pagan ritual. Yet to characterize it in this way is to obscure the fact that the ideologically loaded behavior of Des Esseintes and

Applewhite is a direct tributary of scientific worldviews. Eighteenth and nineteenth-century western science had the dual effect of "naturalizing" the body (we became highly evolved animals, not profane angels) while simultaneously "technologizing" the mind/body equation so that the human organism came to be seen as increasingly machinic. According to this model, the heart is no more than a pump, and the brain an advanced computer.

Long before Arnold Schwarzenegger appeared in *Terminator*, the human body was a cyborg, a techno-organic hybrid. This paved the way for a complex flow of ideas between proto-Freudian models of getting to "the root" of problems, and surgical metaphors suggesting that medicine is really just human mechanics. One implication is the possibility of disassembling the body in order to cleanse it of base sexual urges, whether through castration (as was the case with some Heaven's Gate disciples) or Huysmans's dream of decoking the self.

Gasché discusses Des Esseintes's painful dental experience in such terms:

> [S]ince the result of this operation is a joyful sensation of feeling "ten years younger and taking an interest in the most insignificant things" . . . spiritualization may reveal itself to be a function of a violent extraction of the lower material substratum, here a tooth, whose phallic symbolism is clearly stressed throughout the novel. What this episode establishes is that idealization in fact presupposes extraction, castration, or decapitation, in short, the removal of everything material and sensual from the body. (200)

This sensation was shared by at least one Heaven's Gate follower, who expressed his feeling of liberation after being surgically castrated (Gegax 39).

Huysmans is thus an important hinge between Sade's embrace of sexual artifice and the neomystic impulse to sublimate the sexual, surgically or otherwise. The orgiastic ramparts of Castle Silling are thus linked to the celibate workstations of Rancho Sante Fe.

The degenerate, as portrayed by Nordau, suffers from a pronounced sexual orientation, labeled *erotomania* (169). This affliction is diagnosed as symptomatic of the "morbid exhaustion" (43) of the fin de siècle, and is linked to the explosion (in both senses) of new technologies. The degenerate is depicted as a weak-minded mystic, trapped in a vicious cycle of perverse self-projection. Consequently,

> [h]e attains to a state of mind in which he divines mysterious relations among all possible objective phenomena, e.g., a railway train, the title of his newspaper, a piano on the one hand, and

> woman on the other; and feels emotions of an erotic nature at sights, words, odours, which would produce no such impressions on the mind of a sound person . . . . Hence it comes that in most cases mysticism distinctly takes on a decidedly erotic colouring, and the mystic, if he interprets his inchoate liminal presentations, always tends to ascribe to them an erotic import. (61)

It is thus significant that Richard Wagner—one of Nordau's "higher degenerates"—inspired Nietzsche's *The Birth of Tragedy (Through the Spirit of Music).* In 1872 Nietzsche was captivated by his compatriot's compositions, which he believed displayed the synthetic powers of the great Greek dramatists. But when Nietzsche became more positive and puritanical, his enthusiasm for the fragile condition of being "classically decadent" gave way to his promotion of progress over degeneration, and health over sickness. Wagner's vision of Art as the Sapphic ménage-à-trois of the Muses (Nordau 180) was altogether too romantic for the middle-aged Nietzsche, who detected in such metaphors the sentimental stench of the corpse of Christianity.

Although Weir believes that Nietzsche provided a "complete paradigm of antidecadence" (133), his writings nevertheless constitute the most comprehensive map for exploring decadence and its relation to art and history. With characteristic immodesty, Nietzsche claims to "have a subtler sense for signs of ascent and decline than any man has ever had" (1979: 39). Weir thus aligns himself with Camille Paglia in assuming that "decadent and Dionysian art are contraries." He goes on to state that

> Nietzsche does not *reject* decadence even though he sets himself against it. Rather, it is the decadent who rejects the Dionysian, and a key element of Dionysian art is the quality of overfulness or abundance that can *include* decline, decadence, negation . . . . Again, the decadent and the Dionysian are opposed, but it is the decadent who is "doing" the opposing because of his passive attitude of rejection and negation. (134-5)

Like Nietzsche, however, the French decadents appreciated the transcendental impulse behind the Hellenic fusion of Dionysian themes within Apollonian forms. This is why Huysmans and others often looked to the pagans for answers to the death of God. They also adapted Sade's virulent nihilism to a far more lethargic epoch, when the Enlightenment was beginning to dim. The decadents were thus the most visible in a long line of "panic merchants" who, by perpetuating the mythical powers of the god Pan, explicitly linked the goat-god with an eroticized apocalypse.

To Nordau, Nietzsche was an ego-maniac, and therefore a

degenerate like Huysmans and all the others. Recent scholarship, however, places Nietzsche in direct opposition to such a lineage. Huysmans was a latent Catholic. Obsessed with the superficial transgressions of Satanism, he was thus trapped in the same (albeit inverted) transcendental structure that Nietzsche despised. This shows us that the "red thread" of my Dionysian genealogy inevitably becomes tangled in the footsteps of historical interpretation, and that distinctions between debauchery and refinement cannot account for those antithetical affinities that lie dormant in such texts.

This debate, which is largely semantic, circles around interpretations of artifice, and around its role in either assisting or hindering the perceived flow of time. The key concepts—entropy, degeneration, decadence, and eroticism—form a constellation around the Sadean support of artifice. As a result, any discussion of millenarian ideas are sucked into the dionysian density of such a concept, and *A Rebours*' attempt to consistently foil mother nature leads to Des Esseintes's apoplectic apocalypse.

Technologies of the Flesh

> There is an affinity, or at least a synchrony, between a culture of boredom and an orgiastic one.
>
> Jacques Derrida (1995: 35)

> Sex is worth dying for.
>
> Michel Foucault (1990: 156)

In her chapter on Huysmans, Paglia writes that "*A Rebours* (originally called *Alone*) is Romantically self-contained, its linguistic energy invested in internal sexual differentiation. Its words are thronging multiples, spores of competitive identity. The whole, subdividing into fractious parts, makes love to itself" (436). In its onanistic multiplicity, the text performs a kind of linguistic orgy, enacted through the medium of language. For Huysmans, as for Georges Bataille, eroticism ultimately emphasizes our alienation, solitude, and mortality. It is thus to be used as a (self-)destructive weapon.

In contemplating a painting by Gustave Moreau, Des Esseintes sees Salome, that "goddess of decadence" (Showalter 149), in her true colors:

> [Salome] was now revealed in a sense as the symbolic incarnation

> of world-old Vice, the goddess of immortal Hysteris, the Curse of Beauty supreme above all other beauties by the cataleptic spasm that stirs her flesh and steels her muscles,— a monstrous Beast of the Apocalypse, indifferent, irresponsible, insensible, poisoning, like Helen of Troy of the old Classic fables, all who come near her, all who see her, all who touch her. (53)

Woman, and by association sexuality, represents the traditionally apocalyptic consequences of eroticism. This is elaborated further in the proto-Surrealist nightmare sequence, where Des Esseintes is literally hounded by a woman with a bulldog face and *vagina dentata*. Here the duke's hysterical symptoms spill out into his dreams to confront him in horrific and vivid detail. Visions melt and merge until he finds himself in a "hideous metallic landscape" (92), where Salome's sister-spirit, Syphilis, pursues him into a feverish awakening. A psychoanalytic reading could find a wealth of material here to justify labeling Des Esseintes (and by extension Huysmans himself) a neurotic and hysterical misogynist. I would point out, however, that such a conclusion would depend upon a notional "return of the repressed," which has become far too convenient in the post-Foucauldian theory-scape.

In the first volume of his *History of Sexuality* (1990), Foucault debunks what he calls the "repressive hypothesis": the dominant notion that the Enlightenment centuries attempted to control sexuality through medical and judicial policies of silence, denial, evasion, surveillance, and punishment. As a revisionist historian, Foucault sets out to demonstrate that the nineteenth century actually *produced* what we now call "sexuality", and did so by means of a centerless power structure that operates through horizontal mobility rather than vertical pressure. Far from being silenced, sexuality was compelled to speak, and in increasingly delineated terms. This process, which Foucault calls "the deployment of sexuality" (106), was achieved via the institution of confession. The effect of such "polymorphous techniques of power" (11) is to actually *create* the object of study, rather than reveal it. As a result, "sexuality" is not a secret essence to be prized from our closet, but something actively produced by such a search.

(I make this point not in order to repress the reality of repression, as it were, but merely to emphasize the discursive origins of its undeniable power. In their different ways, post-Franco Spain, contemporary Japan, and the Heaven's Gate cult all provide compelling evidence for the power of released repression. This does not weaken Foucault's argument, however. Because the repressive effect is a major element in the deployment of sexuality, it results in a kind of self-fulfilling prophecy.)

In tracing the history of the "singular imperialism that compels everyone to transform their sexuality into a perpetual discourse" (33), Foucault links the deployment of sexuality to the legacy of Sade: "the most defenseless tenderness and the bloodiest of powers have a similar need of confession. Western man has become a confessing animal" (59). From such a perspective, Des Esseintes's dream—not to mention Huysmans's text—are not pressure valves letting off repressed steam, but part of that "dense transfer point" (103) between people, now known as "sexuality."

The "disfunctionality" of decadent sexuality cannot be overemphasized, especially when viewed through Foucault's framework. Des Esseintes's experiment, however, rejects that proto-Freudian model that views sexuality as the skeleton key to physical and mental health. Instead, it is seen as the source of our degeneration, through revulsion and disease. For William Blake the road of excess led to the palace of wisdom, but for Des Esseintes it led to his own House of Usher.

Huysmans's nightmare vividly rejects the notion that transcendence is to be found in the climactic epiphany of orgasm. Indeed, his waking hours are dedicated to avoiding sexuality and its syphilitic effects. Nordau's organic fatigue makes no exception for the genitals, and Huysmans's tale of libidinal entropy speaks of an apocalypse that comes not with a bang, but a whimper. Death is barely kept at bay in Fontenay, and Des Esseintes lives in those agonizing moments after the orgy, but before the test results.

The Dionysian economy of expenditure is thus forced to keep pace with a new emotional stock market, whereby erotic investments can inflate out of control or render us bankrupt. The legacy of Des Esseintes's experiment can thus be found in today's apocalyptic discourses about the global drop in sperm-counts or the Gen-X game of HIV Russian Roulette. All this leads us back to Nordau, and particularly to his critique of the decadents' perspective on the end of history: "They do not direct us to the future, but point backwards to times past. Their word is no ecstatic prophecy, but the senseless stammering and babbling of deranged minds . . . spasms of exhaustion" (43). And as happens with many deathbed scenarios, repentance isn't too far behind.

In his analysis of *A Rebours,* Stableford discusses the central character's "climactic repentance" (1993: 28) at the end of the novel, which (he believes) foreshadows Huysmans' own conversion to Catholicism. One of Huysmans's contemporaries, Barbey d'Aurevilly, was quoted as saying that "[a]fter such a book, it only remains for the author to choose between the muzzle of a pistol or the foot of the cross" (Huysmans xlix). Huysmans's decision to take the less drastic option resonates with Nietzsche's belief that "one is not 'converted' to Christianity—one has to be sick enough for it" (1982: 637).

On one level, the novel can certainly be read as celebrating the impossibility of living a truly decadent lifestyle, and as thus, echoing Baudelaire's belief that those who seek artificial paradises end up creating private hells (Stableford, 1993: 19). The power of *A Rebours,* however, comes largely from the fact that—like J. G. Ballard's *Crash* (1975)—it is too ironic and ambiguous to be contained within such moral prescriptions.

Perhaps projecting his knowledge of Huysmans's subsequent actions on to the character of Des Esseintes, Stableford seems to mistake defeat for repentance—although there is no doubt that they are closely akin. In the closing pages of *A Rebours,* Des Esseintes deplores the filth and squalor of the fin de siècle in terms remarkably similar to those of his future critic, Nordau, although from an ideologically different position. Forced to return to Paris under doctor's orders, Des Esseintes contemplates his painful reinsertion into the social body. Burdened with the weariness of hereditary hysteria, the duke tries in vain to find solace in apocalyptic visions:

> Could it be that to prove once and for all that He existed, the terrible God of Genesis and the pale Crucified of Golgotha were not going to renew the cataclysms of an earlier day, to rekindle the rain of fire that consumed the ancient homes of sin, the cities of the Plain? Could it be that this foul flood was to go on spreading and drowning in its pestilential morass this old world where now only seeds of iniquity sprang up and harvests of shame flourished? (206)

In the final pages of *Degeneration,* Nordau also presents us with a dystopian vision of the imminent twentieth century, as taken from the fever-charts of the mal du siècle:

> Sexual psychopathy of every nature has become so general and so imperious that manners and laws have adapted themselves accordingly. They appear already in the fashion. Masochists or passivists, who form the majority of men, clothe themselves in a costume which recalls, by colour and cut, feminine apparel . . . . Sadists, "bestials," nosophiles, and necrophiles, etc., find legal opportunities to gratify their inclinations. Modesty and restraint are dead superstitions of the past, and appear only as atavism and among the inhabitants of remote villages . . . on the stage only representations of unveiled eroticism and bloody homicides, and to this, flock voluntary victims from all the parts, who aspire to the voluptuousness of dying amid the plaudits of delirious spectators. (539)

Nordau's prophecy is uncannily accurate. Many of his predictions appear along the decadent trajectory I myself am tracing—from Rimbaud to Rambo, Baudelaire to Baudrillard, *J'accuse* to Jacuzzi (in Todd Gitlin's words), society to satiety, and seminality to senility. All are inscribed with the legacy of libidinal millenarianism.

Unlike Huysmans, however, Nordau depicts an even more degenerated future only in order to destroy it with the "scientific" weight of his optimism. Nordau's optimism rests on two beliefs: first, that the feeble will perish and the strong will survive, and second, that posterity will develop some kind of remote control for coping with the speed of history. If letters were to be suppressed, railways scrapped, telephones banished, papers delayed, and fashion-cycles slowed down, the nerves would have an opportunity to rebuild. By the end of the twentieth century, we would probably see

> [a] generation to whom it will not be injurous to read a dozen square yards of newspapers daily, to be constantly called to the telephone, to be thinking simultaneously of the five continents of the world, to live half their time in a railway carriage or in a flying machine, and to satisfy the demands of a circle of ten thousand acquaintances, associates, and friends. (541)

This generation is certainly with us today. The promised rest period, however, has not been forthcoming (and I don't think that financial crashes are what Nordau had in mind). Although we have our fingers on various buttons—the nuclear, the panic, the fast-forward—no-one can locate the slowdown option.

In our own fin de siècle we encounter discourses of degeneration through a kind of "entropic acceleration." This time, however, they have an even deeper sense of cynicism. If Hillel Schwartz is correct in noting that the last decade is to a century as the last century is to a millennium (xvii), then we can backdate this new phase to the postcoital endism of Huysmans. Thus the industrial revolution, which preempted today's much trumpeted "information revolution," was itself preceded by the printing press and mercantile circulation. These revolutions masked the emergence of yet another—the sexual revolution of the *scientia sexualis*. Such moments are distinct, but not conveniently sequential. It is an old but durable point that revolutions turn like wheels.

Foucault's history of sexuality revolves around these historical revolutions, tracing the "technologies of the flesh" in the nineteenth century to the production of libido through language. Concurrent fears about technological invasions of the body produced a sense of exhaustion and depletion that had an abrasive effect on the soft underbelly of Progress. Decadent subjectivity was thus a cynically flirtatious negotiation between secular pessimism and religious optimism, interpreted superficially as a decaying forward. As Des Esseintes discovered, transgression no longer guaranteed a shortcut to transcendence. Nevertheless, sexuality was still seen as the key to a future that many decadents faced with a combination of boredom, anxiety, and impatience.

Foucault draws attention to the fact that "Today it is sex that serves as a support for the ancient form—so familiar and important in the West—of preaching" (1990: 7). *Preaching*, *prophecy, confession, repression, revelation,* and *liberation,* are thus terms that cluster around "this millennial yoke." When sex becomes inseparable from the problem of truth, all modes of uncovering and revelation become eroticized. As Paglia notes, "Western narrative is a mystery story, a process of detection. But since what is detected is unbearable, every revelation leads to another repression" (7). Is it surprising, then, that when decadents gave up on the Second Coming and the Revelation of God's Truth, they looked for answers in the lascivious dance of Salome and her seven veils? What they didn't realize is that both options issued from the same libidinal tissue.

The 1960s were similarly entranced by libidinal routes to the promised land, and fell into similar traps of complicity, appropriation, and delusion. The "sexual revolution" was primarily a millenarian reading of history, which smuggled much older metaphysical modes into the heart of modernity. As Foucault notes, "[s]omething that smacks of revolt, of promised freedom, of the coming age of a different law, slips easily into this discourse on sexual oppression. Some of the ancient functions of prophecy are reactivated therein. Tomorrow sex will be good again" (1990: 7).

In the 1960s the psychology of belatedness began to give way to a more urgent cultural agenda. The orgy was back.

5

Cosmic Architects

> Maybe it was sentimental, if not actually stupid, to romanticize the sixties as an embryonic golden age. Certainly, this fetal age of enlightenment was aborted. Nevertheless, the sixties were special; not only did they *differ* from the twenties, the fifties, the seventies etc. they were *superior* to them. Like the Arthurian years at Camelot, the sixties constituted a breakthrough, a fleeting moment of glory, a time when a significant little chunk of humanity briefly realized its moral potential and flirted with its neurological destiny, a collective spiritual awakening that flared brilliantly until the barbaric and mediocre impulses of the species drew tight once more the curtains of darkness.
>
> Tom Robbins (248)

Several decades after the event, baby boomers continue to sit behind "the curtains of darkness," trying to shed some light on this magical-mystical decade. This quote from Robbins's *Jitterbug Perfume* (1990) clearly displays the rhetorical double-movement made by many survivors of the sixties counterculture; obliged to dismiss or disown romanticized recollections, and yet, more often than not, doing just that themselves later in the same paragraph. This era (which was obsessed with traditional Western mythical narratives) managed to found an industry dedicated to churning out its own narcissistic myths of the sixties. Even the term *the sixties* functions today—after several nostalgic revivals—as an omnipresent Rorschach blot on to which people project their own meanings and/or memories.

As the steady trickle of memoirs continues into this new millennium, the task of "uncovering" the sixties—of scraping away the sands of time and the misty myths of the media—becomes increasingly archaeological. In *Hippie Hippie Shake* (1995),

Richard Neville presents his book as a "warts and all" analysis, as if most other veterans had forgotten to take off their rose-colored glasses along with their kaftans. To strip away the myth, however, does not uncover some uncut truth or reality, for this is the elusive secret ingredient that held everything together. As Todd Gitlin says in a book simply entitled *The Sixties* (1987), "the outcome and meaning of the movements of the sixties are not treasures to be unearthed with an exultant Aha!, but sand paintings, something provisional, both created and revised in historical time" (433). The sixties was always, and continues to be, a self-conscious conversation with itself.

The mythical glue that was used to fashion that chaotic time into a coherent narrative was reapplied in the 1990s by people as ideologically opposed to one another as Germaine Greer, Camille Paglia, Harold Bloom, Timothy Leary, and Richard Neville. *The Sixties* has consequently become a shorthand term pointing to a multiplicity of contested meanings and moments, and the revisions of these over time. Many social and political battles have since been pushed to the wayside in the artificial process of fitting history in to clearly demarcated, and morally legible, decades. (Did the sixties really end in 1970? Or begin in 1960?)

In this chapter I turn to some very specific texts and technologies that have served as a rhetorical hinge between the decadence of the 1890s and the millenarianism of the 1990s. Some readers may believe it is a little premature—or even ambitious—to be conducting an archaeological expedition into the 1960s. Excavating the libidinal traces of certain rhetorical strategies, however, is an important task in relation to the discussion at hand. Significant figures and struggles are necessarily absent in my selection of voices that speak of the sexual and nuclear revolution, mainly because I seek to uncover a particular stance toward these key moments that qualify as dionysian. Through a recontextualization of Norman O. Brown and Herbert Marcuse, among others, we can forge a greater understanding of the sixties' influence on today's millenarians. (Perhaps it is no surprise then, that such narratives are launched, on the whole, by the characteristic dionysian: male, embittered, American or European, educated, and relatively economically privileged.) To scrutinize the warts of the sixties—and indeed there were plenty—is less important, however, than to understand a turbulent time that spent as much energy on pinpointing a stable collective identity as on trying to dissolve the rigid structures of society.

In terms of historical symmetry, the sixties came a generation too early. As Angela Carter quipped, "the *fin* is coming a little early this *siècle*" (Showalter 1). On the face of it, the sixties zeitgeist had more in common with that of the late nineteenth century than our own.

Certain parallels between the swinging sixties and the naughty nineties have been identified by critics such as Terry Eagleton, drawn to the fact that "[s]exual and political emancipation were once more in the air, late-Victorian Simple Lifers returned in the guise of hippies, the Aesthetes and Decadents were with us again in the shape of consumer hedonism" (1990: 42).

The telescoping of two distinct historical periods is a common journalistic tactic, and presumes the existence of an atemporal cast of characters that move from one century to another like chess-pieces. However, Eagleton goes on to highlight the differences between these epochs, reminding us that we must also resist the temptation to find transhistorical similarities. Because the world changed more in the two or three generations that separate the 1890s from the 1960s than in any other seventy-year period in the whole of human history, we should think carefully before pronouncing the resurrection of cultural "types."

In the 1960s many young people certainly read Charles Baudelaire and Arthur Rimbaud in rooms adorned by William Morris and Aubrey Beardsley. Marcuse tells us that "the new boheme, the beatniks and hipsters, the peace creeps—all these 'decadents' now have become what decadence probably always was: poor refuge of defamed humanity" (1973: 16). Just as the decadents and symbolists had reacted against a hypocritical Victorian morality, so students in the 1960s were challenging the stifling constraints of 1950's prudery. And in another parallel, this new "turn to the subject" was "caught up, sometimes contradictorily, with the emergence of great collective political movements" (Eagleton, 1990: 43).

Many seeds planted in France in the 1880s and 1890s blossomed on the other side of the Channel and the Atlantic in the 1960s. The Flowers of Evil so beloved by European decadents were aestheticized by the flower children into a more traditional and accessible notion of beauty. The torture-garden was weeded and tended until it became a place appropriate for family picnics. The literary obsession with deflowering (symbolized by Hades' sexual attack on Persephone as she gathered flowers) was replaced by a more general interest in *re*flowering. The peace movement's image of the young hippie woman placing a floral tribute in the barrel of a soldier's gun succinctly and symbolically reversed the dominant Sadean fantasy, distorting it into a form of antiphallic penetration. In this spirit, flower-power became the pastoralist alternative to a mechanistic, materialistic and militaristic worldview.

Thus, the language of the fin de siècle was appropriated and adapted for new socio-political contexts. Since similar battles had been waged before, it seemed more appropriate to borrow from a well-established dissident vocabulary than to invent a totally new one. Nineteenth-century writers (most notably Karl Marx) provided a general archive for sixties radicals. Although national boundaries enclosed specific political genealogies, their *lingua franca* was sexual activity and political activism.

Yet, just as some looked over their shoulders to draw inspiration from the past, others nurtured a millenarian appetite to destroy all existing structures and start afresh, as this anarcho-surrealist manifesto makes clear:

> Long live the New Guinea tribe who, aware of the stupidity of technological civilization, massacred the managers of a washing-machine factory, took over the building and converted it into a temple for the marvellous but elusive Rabbit-god . . . . As liberated souls (and we are, for our quest cannot be stopped now) we have necessarily an historically enviable role as cosmic architects armed with hammers, electric guitars, and apocalyptic visions, but more significantly, armed with the exhilarating knowledge that we are able to crush systematically all obstacles placed in the way of our desires and build a new EVERYTHING. (Nuttall 63-65)

This extract dramatizes the unresolved conflict of coexisting desires in this period: the pastoral dream of returning to the garden, and the utopian fantasy of starting afresh on some seductive new planet. Some were in search of an Arcadian Utopia, others a Utopian Arcadia. The dialectical pattern of the sixties was produced by traditional tensions between the *always-already* and the *never-before*.

The most visible sign of these upheavals was the so-called sexual revolution. In a time as idiosyncratic and divided as the sixties, it may seem misguided (or even a little Apollonian) to identify the principal force that galvanized the various agendas of this decade. According to the myth-makers, however, almost all political idealism was refracted through sexual liberation. As a common graffiti of the time phrased it, "Revolution is the orgasm of history" (Grant 172).

Immaculate Contraception

> America's political need is orgies in the parks, on Boston Common and in the Public Gardens, with naked bacchantes in our national forests . . . . I am not proposing idealistic fancies, I am acknowledging what is already happening among the young in fact and fantasy, and proposing official blessing for these breakthroughs of community spirit . . . . What satisfaction is now possible for the young? Only the satisfaction of their Desire—love, the body, and orgy.
>
> Allen Ginsberg (Nuttall 191-192)

> Have you walked down Haight Street at dawn and talked with the survivors? The Street reeks of human agony, despair and death, death, death.
>
> From the Boston *Avatar* (Nuttall 194)

The end of the American sixties also signaled the end of The Orgy in the Baudrillardian sense. It was a time when the carnal fused with the carnivalesque to produce both the "sexual revolution" and its more overtly political configurations. Women in particular began experimenting with a new language that celebrated and encouraged the unprecedented access to, and understanding of, their bodies as specifically and politically sexual. Gay men also began to find a collective voice in which to press for an identity-based sexual politics. From a certain post-AIDS perspective, however, the sexual revolution somehow "failed" to deliver its promise of lasting social change. Enjoyable at the time, it did not succeed in opening exits from sexually restrictive institutions like the state, religion, capital, and family.

In the sixties, emancipatory narratives were still de rigueur, although with the benefit of hindsight we can see that the concerts and love-ins were more concerned about negation than affirmation. They were *against* the war, *against* the church, *against* the politicians, *against* repression and oppression, *against* the older generation, and *against* normalizing moral systems. It followed that they were *for* peace, *for* anarchy, *for* liberation, *for* youth, and *for* "whatever turns you on." To try to identify which came first—action or reaction—is not another chicken-and-egg question. It enables us to understand how the (positive) negation of fear and revolt hatched the (negative) affirmation of the orgy.

The erotic common denominator of collectivity is the organizing principle behind Michel Maffesoli's study, *The Shadow of Dionysus* (1993).[20] "Orgy," in his usage, includes carnivalesque manifestations of the popular, and not just the prosaic permutations of group sex. It denotes the presence of an "obscene constant": a transhistorical means of "stating the problem of sociality or alterity" (2). In tandem with Georges Bataille, Maffesoli presents the orgy as the matrix of an instinctive urge for fusion: "[it is] an 'affective' nebula, a tendency toward the orgiastic or Dionysian. Orgiastic explosions, cults of possession, and fusional situations have existed in all times. But sometimes they take on an endemic allure and become preeminent in the collective conscious. On whatever subjects may be, we vibrate in unison" (xv).

The orgy is presented as a quasi-organic economy, a "red thread" that not only bonds the individual to the community but also ties the past to the present. Maffesoli thus develops Sigmund

Freud's point that the aim of Eros is making one out of many in the drive toward ever larger unities. Like the American Indian potlatch—the sacrifice of a community's wealth in a joyous ceremony—the orgy is a sacrifice of spiritual surplus, a burning of excess libidinal energy. Indeed, "the group expression of desire, as a metaphor for the discarding of privacy and possessiveness, has never seemed more utopian to our acquisitive age" (Grant 129).

Maffesoli attempts to reconcile the individual experience of sexual pleasure with a transcendent communality:

> It is certain that the circulation of sexuality, the initiatory bursting of the self, orgiastic effervescence, and collective marriages all refer to the *ex-stasis,* to going beyond the individual level onto a larger ensemble. It is striking to find that the domestication of mores, individualized culture, diverse socio-economic changes, as well as scientific and technical developments, have in no way lessened this impulse to wander. (6)

In the sixties it certainly increased the instinct to ramble. Rock concerts and love-ins are two obvious examples of the return of the orgiastic. Others include the student activist who, when asked what it was like to be behind the barricades in Paris, May '68, replied, "I fucked 15 girls!" (Neville, 1971: 62). To these instances we could add Jeff Nuttall's interpretation of the Elvis Presley riots as a "revengeful rediscovery of the Dionysian ceremony. He was the idol in a literal sense, a deity incarnate on the old primitive pattern, the catalyst of a rediscovered appetite for community in its fundamental form, orgastic *[sic]* ritual" (30).

Such eruptions represent Maffesoli's "passional logic" which, "like a subterranean switchboard, defracts into a multiplicity of effects that inform daily life" (1). This logic points toward "a confusional order," an orgiastic injunction which, instead of challenging or subverting the Apollonian structures of the social, completely ignores them. But this confusional order, which Bataille found so disorienting, has an almost transcendent potential for Maffesoli:

> In the orgy continuity cannot be laid hold of; individuals lose themselves at the climax, but in mingled confusion. The orgy is necessarily disappointing. Theoretically it is the complete negation of the individual quality. It presupposes, it even demands equality among the participants. Not only is individuality itself submerged in the tumult of the orgy, but each participant denies the individuality of the others. All limits are completely done away with, or so it seems, but it is impossible for nothing to remain of the differences between individuals and the sexual attraction connected with those differences. (129)

Perhaps psychedelic drugs aided the sense of confusion in the sixties, a time now characterized as a concerted (not to mention conceited) groping toward Maffesoli's vision. This orgy should not be considered an atavistic reaction to (post)modernity, but something developing alongside it—society's "shadow part." This new modulation of the Dionysian would understand that "the technological innovation of the future will put itself at the service of the body" (11).

There is no "after the orgy" for Maffesoli because society *always* displays a fusional impulse. Before sex, drugs, and rock 'n' roll there was wine, women, and song (just as today there is intercourse, Internet, and industrial music). As Maffesoli is at pains to point out, the orgiastic is not a rational fantasy of reducing the Many to the One. Instead, it "*allows to be* the different passions that animate everyday life in all their diversity" (1993: 86).

Viewed historically, Maffesoli's study is a sophisticated attempt to transplant the sixties' sexual rhetoric of Brown, James Hillman, Wilhelm Reich, and others, into the more labyrinthine environment of poststructuralist theory. In one sense it is a throwback; in another it illustrates the extent to which the present is still overshadowed by Dionysus. The enemy can no longer be identified as the monolithic targets of Capital or Repression, just as the subject can no longer be considered a stable political agent. The basically Manichaean-repressive model of sixties' sexuality gives way to Michael Foucault's less coherent libidinal landscape, in which all the obvious power-sources and reference-points have been disguised or dismantled. Sexuality continues to nurture subversive potential, but not on the macrocosmic scale it once promised. Instead, "libidinal activism [is now] . . . a practice of jouissance defining a microsphere of resistance and action allowing societies to perdure" (xxiv).

But what prompted this Dionysian eruption of sexuality into the public sphere? To identify it as the inevitable return of the repressed does not answer the question of why the repressed chose to return at *that* particular moment. Any historical contextualization of the extended Summer of Love must take into account two global technologies: the atomic bomb and the oral contraceptive pill. The baby boomers were the first generation who could expect not only to be obliterated in a nuclear holocaust but also to have sex without risk of pregnancy (something former contraceptive methods could not guarantee with such confidence). While it is certainly true that nuclear anxiety characterized much of the late 1940s and 1950s, it is the *combination* of these technologies that becomes decisive in the 1960s. Armageddon was now a military option, always on the brink (outside Japan and colonial test-sites) of spilling out of apocalyptic imagination and into reality. The profound existential fear of a nuclear holocaust coincided with an unprecedented amount of sexual freedom to spawn a unique moment in history, while simultaneously mirroring the liminal excess of other millennial moments.

The promiscuity of this time was predicated on a multiplicity of possible Ends, especially the end of the world and the end of sex as a biological imperative. There was a sense that this could indeed be Apocalypse Now. The bacchic behavior that has come to symbolize the sixties evokes the popular etymology of "carnival" as *carne-vale* (farewell to flesh). Consequently, libidinal millenarianism celebrates the finitude of life, and the miracle of mortality. As Nuttall remarks, rampaging teenagers indulged in "temple ceremonials of the futureless" (30). Whatever route to extinction they took, many boomers decided to live up to their name and go out with a bang.

In the modern era, writes Foucault, "sex became a crucial target of a power organized around the management of life rather than the menace of death" (1990: 147). Both nuclearism and fertility research have been conducted under the sign of scientific advancement, and have quarantined their activities from medieval notions of death. Foucault again makes the salient point: "If genocide is indeed the dream of modern powers, this is not because of a recent return of the ancient right to kill; it is because power is situated and exercised at the level of life, the species, the race, and the large-scale phenomena of population" (ibid.: 137). In other words, the emergence of scientific technologies for prolonging and improving human life created ideal conditions for mass death and even extinction.

Both the Bomb and the Pill were revolutionary devices, conceived by science in order to negate life for some, and enhance it for others. They were technologies invented in a race against both time and the Other. In Peter Jordan's film, *The Sleep of Reason* (1994), the Los Alamos of the 1940s is presented as a "utopian community," led by Oppenheimer in a crusade to save the (civilized) world. Similarly, Sanger and Pincus believed that their work had the potential to save the West from a devastating population explosion, also located east of the United States.

Sexless Hydrogen: The *Frisson* of Fission

> [T]here appears in many cities a kind of helplessness once they begin to realize that they are objects marked for destruction.
>
> The Mayor of Milwaukee (1950) (Boyer, 1985: 282)

Nuttall's book *Bomb Culture* (1972) is a fascinating textual artifact of that decade. It documents the antibomb movement in England,

and its intellectual and artistic allies and influences. Nuttall's genealogy is very similar to my own, following that chaotic trail of ideas from Sade through Friedrich Nietzsche to the Surrealists and Situationists. He argues that there was a Copernican shift after Hiroshima, and that the Bomb terrified the young into a kind of frenzied nihilism, which left them incapable of conceiving that life had a future:

> The question then was practical. How best could one go about the business of waiting in humiliation for the end of man? One could, to begin with, become more passive . . . . Another thing we could do was live for sensation . . . live for sex rather than love, for speed rather than safety, for kicks. It is my experience that a large number of teenagers became then, and remain, incapable of thinking more than half an hour ahead. (105-106)

Nuttall identifies this as part of an "anti-gestalt," the "instinct to leave nothing complete" (ibid.).

The young—or at least those wealthy enough to engage in such apathetic posturing—were thus straddling a pendulum that swung between a panicked energy and what Paul Boyer labels an "ominous terminal lassitude" (1985: 263). Nuttall's assertion that the generation gap was opened up by bomb-culture undermines those "boomer vs generation x" or "hippie vs punk" clichés that continue to circulate in the media. Johnny Rotten's catch-cry, "No future," speaks of an anxious continuity across the decades. Popular readings of the alleged generation gap contrast today's solipsism and apathy with the sixties' energetic engagement with the world. But these tend to forget that "the pale face of Juliette [Greco], without make-up except around the eyes, with whited lips, has been the mask for female middle-class rebels ever since. The style, with its necrophiliac overtones, constitutes another device for living with the possibility of death. Boredom was a mode" (Nuttall 37).

Nuttall's description still applies, conjuring up the ubiquitous image of the goth in the 1980s and 1990s. Here too, boredom and the possibility of death fuse into a subcultural identity. The cultural climate of the sixties, however, was unprecedented. For the first time, a man-made secular dread permeated the social fabric with quasi-religious consequences. For Paul Virilio, consciousness of nuclear danger is stimulated less by the risk that nuclear weaponry will be deployed then by the fact that "it exists and is imploding in our minds" (1986: 150).

This ominous Eschaton also became the basis of that kind of inverted liberation that Andrew Milner calls "apocalyptic hedonism" (36). In a Sadean aftershock, influential writers such as J. G. Ballard produced near-futuristic fables predicated on the belief that "the hydrogen bomb was a symbol of absolute *freedom*. I feel it's given me the right—the obligation even—to do anything I want" (Pringle 133). Norman Mailer's advice for the atomic age is just as relevant now as it was then, when he said that "the only life-giving answer is to accept the terms of death, to live with death as immediate danger, to divorce oneself from society, to exist without roots, to set out on that uncharted journey into the rebellious imperatives of the self" (Nuttall 17). So much, then, for the claim that the sixties rejuvenated the idea of idealistic community.

Nuttall believes that "the mass of young people would probably not have registered their insecurity so thoroughly, would not have divided themselves off so completely as a cultural group, had they been conscious of the origins and content of their unease" (11). The origin was Hiroshima, and the content was irrational mass death. To consciously focus on this "unease," whether politically or personally, proved too much for this and subsequent generations to bear.

In the early 1970s, Neville maintained that people don't care about dying if everybody else is going to die too: "Duffle coats and CND [Campaign for Nuclear Disarmament] badges symbolized a new generational identity. For the young, being sad about the Bomb was fun" (1971: 26). Although directed against people like Nuttall, such remarks do nothing to weaken the argument of *Bomb Culture*. The loaded word here is *fun,* for Neville seems to believe that terror and fun are mutually exclusive. Yet both can coexist in the one psyche (or subculture), each shaping the other in a complementary conflict.

Nuttall's narrative vibrates with the tension between a desire for macrocosmic political change and a belief that salvation is to be found in hedonistic excess—between what Neville dubbed the "hard-line lefty" and the "hard-on hippy" positions (ibid.: 224). Kerouac provides us with a typical example:

> It's the great molecular comedown. Of course that's only my whimsical name for it at the moment. It's really an atomic disease, you see. . . . It's death, finally reclaiming life, the scurvy of the soul at last, a kind of universal cancer. It's got a real medieval ghastliness, like the plague, only this time it will ruin everything, don't you see? Everybody is going to fall apart, disintegrate, all character structures based on tradition and uprightness and so-called morality will slowly rot away, people will get the hives right on their hearts, great crabs will cling to their brains . . . their lungs will crumble. But now we have only the symptoms, the disease isn't really underway yet—virus X. (Nuttall 113)

This "disease" is certainly with us now, whether we call it "AIDS", "market correction", "the digital divide", "postmodernism" or whatever. These doomsday images were as much Oppenheimer's creation as Kerouac's. It is clear from the tone of his conclusion that Kerouac does not write out of resignation and fear. "Whatever it is, I'm all for it," he says. "It may be a carnival of horror at first—but something strange will come of it, I'm convinced" (ibid.). In the sixties, the Grim Reaper of immanent extinction said "check" to the collective life force of the libido; the young, instead of pondering the strategic options on offer, did the equivalent of tipping over the chess-table. The Bomb and the Pill seemed to be sitting on either side of a giant seesaw, with the world watching on.

Herbert Marcuse has noted that "the mere anticipation of the inevitable end, present in every instant, introduces a repressive element into all libidinal relations and renders pleasure itself painful" (1973: 162). Jonathan Swift also understood that such a debauched reaction to imminent destruction was inevitable. Imagining the reaction of Londoners to the arrival of a doomsday comet, Swift wrote: "They drank, they whored, they swore, they lied, they cheated, they quarrelled, they murdered. In short, the world went on in the old channel" (Boyer, 1985: 240).

Boyer shares Nuttall's conviction that the Bomb had an unprecedented and underrated impact on the psychocultural landscape in the second half of the twentieth century. In his study of early reactions to the dawning of the nuclear age, *By the Bomb's Early Light* (1985), Boyer writes, "It is as though the Bomb has become one of those categories of Being, like Space and Time, that, according to Kant, are built into the very structure of our minds, giving shape and meaning to all our perceptions" (xviii).

In the late 1940s America was terrified by the Frankensteinian power it had unleashed on its enemies, and believed it was only a matter of time before a new enemy would inflict it on them. The billboard promise of a safe and clean nuclear-fueled suburban utopia barely veiled the anxieties provoked by this scientific revolution. Repentant atomic scientists seized on this fear and manipulated it politically in a strategic campaign to return the Horror to its Pandora's Box; for as Boyer notes, "the politicization of terror was a decisive factor in shaping the post-Hiroshima cultural climate" (66). These scientists toured the nation to alert people to the sinister subtext of the government's assurances that nuclear power would "set man on the road to the new millennium" (126). They were criticized for pushing the nation "toward a state of near panic" in the attempt to realize their objective. In 1946 the historian Erich Kahler delivered this warning to the atomic scientists:

> The general fear, on which so many people count as a restraining

> influence, is a questionable defence. Between fear and its object there exists a menacing and magic interaction which tends to gradual intensification, and eventually to a *panic merging* of the two. In a crisis, help has never come from fear, but only from calm and careful consideration. (73—my emphasis)

The political mobilization of fear by scientific activists created a powerful legacy that had a major impact on the (counter) culture of the sixties. This "panic merging" was realized in an orgiastic fusion of the young with an imagined apocalypse. Living in the shadow of not only Dionysus but also of instant destruction, they experienced the "orgy" in Maffesoli's sense, namely, as "death collectively lived."

Right from the beginning, commentators contextualized the atomic bomb in long established apocalyptic narratives. Certain biblical phrases—such as "the heavens shall pass away with a great noise, and the elements shall melt with fervent heat, the earth also and the works therein shall be burned up" (2 Pe. 3:10)—suddenly seemed chillingly significant. After combing the world's literature for similar prophecies, the Manhattan Project seemed to be merely fulfilling something that had been foretold many centuries before. As far back as 1681, Thomas Burnet had predicted in his *Sacred Theory of the Earth,* that "Seeds of Fire" were sealed within atoms in the center of the earth, and that on the last day God would release the "Chains" holding these fires in check (Boyer, 1985: 240). Bataille framed his own reaction in similar terms: "Truman would appear to be blindly fulfilling the prerequisites for the final—and secret—apotheosis. It will be said that only a madman could perceive such things in the Marshall and Truman plans. I am that madman" (Brown 1991: 181). But many others were equally "mad."

Put simply, panic was the initial reaction to this situation. The herd-instinct to flee was very powerful, according to Boyer, in the days following the destruction of Hiroshima and Nagasaki. The sixties were seeded not only by the resonant headlines of the times, but also by the rash of science-fiction novels that followed this unprecedented event. Stories such as Ward Moore's *Greener than You Think* (1947) became allegories for a civilization that first greeted imminent destruction with hedonistic hysteria and then lapsed into numbing apathy—a move that in many ways maps the trajectory from the 1960s to the present: "Panicky survivors scavenge in supermarkets, copulate randomly, drink themselves into a stupor, or go quietly insane" (Boyer, 1985: 262). Pan was back in town after a lengthy absence, and inciting the riotous against the righteous. Even Cornell University scientists who were testing for "human susceptibility to crack-up and panic" (ibid.: 323) conducted their experiments on "psychoneurotic goats" placed near the Marshall islands nuclear test site.

Nearly two decades later, those children who had crouched under their desks during nuclear drills began pooling the precarious flame of life which flickered within them. This was now a culture in which a fourteen-year-old schoolboy could write; "The hydrogen bomb reeks with death. Death, death to thousands. A burning, searing death, a death that is horrible, lasting death. The most horrible death man has invented; the destroying annihilating death of atomic energy. The poisoning, killing, destroying death. Death of the ages, of man, the lasting death" (ibid.: 350). Registered in this paragraph is not the timeless, universal, and profoundly mortal fear of death, but hysteria caused by the possibility of mass extinction. Such kids began to realize Lewis Mumford's fear that in its attempt to escape or deny Armageddon, society would turn toward "fantasy . . . purposeless sexual promiscuity [and] narcotic indulgence" (ibid.: 287).

Significantly in terms of my study, Michel Foucault situated himself in this nuclear genealogy, which created the psychosocial conditions for what has since been swept under the carpet of "the Sixties." He admitted having

> very early memories of an absolutely threatening world, which could crush us. To have lived as an adolescent in a situation that had to end, that had to lead to another world, for better of worse, was to have the impression of spending one's entire childhood in the night, waiting for dawn. That prospect of another world marked the people of my generation, and we have carried with us, perhaps to excess, a dream of Apocalypse. (Beachy 27)

During the Cuban Missile Crisis of 1963, Bob Dylan wrote "A Hard Rain's a Gonna Fall", and explained that his convoluted lyrics were really a collection of first lines for songs that may not have the opportunity to be written. In contrast to Michael André Bernstein's belief that apocalyptic fantasy affords pleasure in "direct proportion to its improbability" (1992: 39), the forty years of cold war nuclear anxiety ensured that a period of artistic potlatch was at hand; a public burning of emotional and psychological baggage. Contributing to this not-so-improbable end-pleasure, Brown strove for a "fiery consummation" in metaphoric rather than nuclear terms, noting that "the Loins [are] the place of the Last Judgement" (1990: 178).

These various responses to the Bomb all question Ginsberg's famous description of Hydrogen as *sexless*. If Ginsberg used the term to mean nonspecific gender, then he did so against the grain of a contemporary feminizing and masculinizing of the Bomb by different parties for different purposes. When we split the hydrogen atom, are we creating yet another discontinuity that Mother Nature cannot abide, and will consequently punish with a holocaustal howl?

Will they rush to reunify, like Plato's divided beings? Brown warns us that "in the twentieth century, in this age of fission, we can split the individual even as we can split the atom" (ibid.: 82).

Dionysus in '69

> As all the living forms of life are the lineal descendents of those which lived long before the Silurian epoch, we may feel certain that the ordinary succession by generation has never once been broken, and that no cataclysm has desolated the whole world. Hence we may look with some confidence to a secure future of equally inappreciable length.
>
> Charles Darwin (489)

Since Apollo is often described as an artificer, it is not impossible to think of technology as inspired by Apollo and infused with Apollonian values. "Nature," on the other hand, is the realm of Dionysus, and never the twain shall meet. We would indeed be living in a drastically different world if the first men to walk on the moon had got there in the rocket ship *Dionysus*. This begs the question of whether there is such a thing as *Dionysian artifice*. Is this term oxymoronic? I have already argued that cybersex is an example of this fragile fusion, and at this point I offer the Pill as another possibility.

In her study of libidinal millenarianism, *Sexing the Millennium* (1993), Linda Grant provides evidence in support of the oral contraceptive pill as an Apollonian artifact. As an instant relic of both "the god of all plastic powers" (Nietzsche, 1956: 97), the Pill was designed to help solve what was perceived (and indeed still is) as one of the greatest challenges facing humanity: overpopulation. While some saw nuclear bombs as a solution to the problem, the majority believed in less drastic alternatives. Technology, however, can be put to uses other than those intended by its inventors. The Pill would turn out to be yet another Frankenstein's monster in that strange utopian community that crystallized around Katherine Dexter McCormick, Margaret Sanger, and Gregory Pincus only four or five years after its introduction into the United States in 1960.

This Apollonian artifice was invented in the interests of controlling the population explosion in the Third World. In addition to the racist implications inevitably harbored by such a project, it had unforeseen Dionysian effects at home. As with the atom bomb, the Pill was developed in a climate of passionate optimism, when science was allegedly poised to solve all social and economic problems. In both cases, a technology devised to keep the "yellow peril" at bay came back to haunt the West, this time in the milder form of a moral apocalypse: "The Pill was to become one of the most potent symbols of the sixties' faith in progress, an iconic representation like the inner-city tower block of the failure of technology to fulfill our dreams" (Grant 59).

It is ironic, then, that this product of a belief in scientific progress would fuel the fire already started by those who were working against the rational, the imperialistic, and the teleological. Nuttall acknowledges the pervasiveness of new technologies in the counterculture, and like Grant, he remembers the sexual revolution as a collage of "zippers, leathers, boots, PVC, see-through plastics, male make-up, a thousand overtones of sexual deviation, particularly sadism, and everywhere, mixed in with amphetamines, was the birth pill" (34).

Grant sees the prophecies of the hippies as echoing various millenarian movements such as the seventeenth-century Ranters, who preached a doctrine of sexual freedom, and thus linked erotic emancipation with demands for social and political changes. For Grant, sexuality is a highly significant site of contestation which consistently resurfaces in turbulent times. She quotes an anonymous "witness":

> In the sixties you almost had to fuck for the good of the human race. It was your moral duty to keep this thing going like a transcendental chain letter, in order to improve our lot and save the planet. There was a general idea that people who controlled the world and created all the evil, did so because they couldn't fuck . . . . It was loosely, sloppily but definitely messianic and programmatic. (130)

Here sexuality is seen as a healing and benevolent force, without the darker connotations conferred upon it by Bataille or Sade. But if it was a messianic programme, who was the messiah? Was it, like the Free Spirit, that god within which exiled sin? (Considering this context, it is significant that Norman Cohn's classic study, *The Pursuit of the Millennium* [1957], was itself a cult book at the time.)

The most visible Dionysian cult of the sixties in Europe and America included those hordes of young people who worshiped at the technologically enhanced altar of rock 'n' roll. Messianic figures such as Jim Morrison and Mick Jagger spun apocalyptic tales of terror and transcendence, while tabs of LSD dissolved on pious tongues like communion wafers. If wandering bands of flagellants excited millenarian fever in the eleventh and thirteenth centuries, then traveling bands of rock musicians were the most prominent prophets in the 1960s, enciting carnivalesque confusion. Whereas literature had been the main site for angst and ennui in the nineteenth century, rock 'n' roll became the dominant form of expression for transgressive impulses in the time of the pill.

"Human culture is human sacrifice," Brown reminds us, and we must therefore come to terms with "that heroical frenzy which was the life of . . . Jimi Hendrix" (1991: 197). A popular explanation of the deaths of Jimi, Janis, and Jim, is that the "battered Gods of the old order" still needed sacrifices to placate them. The music and lyrics of the time compose an extensive archive of fin de siècle decadence. But as Gitlin points out, "music couldn't stay at millennial pitch any more than politics" (428).

Music has enjoyed an undisputed status as the younger generation's most popular medium of Dionysian expression. In the sixties, however, live dramatic performance was one of the most intense and subversive art forms. At this time, alternative theatre peddled an explosive concoction of anarchistic ideas imported from Antonin Artaud, Alfred Jarry, and Bertolt Brecht, as well as from surrealists and situationists. The German wing of the Mexican PANic group mounted chaotic guerrilla performances to spread their absurdist orgiastic gospel, as did collectives such as the Vienna Institute of Direct Art and the Japanese Zero Dimension Group (Nuttall 119, 178).

In 1968 the innocuously named Performance Group—which was later to become Julian Beck's Living Theater—produced its own mythology of the sexual revolution by reinterpreting Euripides' *Bacchae* as a hip exploration of the erotic apocalypse, called (and the pun was undoubtably intended) *Dionysus in '69*. In his review, Stefan Brecht describes "[t]he women on top, standing separate and self-contained in ecstasy. The men on the floor are undulating, a wave-motion in masturbatory or coital flexions, the women above them in the pelvic thrusts of coitus or orgasm" (156). The unintentional pathos of this performance provoked Brecht to question why, in a late capitalist environment, the orgy is inevitably pornographic, and whether its political and aesthetic impact is diluted under the auspices of art: "The choreography of these anonymous couplings suggests the impersonality of street prostitution. Their intensity, duration, realism . . . make the play a sex show: a play of unsentimental enthusiasm; unbridled, glandular" (163). This reincarnation of Nietzsche's beloved art minimizes Apollonian order and structure: scripts were rarely followed, and spontaneity and unpredictability were encouraged by audience participation: "we are shown individuation as incidental to humanity, humanity as a block of self-procreating spasmic meat. The message seems to be: let us not deny within us or within others this origin, our true identity—flesh out of flesh, issue of sperm, orgasm, spasm" (ibid.: 157).

Brecht's evocation of *Dionysus in '69* serves to remind us once again that Eros and Thanatos are inseparable. He writes that this play swings between "jejune hedonism and panic," creating "a theatre of fear disguised . . . a universe of joylessly egoist obsession acted out in endless repetition in an atmosphere of dread" (166, 168). Because it takes place in the nuclear climate, "[i]ts kinetics intimate the apprehension of combat missions and the orgiastic *mise-en-scène* submerges the fable-nexus between death and orgiastic ecstasy" (165).

Dionysus in '69 was a sign of the times, in that it proposed screwing as a political alternative to war. In a curiously puritan twist, however, it was not presented in a joyous fashion. For if we can trust Brecht to speak for the audience as a whole, the general effect was a "stunned introspection, the sadness, the desperation of taking stock of oneself. The attitude promoted . . . is frantic lust for lust" (164). Here we find the seeds of Baudrillard's simulated and postalienated narcissism; the sense that the orgy was over before it had begun.

If the orgy was so traumatic in 1969—that allegedly utopian window of light—was it ever the vital communion that we have been led to believe? If Ginsberg's nymphomaniac portrait is indeed just an idealist fancy, then perhaps we cannot discount the fact that every era since the Fall has come "after the orgy." Perhaps we should refigure the sixties, like the premillennial nineties, as simultaneously before, during, and after the Orgy. As an ideal, the orgiastic thus becomes a caricature, a carrot which—in typical cart-before-the-horse fashion—we dangle behind us rather than in front. It makes me wonder whether the cults of the Free Spirit, Ranters, Adamites, and the Taborites—romanticized in the sixties as Edenic fuck-fests—were also held inside the Grim Reaper's brothel.

Other narratives from the 1960s are certainly not so explicitly morbid. *Bliss Apocalypse,* a play written by Daniel Moore for the Floating Lotus Magic Opera Company, was also performed in 1969. Its eschatological perspective is more mystical, in emphasizing the rebirth inherent in death. This Lawrentian fascination with the Phoenix reflects the millennial sixties in a more optimistic mood:

> Our thirst for the primordial kept us from using electricity to amplify any of the instruments or actors. The whole vision was designed to be performed outside in the raw air of IT, on a hillside after civilization blow all their plugs and still the Spirit dancing and approachable and manifestable within us! Haunted by feelings of cultural hopelessness, we created out of cardboard and cloth the rippings of eternal music, flute-flashes in the smoldering

> dark! To approach men with mouths abruptly open, to let sincerities flow in this marketplace of violent madmen kicking over the vegetables! (53)

The sacredness of sexuality is replaced by the sexuality of sacredness, for nothing overtly libidinal takes place in *Bliss Apocalypse*. Rapture is achieved via a direct connection with IT—God, Life, Love, and the Eschaton . . . whatever you want to call it. The End is normalized and domesticated in the concept of rebirth and its accompanying ecstatic state:

> The Dead are hopelessly confused
> The Dead do not know they are dead . . . .
> They believe they still live in Bodies
> But their bodies are heaped like papers
> Their spirits float like leaves!
> Oh this is Transformation of Death Consciousness
> Through Underworld Tunnels to Sunrise
> We descend to the Place of Shades
> To Transform Death-Wish Falcons into Light! (65)

These Death-Wish Falcons could be seen circling the Trinity Nuclear Test site in the Alamogordo desert in 1945. One witness of the first atomic explosion coped with the enormity of its impact by returning to familiar notions of rebirth: "[o]n that moment hung eternity. Time stood still, space contracted to a pinpoint. It was as though the earth had split . . . . The big boom came seconds after the great flash—the first cry of a newborn world" *(Sleep of Reason)*. William Laurence, having witnessed the same explosion, appropriated the erotic climax of Molly Bloom's narrative for his own purposes: "The hills said yes and the mountains chimed in yes. It was as if the earth had spoken and the suddenly iridescent clouds and sky had joined in one affirmative answer. Atomic energy—yes" (Boyer, 1985: 250). By transgressing the laws of nature we had transcended ourselves.

The cold war context of *Bliss Apocalypse* is unmistakable, its response being more concerned with sublimation than subversion. It refuses to engage with various problems, one of which is that the existence of nuclear weapons automatically negates any concept of rebirth that includes the human: hence its retreat into mysticism. This ageless story of a plea for supernatural assistance depoliticizes apocalypse by recycling it as myth. But I guess a happy ending is necessary for a play that invites "communes . . . to do comic versions of *Bliss Apocalypse* with children" (70).

Echoing the quote from Tom Robbins at the beginning of this chapter, Grant notes that "for twenty years, between the invention of the Pill and the beginning of the AIDS epidemic, there was a moment which had never occurred in history before, when sex was free from the threats of both pregnancy and disease. What, if anything, were the lasting effects of that window into the light?" (20). Once again the sixties are portrayed as one last moment of illumination before the dark curtains of the late twentieth century are drawn. Unfortunately, this "window of light" metaphor obscures the more gruesome aspects of the period. AIDS was the final nail in the coffin of an already ailing sexual revolution. Grant documents the "almost cosmic sense that there is a conspiracy against sex at work in the world," for every time we seek to quench the thirst of Eros, "something keeps poisoning the well" (132).

Jean Baudrillard dates the rise of AIDS with the demise of sexual liberation, although he doesn't see it as simply a case of the virus gate-crashing the orgy. He regards AIDS as a paradoxical result of "the very success of prophylaxis and medicine" (1993b: 64). The extermination of humanity, he argues, begins with the extermination of humanity's germs, for "under the reign of the virus you are destroyed by your own antibodies. This is the leukaemia of an organism devouring its own defences, precisely because all threat, all adversity, has disappeared" (ibid.).

In a politically dangerous balancing act, Jean Baudrillard views AIDS as neither divine punishment nor a CIA plot. Instead, it is an internal mechanism that prevents the system from plunging us "into the void" (ibid.: 69), a total circulation that leads to dispersion. Thus, in a typically Baudrillardian twist, AIDS does not so mucy *destroy* sex as *preserve* it. AIDS is a form of resistance: it saves us from the "even worse eventuality" of a "total promiscuity," in which "sex itself would self-destruct in the resulting asexual flood" (ibid.: 68). This is not a moral argument, although it is highly susceptible to interpretation as such: "[a]t present we live according to at least two principles: that of sexual liberation and that of communication and information. And everything suggests that the species itself, via the threat of AIDS, is generating an antidote to its principle of sexual liberation" (ibid.: 66).

But in 1969 the deadly side of sex was still only metaphoric, falling as it did between syphilis and AIDS. In that same year Germaine Greer, Jean Shrimpton, and Heathcote Williams started a magazine entitled *Suck,* which attempted to create an alternative and liberating pornography free from the banal and sexist trappings of England's Soho. Even at the time, Greer had to admit that much of it "derived from the *fantasy machines* developed by commercial pornography to reinforce the sexual status quo" (Grant 212). Long before sex became fatal, the material was still "heavy with hatred and cruelty and [the] desire of death" (ibid.), reinforcing Julian Pefanis's point that "[p]ornography ultimately is more about death than it is sex; Thanatos surpasses Eros [in] an 'erotics of agony'" (137). The opaque plastic wrappers of porn magazines merely masked the creeping suspicion that the sexual revolution would leave only a market in its wake.

In the 1964 film *Dr Strangelove: Or How I Stopped Worrying and Learned to Love the Bomb*, Stanley Kubrick explicitly identifies the fear of sexuality as the possible trigger of a nuclear attack. General Ripper—who has clearly let his cold war paranoia get the better of him – explains his theories on fluoridation:

> General Ripper: "It's incredibly obvious isn't it? A foreign substance is introduced into our precious bodily fluids without the knowledge of the individual, certainly without any choice. That's the way your hardcore commie works."
>
> Mandrake: "Tell me, when did you first become . . . develop this theory?"
>
> General Ripper: "Well, I . . . ah, I . . . I first became aware of it, Mandrake, during the physical act of love. Yes a profound sense of fatigue, a feeling of emptiness followed. Luckily I was able to interpret these feelings correctly: *loss of essence.* I can assure you it has not reoccurred, Mandrake. Women sense my power and they seek the life essence. I do not avoid women, Mandrake, but I *do* deny them my essence."

General Ripper translates the external, political "threat" of communism into a model of contagion bearing directly on the body. The irony, of course, is that his *life-essence* is the libidinous energy that unleashes mass death and destruction on the world. The climax that he has been stoically denying himself in his relations with women explodes in a momentous "wargasm," a "pornography of violence" (Ruthven 38). It is indeed a telling indicator of the sixties zeitgeist that *Dr. Strangelove* ends with a full-scale nuclear war instead of a more optimistic Hollywood compromise.

Libidinal links between sex and the legacy of the Manhattan Project are not restricted to fiction, however. In his monograph on *Nuclear Criticism* (1993), Ken Ruthven cites a few examples of how the Bomb was eroticized in the mid-1940s. The actress Linda Christians was described as "Hollywood's Anatomic Bomb" in a necrophiliac publicity shot, just as Rita Hayworth was stenciled on one of the "devices" dropped on the Marshall islands in 1946. The bikini—which has become the quintessential symbol of female sexuality—was invented by the French engineer Louis Reard, and named after the Bikini Atoll testing zone. Ruthven also wonders what gang-rape fantasies lurk behind the title of W. C. Anderson's book on these tests: *12000 Men and One Bikini* (63). (A phallic trope that has since been appropriated by the cartoon character Tank Girl, who sports a bikini actually made out of missiles.)

Dr. Strangelove and *Bomb Culture* point to the undercurrent of pessimism in the sexual revolution. My point in drawing attention to them is not to deny the utopian and hedonistic aspects of the sixties, but to observe that these festive spectacles were predicated on —and inextricably bound to—a profound fear of apocalypse. Both the cold war and the Vietnam War are often portrayed as external conflicts that significantly influenced domestic affairs in the United States. But in fact the hippies made love not as an alternative to war, but as an extension of it: they fucked with the taste of death in their mouths.

Such matters run counter to media clichés of the sixties through images of frolicking nymphs and satyrs at Woodstock. Although that festival began as a model of utopian possibility, by the third day it had deteriorated into a nightmare of hunger, bad trips, disorientation, and exhaustion: Pan-ism turned into panic. The Rolling Stones' concert at Altamont was an inevitable inrush of oxygen in the utopian vacuum of 1969. As Stefan Brecht notes, "the flower child and the Hell's Angel are two sides of a coin," and the "loving hip" is apt to turn into the "vicious hip" (161). Interpretations of Woodstock as a utopia degenerating into chaos and confusion—seen as symbolic of the sixties themselves—fail to take into account the horror and panic that encouraged the "free love" in the first place.

The Politics of Play

> The politics of play: international, equi-sexual, inter-racial survival strategy for the future, the laughing gas to counteract tomorrow's Mace. Onward to the eighties, Motherfuckers!
>
> Neville (1971: 228)

> Is there life before death?
>
> Virilio (1983: 140)

In the 1940s and 1950s, the eccentric philosopher Wilhelm Reich believed that the woes of civilization could be remedied by "unleashing" Eros in the form of Orgone energy. By the 1960s, however, Reich's "cult of the orgasm," was rejected by the popular front of the sexual revolution: "Out goes Reich's fuddy duddy orgone box," writes Neville; "in comes happy, hippy playful sex" (1971: 224-225). Brown also saw little prospect of redemption in the orgasm, mainly because he believed it to be a strategic effect of "genital tyranny" (an observation more recently refined in the breathtaking writings of Leo Bersani). Brown exposed Reich's pseudo-subversive solution as an ally of that "exaggerated concentration on one of the many erotic potentialities" upon which Apollonian culture depends (Brown, 1970: 27).

For Brown, the issue must always be framed by eschatology. "The question is: What shall man do to be saved?" (57). Taking a tip from detective novels, he seeks the answer to this question where you would least expect to find it; in the death-drive:

> Freud was right: our real desires are unconscious. It also begins to be apparent that mankind, unconscious of its real desires and therefore unable to obtain satisfaction is hostile to life and ready to destroy life itself. Freud was right then in positing a death instinct, and the development of weapons of destruction makes our present dilemma plain: we either come to terms with our unconscious instincts and drives—with life and with death—or else we surely die. (x)

According to Brown, this knowledge leads to a condition we all suffer from: "death-in-life," a direct result of civilization's artificial separation of being and not-being. Such an existential split, he argues, prompted an immense withdrawal of libido from life. "Whereas in previous ages life had been a mixture of Eros and Thanatos," writes Brown, "in the Protestant era life becomes a pure culture of the death instinct" (ibid.).

Brown believes that our anxiety about death has been constructed historically, and is not (as we are led to believe) instinctual or metaphysical. As a consequence, life and death are united on the organic level, but split on the psychic level, and this cultural fracture is discernible in everything we do, say, or think. Brown disagrees with prophets of doom such as Arthur Schopenhauer because they "spuriously" affirm death over life, as if the two could ever be judged separately. As Rainer Maria Rilke says, "Whoever rightly understands and celebrates death, at the same time magnifies life" (ibid.: 108).

In staring death in the face, Brown aligns himself more with decadent than romantic strains of thought. "Romanticism is infantilism," he argues, "because it ignores the demands of the reality-principle" (39), and therefore offers no solution. The natural process of death must not be excluded from the ego, but incorporated within it, so that *discontinuous being* (to use one of Bataille's terms) can be integrated with existence.

It soon becomes clear that Brown's embrace of Thanatos follows the biblical trajectory towards revelation and millenarian transcendence:

> For the therapist and humanitarian, a philosophy of history has to take the form of an eschatology, declaring the conditions under which redemption from the human neurosis is possible . . . . The reunification of life and death . . . can be envisioned only as the end of the historical process . . . history, as neurosis, press[es] restlessly and unconsciously toward the abolition of history and the attainment of a state of rest which is also a reunification with nature (1970: 86, 91).

Brown thus manipulates Hegel's belief that "history is what man does with death" (102), namely, repress it. According to such a scheme, humans are neurotic animals trapped within time. But if we were able to reconcile and reunify those instinctual opposites, life and death, then history itself would end, for it is that conflict that produces "time" in the first place. We would then be free, for "only repressed life is in time and unrepressed life would be timeless or in eternity" (93). Brown thus sees repression as generating not only culture but also its vessel, namely, historical time. By seeking salvation in the timeless id, psychoanalysis therefore harbors age-old religious aspirations for a Sabbath of Eternity.

This is all very well as a messianic program for the sixties. But how are we go about the enormous task of reunifying the instinctual opposites of life and death? For Brown, the solution to this all-pervading Apollonian denial is, quite simply, a return to Dionysus. Insisting on the bodily foundation of all human endeavor, Brown's psychoanalytic prophecy foresees the evolution of a Dionysian "consciousness":

> The human ego must face the Dionysian reality, and therefore a great work of self-transformation lies ahead of it . . . . As long as the structure of the ego is Apollonian, Dionysian experience can only be bought at the price of ego-dissolution. Nor can the issue be resolved by a "synthesis" of the Apollonian and the Dionysian; the problem is the construction of a Dionysian ego. (175)

While Brown admits the immensity of such a project, he detects signs of its emergence not only in "the sexology of de Sade and the politics of Hitler" but also in "the romantic reaction" (176).

Neither provides an inspiring model for the new man. But Brown's point (supported by thinkers such as Marcuse) is that such "monsters" are spawned by the "sleep of reason," and would not have assumed such horrific forms in a more directly Dionysian culture. The Dionysian exuberance proposed here is more than just a safety-valve for preventing such organized atrocities as the death camps and hydrogen bombs. It is the very basis of communal experience.

Brown's unrepressed subject would be someone strong enough to live, and therefore strong enough to die. He (and there is no doubt that this subject is gendered masculine) would be "what no man has ever been, an individual" (291). Because the Dionysian consciousness would neither observe the limit, nor "*not negate any-more*" (308), it shares certain qualities with Nietzsche's Overman (*Übermensch*). Both are comfortable with the idea that "what has become perfect, all that is ripe—wants to die" (292). Brown's over-man thus takes his place in that gallery of "new subjects" or "posthumans" described by everyone from Plato to Donna Haraway, D. H. Lawrence to Stelarc, and Timothy Leary to Terrence McKenna.

Whether the hippies of the sixties were consciously trying to subvert the whole of history, or just trying to get their rocks off, is a moot point. No doubt both the cold war and the Vietnam War helped Brown's words to resonate more widely than in a less fear-ful period. With the benefit of hindsight it is easy to see Brown, and indeed Marcuse, as nuclear theorists responding to R. D. Laing's dictum that insanity is the only sane response to an insane world. Modernity's more general obsession with apocalyptic and orgasmic closure became intensified in the writings of those who recognized the libidinal aspect of this millenarian climate, exacerbated by the Pill and the Bomb. It wasn't long before several historical develop-ments, including the elevation of Governor Reagan to president, and the concurrent AIDS moral panic, combined in the 1980s to stretch and disfigure the dionysian themes of the 1960s—and set the scene for the thanatic '90s.

6

Playing at Catastrophe

Prêt-à-Mort: Necrophilia and Death Fashion

> A human race has to invent sacrifices equal to the natural cataclysmic order that surrounds it.
>
> Jean Baudrillard (1989: 3)

> You know that feeling you get when you're leaning back on a chair and you feel that you're just about to fall and then you catch yourself? . . . . I feel like that all the time.
>
> Steven Wright

In the final years of the twentieth century a new "look" emerged from the eternally recurring spectacle of the fashion world. Mimicking the corpse, it was referred to as "death fashion" or "heroin chic." Beautiful young models are arranged in mortified postures, and a fabricated autopsy report listed alongside the label and price ("black chiffon dress, internal trauma arising from severe beating").

This phenomenon represents an ironic response to an earlier and more naive epoch, the 1950s, when advertisements exploited the fear of nuclear attack by offering fashion tips for the apocalypse: "Men should wear wide-brimmed hats, women stockings and long sleeved dresses" (Boyer, 1985: 310). Illustrating what Frederic Jameson calls "one of those extraordinary postmodern mutations where the apocalyptic suddenly turns into the decorative" (1991: xvii), such images are saturated with both the black humor of hindsight and the anxiety of anticipation.

Death fashion is certainly a last-ditch attempt to whip up controversy (i.e., profitable attention) in an unshockable age. But it is also the inevitable end point of the necrophilic logic behind "panic sex," whereby "sexual activity is coded by the logic of exterminism" (Kroker & Kroker 14). In the "late" AIDS-era, death fashion recuperates the escapist impulse of heroin use, before fusing it with the Russian roulette mentality of "postorgy" sex. It depicts the aftermath of the devastating plague, "that common millennial trope now rendered sexual" (Kingwell 200). Hence the Krokers' claim that "[w]e have reached a fateful turning point in contemporary culture when human sexuality is a killing-zone, when desire is fascinating only as a sign of its own negation, and when the pleasure of catastrophe is what drives ultramodern culture onwards in its free fall through a panic scene of loss, cancellation and exterminism" (13). Centuries of romantic poetry have eroticized the corpse, and in this sense death fashion is merely a development of the gothic and decadent fascination with decomposition. "Fashion has become our contemporary mode of being in the world," writes Gail Faurschou, "and our contemporary 'mode' of death" (82).

The brief controversy provoked by death fashion pictorials suggests that many people viewed this trend as an abhorrent perversity, but this does not mean that it was automatically "transgressive" or even "dionysian." Heroin chic may well *appear* transgressive, by aestheticizing the logic of libidinal millenarianism, however it is far too implicated in the machinations of capitalism to be labeled as such. As Baudrillard reminds us, "the desire for death is itself recycled within fashion, emptying it of every subversive phantasm and involving it, along with everything else, in fashion's innocuous revolutions" (1993: 88). Mark Kingwell similarly believes that when "stage-managed with great care, transgression functions paradoxically to reaffirm the value of the norms it would transcend" (185). Although the possibilities for transgression multiply in an increasingly taboo-laden culture, they are short-circuited by the commodification of narcissism. (Indeed, as I write, the Australian government is considering plans to place general health warnings on advertising images that feature skeletal models [*Warning: Death Can Be Fatal*]. Certain sectors of the fashion industry may soon find themselves stigmatized in the same way as tobacco magnates.)

Such images do not evoke the specters of the already dead, who are banished from contemporary consciousness. Instead they denote Norman O. Brown's "death-in-life." They are more a parody of our cosmetic notions of death and decay, rather than a symbolic acknowledgment of our mortality. As such, death fashion represents an epoch whose commercial products include "Lyf-Lyk" funeral makeup and Trans Time Inc. Cryogenics (Chidester 278, 287).

Death fashion's fusion of banality, disgust, violence and eroticism simulates the sacrificial gesture of Bataille's millennium. The secret of its particular eschatology lies once again in an ambivalent artifice. For these are not snuff pictures. The models are not dead; they merely *simulate* death. Such images are generated for profit, not loss. If "death fashion" is a sacrifice, then the models have been slain for gain on the altar of the dollar (which is not to privilege a pure realm reserved for works of "art").

The advertising campaign by Bennetton, which included journalistic photos of soldiers crushed by tanks, marks the limits of this logic. By splicing their brand-name into horrific newsreel footage, this company transcended questions of the "immorality" of advertising, and became amoral precisely through its "transgression" of decency. Its flagship magazine, *Colors*, shows how Benetton has digested postmodern media theory and excreted a campaign based on mute realism. Paradoxically, this has resulted in yet another level of hyperreality in Baudrillard's Inferno. Indeed, Nike showed admirable restraint in not adding its name to photographs of those Heaven's Gate suicides who wore its shoes. Perhaps they were even more canny than Benetton in not drawing attention to the free advertising they were receiving through the news media.

Death fashion is merely the latest manifestation of the tumultuous relationship between Eros and Thanatos. As long ago as 1824, Giacomo Leopardi recognized this kinship by depicting them as sisters in his moral tale, "The Dialogue of Fashion and Death." "You from the very start went for people and blood," Fashion tells Death,

> while I content myself for the most part with beards, hairstyles, clothes, furniture, fine houses and the like. But in fact I have not failed . . . to play a few tricks that could compared *[sic]* with yours, as for instance to pierce ears, lips and noses, and to rip them with the knickknacks I hang in the holes; to scorch the flesh of men with the red-hot irons I make them brand themselves with for beauty's sake; to deform the heads of infants with bandages and other contraptions, making it a rule that everyone in a certain country has to have the same shape of head . . . to cripple people with narrow boots; to choke their breath and make their eyeballs pop with the use of tight corsets. . . . I persuade and force all civilized people to put up every day with a thousand difficulties and a thousand discomforts, and often with pain and agony, and some even to die gloriously for the love they bear me. (Faurschou 58)

The conceptual tentacles of this phenomenon originate in the writings of the Marquis de Sade, Friedrich Nietzsche and Bataille, and then filter through Marshall McLuhan, Guy Debord and—most rigorously—

Baudrillard. In order to understand what "necro-spectacles" such as death fashion contribute to our neodecadent moment, it is necessary to sift through some of the entrails of our sacrificial culture.

As we have seen, Baudrillard reduces the dilemma of a sexually saturated society to one question, "What are we to do after the orgy?" He may, however, be jumping the gun. The mechanical (i.e., Sadean) logic of the industrial revolution continues to define both sexual monotony and erotic excess up to and including the electronic era. In this case, the orgy will continue indefinitely; only the participants will change or die. Like the cogs of a machine, orgiastic participants are expendable by being replaceable. This is merely another version of what Gilles Deleuze calls "machinic desire." Even in the age of computers, each part can be replaced, upgraded or rerouted through the system. It may thus be time to rephrase Baudrillard's question to, "How do we *stop* the orgy?" Will it grind to a halt and explode with its own frictional heat, or will it succumb to its own viruses? Or must the softer surfaces of the flesh endure the legacy of the Luddites?

Those glossy fashion spreads that depict young men and women—traditionally considered to be in the prime of life—strangled in baths or bleeding from bullet holes on escalators, capture the static horror of the Marquis de Baudrillard's fatal orgy. Like the copulating shadows on the walls of Castle Silling, or the seared portraits of the Hiroshima streets, they delineate holographic afterimages of the event. We become hypnotized by the absence that simulation entails. Charles Levin, who believes that the theory of postmodernism may best be described as "a social theory of the after image, a theory of collective life as an aftermath," thinks that "postmodernism is really a kind of '*postmortemism*'" (1988: 104). To realize that we are living not only after the orgy, but also after an insidious apocalypse, induces rigor mortis of the spirit. Suddenly we are all potential mannequins for a death fashion shoot.

Close Encounters of the Third Kind: the Joachite Structure of Baudrillard's Philosophy

> It would be stupid to prophesy an apocalypse in the literal sense of the term. My idea is that the catastrophe has already happened, it's here already. What interests me is precisely beyond the catastrophe, what I would call its hypertelia . . . . I would prefer not to play the role of the lugubrious, thoroughly useless prophet.

Baudrillard (Gane, 1993: 43, 99)

Although Baudrillard continues to deny that he is a doomsayer, he can do little to alter the fact that this is how he is consistently framed (and the pun is intended). The rhetorical power of his convictions, the poetic momentum of his prose, and the eschatological targets of his intellect, all combine to create an oeuvre whose "truth-effect" places him in the position of a postmodern Nietzsche. Brian Rotman is certainly swimming with the current when he describes Baudrillard as the "prophet of apocalypse, hysterical lyricist of panic" (ibid.: 7). In one of those metaphoric feedback loops he is so fond of, Baudrillard's philosophy has permeated popular culture to such an extent that he is perceived and represented as both a prophet and *symptom* of the apocalypse—the man who narrates the end so eloquently as to bring it about, or at least accelerate its arrival: *In the end was the word, and the word was Baudrillard.*

The more sensational aspects of his writing have been emphasized by the media and not discouraged by Baudrillard's own role-playing as provocateur. This has resulted in a heady mixture of hostility, indifference, mild amusement, and even embarrassment within the academy and other intellectual institutions. Functioning as a kind of demonized trickster figure, Baudrillard is often ruthlessly simplified or foolishly taken at face value. Consequently he is frequently dismissed as a charlatan, which is akin to accusing politicians of hypocrisy or prostitutes of insincerity. Those who discount Baudrillard's more recent work have not usually read *Symbolic Exchange and Death* (1993), which in effect—as his most rigorous, erudite and original work—forms a durable safety net for his later and more audacious intellectual acrobatics. This is not to deny that Baudrillard can be infuriatingly oblique, mind-numbingly repetitive, morally reprehensible, and plainly inconsistent. The trouble is that such accusations are beginning to eclipse his valuable insights.

Baudrillard's name is associated also with a mid-1980s American appropriation of French "postmodern" theory, which leaves him vulnerable to the charge of being an anachronism. This is somewhat ironic, considering that it was Baudrillard who suggested "that we go directly from 1989 to 2000" for there is no good reason "to languish for another decade in this hellish atmosphere" (1993a: 93). Baudrillard thus not only provides the title of this book, but the postcoital historical model which has inspired my own exploration of a specifically libidinal millenarianism.

As a veteran of both the sexual revolution and May '68, Baudrillard is well-qualified to speak of living "after the orgy." Such formative experiences inject a faint but continuous note of nostalgia into his rigorously antisentimental agenda. Like Tom Robbins, Linda Grant and Camille Paglia, Baudrillard speaks of the 1960s as a period that "opened a gap" (Gane, 1991: 159) in the sociocultural curtain. "Sometimes," he admits, "I find myself longing for that lightness of spirit we had in the sixties, when people had more zest for collective interventions and group action" (1993: 190). Baudrillard would regard such a biographical reading of his work as theoretical violence of the worst kind. Yet his reference to "mourning" the sixties (ibid.: 20) needs to be kept in mind by anybody attempting to connect sexuality with the *thanatopraxis* (Baudrillard's own term) of millenarian ideologies. It is surely significant that, in the watershed year of 1968, Baudrillard translated W. E. Mühlmann's *Messianismes Revolutionnaires,* indicating an empathy with end-of-the-world heretics.

Accused of passive nihilism, Baudrillard responds with a nutshell account of his personal approach to eschatology:

> To look ahead in this way requires a somewhat metaphysical and a somewhat transcendental curiosity. People have spoken so often about the end of things that I'd like to be able to see what goes on the other side of the end, in a sort of hyperspace and transfinity. And even if things are not really at their end, well! Let's act as if they were. It's a game, a provocation. Not in order to put a full stop to everything but, on the contrary, to make everything begin again. So you see, I'm far from being a pessimist. (ibid.: 133)

Indeed, when asked by *Le Journal des Psychologues* whether one should speak evil and think negatively in order to avoid catastrophe, Baudrillard answered, "Yes, that seems to be the only recourse, at least in terms of immunity" (ibid.: 175). Such a strategy sustains not only many of those disillusioned with the outcome of the 1960s, but also that younger demographic once labeled *Generation X.* A brief recontextualizing of his thought, therefore, will help us to map the politics of exhaustion into the present.

The figurehead of Baudrillard's philosophy is his theory of simulation, which, "out of some obscure need to classify" (1993a: 5), forms the third stage in his historical development of the sign. Loosely speaking, the first stage of the sign involves a direct reference to some kind of "meaning," the second stage to a masking or mimicry of this meaning, and the third stage to an usurpation and evacuation of meaning. In this last scenario, the sign breaks loose from its referent, no longer anchored to anything in "reality," and becomes a hyperreal satellite orbiting a world without any coherent connections. This is the postmodern stage, where mass-reproduction results in a world full of copies without an original. Organized chaos reigns. Baudrillard captured the attention of a spectacle-saturated United States by theorizing the vertigo of this simulated situation, of which the North American media is the prime example. According to his model, then, this third stage heralds a virtual apocalypse.

At this point it is worth remembering that the stock-in-trade of (pre)millennial prophets is to map historical epochs on to an apocalyptic time line. Norman Cohn has amply demonstrated that the most influential historical schema during the Middle Ages and the Renaissance was the tripartite model of the great prophet Joachim of Fiore (1145–1202). From this point on, no apocalyptic history was taken seriously unless divided into three stages, confirming the old saying that "bad things comes in threes." Frank Kermode detects Joachim's structural powers at work in the modern era, and believes it "may well have contributed more than a little to the thought and feeling of the late-nineteenth-century 'Decadence'" (1995: 256). Elsewhere he notes that "the Third Reich" is itself a Joachite expression (1975: 13).

Cohn credits Joachim with being the first to break with a primarily moral or religious concept of chronology by inventing a method of specifically *historical* interpretation. This enabled the development of a new prophetic system, "which was to be the most influential one known to Europe until Marxism." Cohn argues, "it is unmistakably the Joachite phantasy of the three ages that reappeared in, for instance, the theories of historical evolution expounded by the German Idealist philosophers Lessing, Schelling, Fichte and to some extent Hegel" (1993: 109). Even Marx did not dispense with this tripartite structure, in so far as his three successive epochs (primitive communism, class society, and utopian communism) mirror Joachim's sequence of fear, faith, and freedom.[21]

Indeed, the dynamic properties of the number three appear irresistible to those who try to map the meaning of time. Prophets seem drawn to the historical angles of the triad. It is thus more than likely that Baudrillard's obscure need to classify (which itself issued from a Marxist orientation) reflects this deeply entrenched proleptic pattern. The conceptual grids of Western metaphysics thus form the limits of Baudrillard's thought, no matter how contemptuous he is of philosophies that take the human subject as the subject of history.

One major difference between Baudrillard and Joachim is that the former feels no compulsion to adhere to his own models or formulas. To rigidly follow one chronological scheme seems a quaint notion to Baudrillard, for he sees no contradiction in presenting a three-stage time line on one hand, and a fractal-pattern on the other. Happily, his dionysian intellectual heritage allows such anti-Apollonian logic.

In his most programmatic attempt to explain his philosophy, *Symbolic Exchange and Death*, Baudrillard identifies the closest thing to an absolute term in his thinking:

> Everywhere, in every domain, a single form predominates: reversibility, cyclical reversal and annulment put an end to the linearity of time, language, economic exchange, accumulation and power. Hence the reversibility of the gift in the counter-gift, the reversibility of exchange in the sacrifice, the reversibility of time in the cycle, the reversibility of production in destruction, [and] the reversibility of life in death . . . . In every domain it assumes the form of extermination and death, for it is the form of the symbolic itself. Neither mystical nor structural, the symbolic is inevitable. (2)[22]

Power is seen as an objective force that follows the rules of reversibility, and can therefore be regained or reduced through acts of symbolic violence. Examples include both the irreverent absurdity of pataphysics (the "science of imaginary solutions") and the systematic cruelty of terrorism. Both recognize the power of the symbolic as a means of reclaiming our own death in defiance of the state monopoly on mortality (and indeed, immortality).

For Baudrillard, as for generations of medieval monks, the meaning of existence comes down to cracking "the code" that then reveals the secret of the End. Social control in this current "neo-capitalist cybernetic order" (ibid.) thus becomes a secular form of apocalyptic prognosis based on the proliferation of signs. (Think, for example, of market analysts.) These replace those traditionally prophetic modes associated with symbolic *ends*. Consequently, sacred prediction yields to secular forecast.

Baudrillard's reading of history thus anticipates the findings of "chaos theory," whereby random elements begin to follow their own inscribed patterns. Our overs(t)imulated society begins to fall for its own media-made decoys. The question becomes; What does it mean to look for a sign when the world is plagued by them? Even the apocalypse itself can lose its symbolic power through its excessive use as an omen of the end by those who ignore the rule of reversibility. "What we must fear," remarks Baudrillard in an interview, "is not the term date of the year 2000 (which is itself a symbolic end); it is that this term date even has been rendered impossible or useless, like all other symbolic term dates . . . . That would really be the end of the end (Gane, 1993: 164).

In discussing *King Lear* and *Macbeth*, Kermode refers to the history of "researches into death in an age too late for apocalypse, too critical for prophecy" (1975: 88). He believes Shakespeare's world exhibits "all the symptoms of decay and change, all the terrors of an approaching end, but when the end comes it is not an end, and both suffering and the need for patience are perpetual" (ibid.: 82). Libidinal millenarianism connects directly to this endlessness of the end. Baudrillard's apocalyptic asymptote differs from Shakespeare's, however, because it is rooted in a very different epoch. Obsessed with the unprecedented nature of our age, Baudrillard ignores the fact that the "end of the end" has been considered before the era of simulation.

In fact, Baudrillard's philosophies of ideological exhaustion develop from a kind of antirevelation. Our postalienated situation leads to what he calls "horizontal immortality," an impoverished state not unlike Brown's death-in-life or Marcuse's one-dimensional man. All exemplify libidinal entropy. Yet Baudrillard rejects transcendence as a solution, since he blames the Christian monopoly over verticality as the root of the problem in the first place. When human history hit "escape velocity," it left us adrift in a symbolic antigravitational field. Social relations started to drift free of any reference point, moral, legal or otherwise. A reading of Elias Canetti's *Human Province* persuades Baudrillard that at

> a precise moment in time the human race . . . dropped out of history. Without even being conscious of the change, we suddenly left reality behind. What we have to do now . . . [is] find that critical point, that blind spot in time. Otherwise, we just continue on with our self-destructive ways. This hypothesis appeals to me because Canetti doesn't envisage an end, but rather what I would call an "ecstasy," in the primal sense of the word—a passage at the same time into the dissolution and the transcendence of a form. (ibid.: 99)

Baudrillard exercises considerable latitude in dating this ironic rapture, which roughly accompanied the Apollo moon landings. It occurred at the close of the Second World War or alternatively at "some point in the 1980s" (1994: 10). Canetti's metaphor prompts Baudrillard's own variation on the "end of history" theme, an apocalyptic motif recently popularized by Frances Fukuyama (1992).

According to Fukuyama, (upper-case) History ended with the fall of the Berlin Wall, culminating in the ultimate "victory" of liberal democracy. Baudrillard's account is less humanistic. Although at some point we "dropped out of history," history continues unabated, and we follow in its wake like a sonic boom that will never have the opportunity to be heard. In J. K. Huysmans's *A Rebours,* this state of affairs is only a latent possibility, but Baudrillard completes the idea by stretching it across the twentieth century:

> The end is, in fact, only conceivable in a logical order of causality and continuity. Now, it is events themselves which, by their artificial production, their programmed occurrence or the anticipation of

> their effects—not to mention their transfiguration in the media — are suppressing the cause-effect relation and hence all historical continuity . . . . We may perhaps even see this as an adventure, since the disappearance of the end is in itself an original situation. It seems to be characteristic of our culture and our history, which cannot even manage to come to an end, and are, as a result, assured of an indefinite recurrence, a backhanded immortality. Up to now, immortality has been mainly that of the beyond, an immortality yet to come, but we are today inventing another kind in the here and now, an immortality of endings receding to infinity. (1994: 115)

This "immortality of endings receding to infinity" brings forward Nietzsche's eternal return into the cybernetic era, and crystallizes it within Sade's or Huysmans' definition of artifice. Baudrillard believes computer-networks are "the particle accelerator which has smashed the referential [read "natural"] orbit of things once and for all" (ibid.: 2). As such, postmodernity is witness to "the most degenerated, most artificial, and most eclectic phase" (Gane, 1991: 158). Traumatized by a century of unprecedented technological progress and political violence, our epoch breaks its neck trying to follow the Doppler effect of history.

Our response to this general disorientation is to renovate the ruins of the past, both literally and metaphorically. We are thus, according to Baudrillard, in the midst of effacing all the ideological signs and political accomplishments of the modern era. This "enthusiastic work of mourning" whitewashes every significant event of the century, including revolutions, wars, colonialism, and nuclearism. Through a ritual of remembrance we are in fact rewinding the tape in order to erase it; lest we *really* remember. Everybody is now undoing history with the same enthusiasm that went into making it (ibid.: 32)—a process seen by Baudrillard as both sinister and comic.

Many proponents of the postmodern condition have been excited by such a notion, mistaking it as the premise for a new beginning. They argue that postmodernity is actually the galaxy of alternative histories resulting from the big bang of an infinitely dense History. But the melancholic Baudrillard sees no cause for celebration. To Baudrillard's Gallic nose, the present state of affairs reeks of the millenarian reflex to repent. Indeed, repentance is symptomatic of postmodernity, and discernible in "the recycling of past forms, the exalting of residues, rehabilitation by bricolage, eclectic sentimentality" (ibid.: 35). Whereas bands of blood-spattered self-flagellators roamed the land in the Middle Ages, today we burn with "archive fever" (Derrida) and the mania to mummify the past.

Given such a cultural climate, our symbol of the apocalypse ought not to have been the Four Horsemen, but Pee-wee Hermann, that ironically infantile comedian whose career was ruined when found masturbating to a flickering porno screen. The late twentieth century was consumed by a Kleenex-ideology, sopping up the effluvia of previous decades to prepare for the corrosive stains of the second coming. Baudrillard writes;

> We used to ask what might come after the orgy—mourning or melancholia? Doubtless neither, but an interminable clean-up of all the vicissitudes of modern history and its processes of liberation (of peoples, sex, dreams, art and the unconscious—in short, of all that makes up the orgy of our times), in an atmosphere dominated by the apocalyptic presentiment that all this is coming to an end. Rather than pressing forward and taking flight into the future, we prefer the retrospective apocalypse, and a blanket revisionism . . . . Celebration and commemoration are themselves merely the soft form of necrophagous cannibalism, the homeopathic form of murder by easy stages. This is the work of the heirs, whose ressentiment towards the deceased is boundless. Museums, jubilees, festivals, complete works, the publication of the tiniest of unpublished fragments—all this shows that we are entering an active age of ressentiment and repentance. (ibid.: 22)

These undoubtably neo-Nietzschean words resonate loudly within the echochamber of popular culture, informing death fashion, modern primitives, techno-pagans, and the cyberians of the new millennium.

"Maybe after all the year 2000 will never occur," Baudrillard concludes, for the simple reason that we cannot escape this "fatal asymptote which causes us . . . to rewind modernity like a tape?" (1994: 11). In such a metaphor we can detect not only the geometry of the orgy and the "red thread" of Dionysus, but also the "thanatic asymptote" on which my notion of libidinal millenarianism depends. Bataille's interpretation of eroticism—plunging towards extinction, yet cleaving to life in order not to extinguish the experience—is thus paralleled by our constant deferral of global suicide.

Speaking specifically of nuclear annihilation, Baudrillard entertains the possibility that "there is no strategic guarantee in deterrence, nor, furthermore, any survival instinct of the species" (1990: 186). What protects us from a nuclear holocaust, he argues, is not the balance of terror, but the possibility that we will miss out on the media spectacle of Armageddon. That the apocalypse will not be televised. "*That is why it won't happen* . . . the drive to spectacle is more powerful than the survival instinct, we can count on that" (ibid.).

Such an assertion extends Walter Benjamin's statement that humanity can now "experience its own destruction as an aesthetic pleasure of the first order" (1992: 235). In the twenty-first century we have become aware of a fundamental tension between the urge to destroy ourselves in the "ultimate spectacular," and the knowledge that this is impossible, that we will be consumed by it. This is yet another version of the thanatic asymptote, this time on a macrocosmic scale. We yearn for the aesthetic thrill of Apocalypse, and yet we cling to life, for we can't satisfy our voyeuristic desire if we are in fact dead. The one balances the other in a metaphysical parody of the nuclear deterrence theory, and with the same profound consequences. Our only option appears to be homeopathic: we consume the mini-apocalypses hurled at us each day through the media *as if* each were the Big One.

The younger generation's *penchant* for black is a sign of the frustrated mourning that this situation demands, the recognition that the body is merely a "corpse full of cravings" (Kermode, 1975: 117). It is analogous to the drag queen's strategy of denial through exaggeration or overcompensation. The nirvana-principle—uncannily enacted by grunge-icon Kurt Cobain—is thus sifted through the street-languages of subcultural style. Kingwell observes that

> [w]hereas the flagellants of other end-times tied their public suffering to religious purification, and met the uncertainty of the Second Coming with self-abasement and violent denial, the young extremists of our own day link body decoration to a purification of social expectations, and meet the uncertainty of their own futures with a refusal to invest that future with expectation or meaning. (184)

The heart of darkness becomes refigured through popular culture, so that Kurt's, "yeah, whatever nevermind," supplants Kurtz's, "The horror! The horror!"

The most recent fin de siècle thus merely extended the bomb culture of the 1950s and 1960s. Eyes skyward and bowels empty in anticipation, we witnessed that fatal asymptote dangling over our heads like Pynchon's apocalyptic rainbow. Exhausted and underpaid, the erotic gravity of the situation forced us to become frozen in an obscene, pornographic parody, waiting with open mouths for that orgasmic impact (which itself parodies the nebulous desire of a sign-saturated society). "Panic in slow-motion," Baudrillard calls it; or in Steve Wright's image, feeling like you're constantly falling backward but never actually hitting the floor. This is the gut-wrenching moment of panic: to be caught in the headlights of history as it speeds toward oblivion.

"A Biocybernetic Self-Fulfilling Prophecy World Orgy I":

Or Surviving the Necropolis

> For all we might strive to forget the problem of the end, then, or circumvent it by artificial technical solutions, the end does not forget us.
>
> Baudrillard (1994: 91)

> Prophecies are ragged and dirty.
>
> Vaughan in David Cronenberg's *Crash* (1996)

Having long meditated on the shortcomings of the so-called *sexual revolution,* Baudrillard concludes that it did not so much *fail* as succeed only too well. Developing the insights of Brown and Marcuse, Baudrillard exposes this particular orgy as an ally of the same antisymbolic forces it claimed to oppose. The 1960s' embrace of Eros accompanied a general denial of Thanatos, producing an unbalanced state of affairs. Consequently, sex could never be truly "subversive" or "transgressive," for it acted like a Trojan horse for smuggling in the ideologies of immortality, that secret weapon of the church, the economy and the state. As Baudrillard notes, "all 'historical' societies are arranged so as to dissociate sex and death in every possible way, and play the liberation of one off against the other—which is a way of neutralizing them both" (1993: 184).

Viewed from such a perspective, Wilhelm Reich's orgone energy becomes a conservative force, giving the orgasm a *function,* and coercing it to align with productivity, utility, and other identity-based agendas. This is why Baudrillard believes that the "slogan of sexuality is in solidarity with political economy," because both aim "at abolishing death." Those who opt for sex "have only exchanged prohibitions" (ibid.: 184-185).

Here Baudrillard fails to acknowledge that "sexuality" should not be isolated as a theoretical construct, principally because it cuts across many other grids of experience—metaphysical, cultural, linguistic, economic, and so on. Consequently, sex (like death) is both everywhere and nowhere, a transparent membrane covering everything like clingwrap, and stretched to a breaking point. This does not mean, however, that we can no longer talk about it; rather, it must find a conducting medium in order to make sense. A proper context must be found before "sexuality" can trace the shape of its own disappearance. In other words, we cannot discuss sex as a discrete mode or structure because the word *sex* is meaningless until it hooks onto some other valency. It is for this reason that Baudrillard is drawn to the orgiastic conjunction of sexuality with some other millenarian seduction, for instance death or technology.

Dionysus thus morphs into the Grim Reaper as *the* symbolic other. Since death is no longer experienced as a collective social phenomenon, it fascinates only in its sacrificial artifice:

> All passion then takes refuge in violent death, which is the sole manifestation of something like the sacrifice, that is to say, like a real transmutation *through the will of the group.* And in this sense, it matters little whether death is accidental, criminal or catastrophic: from the moment it escapes "natural" reason, and becomes a challenge to nature, it once again becomes the business of the group, demanding a collective and symbolic response; in a word, it arouses *the passion for the artificial,* which is at the same time sacrificial passion. (Baudrillard, 1993: 165)

"Sacrificial passion" was illustrated vividly in the weeks following the "artificial" death of Princess Diana. Paradoxically, "natural" death is interpreted as an artificial invention of western science, its "objective and punctual character" being the collective projection of a linear, apocalyptic culture. As the Situationist Raoul Vaneigem states, "We do not die because we must, we die because it is a habit, to which one day, not so long ago, our thoughts became bound" (ibid.: 144).

It may seem willfully contradictory of Baudrillard to discuss the modern metropolis as a "culture of death" after lamenting society's denial of its very existence. But this is just another example of his dionysian fondness for the reversible. "The cemetery no longer exists because modern cities have entirely taken over their function: they are ghost towns, cities of death" (ibid.: 127). Subsequently, death is everywhere for the simple reason it has been swept under the carpet. Like the pervasiveness of "crime" in a culture obsessed with eradicating it, death lurks around every corner, so that in our unprecedented age, "death is a delinquency" (ibid.: 126).

From Baudrillard's self-confessed necrospective, all sexuality is necrophilic, because we refuse to acknowledge our symbolic debt to the dead: "Death is ultimately nothing more than the social line of demarcation separating the 'dead' from the 'living': therefore, it affects both equally" (ibid.: 127). Life is thus merely a surplus value (a survival) according to which we measure the profits/prophets of our spiritual bankruptcy. Life becomes a matter of economic management, of how we *spend* our time. Existence is seen increasingly in terms of accumulation, for which death is due payment. Baudrillard's crucial realization is that "the emergence of survival can therefore be analyzed as the fundamental operation in the birth of power" (ibid.: 129).

The concept of immortality thus emerges simultaneously with the symbolic apartheid of the dead. Modern millenarians must therefore take advice from medieval heretics, and take life back into their own hands. Rather than be blackmailed by the immortality of the soul (Christianity), or seduced by the Darwinian imperative to survive (the Michigan Militia and other renegade para-military organizations), they must commune with the dead while living in the symbolic space-time continuum of this "divided space."

Raoul Vaneigem also believes that the ethical imperative to survive is the most powerful tool of the modern state. His historical polemic, *The Movement of the Free Spirit* (1994), complements Baudrillard's thoughts on the symbolic power of commandeering one's own fate. Beginning with the premise that "the Middle Ages were no more Christian than the late Eastern Bloc was communist" (10), Vaneigem documents the trials of medieval heretics from the perspective of the present, and seeks to demonstrate the now familiar dionysian assertion that "the economy is everywhere that life is not" (17). Sounding remarkably like Baudrillard, Vaneigem states that

> [t]he apocalypse has been announced so many times that it cannot occur. And even if it did it would be hard to distinguish it from the everyday fate already reserved for individual and community alike. Is it hard to imagine a more sinister dance of death than war, torture, tyranny, disaster, sickness, boredom, guilty pleasures, and the kind of gratification that prefers self-torture to self-enlightenment? Is not survival cut from the very same cloth of apocalypse? (19–20)

Vaneigem realigns Ingmar Bergman's chessboard, so that death *and* life both oppose survival. This theoretical move is informed less by Baudrillard's cool and ironic postalienation than by his own political passion, which continues to voice the genuinely transgressive demands of adversary culture:

> The millenarian incitement to produce one's own unhappiness has so thoroughly impregnated the world of the imagination that everything from art to daydreaming consists of negative scenarios, doomed love affairs, inevitable failures, inevitable obsolescence, bitter victories or bliss in ignorance. The only way to remedy the lassitude brought on by survival is through a treatment, focusing on negativity, that uses alchemy to rid life of the effects of survival, radically remaking the human from what is most human: namely the search for pleasure. (248)

The most profound response to the supremacy of a deferred eternity is thus to appropriate the afterlife libidinally in the present. Vaneigem's project rests on his belief that "[t]he end of the world, with or without renewal, is profitable only in its anticipation. The economy prophesies the apocalyptic horror of the world's disappearance only on the condition of the horror of an already ruined life" (88).

The answer, according to Vaneigem, is certainly not vulgar hedonism, which inevitably results in the aftertaste of death (a result of failing to address the libidinal atrophy of the market). Nor is it Bataille's vision of nostalgic continuity, but rather in a spiritual "alchemy" that inhabits the space between transgression and transcendence. Such a vision, however, is far too esoteric, oblique, and romantic (read "sixties-ish") to be adopted by those he expects to live it out, namely the Maffesolian neotribes of the urban centers. Nevertheless, Vaneigem insists that "nothing can stop [him] from searching out that strange crowd of people who inhabit the shadows of the scaffolds, the darkness of prisons and factories, the secret places of the city . . . [for] . . . . It is they who have lived and are still trying to live by forsaking the imperatives of survival" (257).

Today's "strange crowd" consists of those "idlers of the Apocalypse" (Virilio, 1986: 69) who seem to instinctively appreciate the symbolic power of controlling their own bodies (and by extension, their own death) in the interests of "living truly." By cutting and piercing their flesh, these neopagans oppose the alienated spectacle of death fashion, as well as the survivalist mentality of cosmetic surgery. The ideas of Baudrillard, Vaneigem and Michel Maffesoli are inscribed in the bloodletting and branding of these (perhaps only slightly) less mediated bodies. Indeed, the "self as counterdiscourse" (John Walker) seems to be an ironic return to decadent notions of art and artifice.

Baudrillard likewise sees something subversive in this postmodern tendency to equate adornment with transcendent pain. Observing an almost organic empathy between graffiti-scrawled trains and tattooed flesh, Baudrillard comments that "[s]omething about the city has become tribal . . . before writing, with these powerful emblems stripped of meaning. An incision into the flesh of empty signs that do not signify personal identity, but group initiation and affiliation: 'A biocybernetic self-fulfilling prophecy world orgy I'" (1993: 82).

The contemporary obsession with survival is, for Baudrillard, "the most worrying sign of the degradation of the species" (1989: 43). It represents the flip side not only of the decadent's meticulous self-abuse, but also of the heroin-fueled "thanatoids" of our own time. Yet Baudrillard, as always, jolts us out of such Apollonian earnestness by reminding us that "[e]verywhere survival has become a burning issue, perhaps by some weariness of life or a collective desire for catastrophe." Nevertheless, "we should not take all this too seriously," because it is "also a playing at catastrophe" (ibid.: 42).

Temporary Autonomous Zones and the Archaic Revival

> . . . the mass of people oughtn't even to try to think—because they *can't*. They should be alive and frisky, and acknowledge the great god Pan. He's the only god for the masses, forever. The few can go in for higher cults if they like. But let the mass be forever pagan.
>
> Oliver Mellors, *Lady Chatterley's Lover*
> (Lawrence, 1994: 300)

> The twentieth century does not make sense whatsoever unless it ends in a complete transformation of the species. And the nuclear death and the life-affirming factors are so inextricably intertwined that it will remain a horse race right up until the last moment.
>
> Terence McKenna (20)

> When are a few lumps going to appear in this smooth time? Hard to believe in the return of Carnival, of Saturnalia. Perhaps time has stopped here in the Pleroma, here in the Gnostic dreamworld where our bodies are rotting but our "minds" are downloaded into eternity. We know so much—how can we not know the answer to this most vexing of questions?
>
> Hakim Bey (1994)

Baudrillard not only believes that utopia exists, but that it lies conveniently across the Atlantic ocean. In his travel book, *America* (1989), he squints into the "mirror of our decadence" in a Swiftian journey of surreal discovery and philosophical reflection. While "we" Europeans (and colonial mimics) philosophize on the end of anything and everything, in America things are actually *coming* to an end.

(In fact, Baudrillard and Fukuyama are merely the most recent intellectuals to perceive historical stagnation in the United States. Julian Pefanis reminds us that, for Alexandre Kojève, "the American way of life prefigures a life at the end of history" [1991: 13]; similarly Huysmans's *A Rebours* was written "[o]ut of disgust with [the] American lifestyle" [in Beaumont 44]. Indeed, this nation's violent inception was explained by Christopher Columbus in millennial terms: "God made me the messenger of the new heaven and the new earth of which he spoke in the Apocalypse of St. John after having spoken of it through the mouth of Isaiah; and he showed me the spot where to find it" [in Boyer, 1992: 225].)

The model citizens of this modern utopia are joggers, who, according to Baudrillard at least

> are the true Latter Day Saints and the protagonists of an easy-does-it Apocalypse. Nothing evokes the end of the world more than a man running straight ahead on a beach, swathed in the sounds of his walkman, cocooned in the solitary sacrifice of his energy, indifferent even to catastrophes since he expects destruction to come only as the fruit of his own efforts, from exhausting the energy of a body that has in his own eyes become useless. (1989: 91)

Of course the irony that propels Baudrillard's narrative is the realization that this utopia is simultaneously a nightmare. The old Chinese proverb—"May you get what you want"—has come true. Affluent liberation has produced a kitsch prison.

The pragmatic difficulty of sustaining and maintaining the utopian state is that it always threatens to flip into dystopia. As most communes discovered in the 1960s, utopia is "no-place" on account of its tendency to fall apart, given the elusiveness of perfection (at least since the Fall). Not everyone will agree with Baudrillard's provocative assertion that the American experience is "the crisis of an achieved utopia." But we can certainly appreciate the hypothetical dilemma of America having to confront "the problem of its duration and permanence" (ibid.: 92).

In Western eschatology the millennium is often a synonym for utopia. (Thomas More's *Utopia* was subtitled *Millennium* in some editions.) This equation was reinforced by the biblical anticipation of Christ's thousand-year reign, and its attendent spiritual perks. Armageddon, the Second Coming, and the last days leading to Judgment Day, convey a powerful sense of imminence while, simultaneously locating it in the "no-place" of the future. In this scenario, tomorrow never comes. Situating utopia within the hyperreal coordinates of American commodity culture, Baudrillard claims that, "[u]topia is no longer the domain of transcendence, it is the domain of simulation" (ibid.: 27).

From More and Jonathan Swift to H. G. Wells and Baudrillard, speculative literature has tended to equate social utopias with entropy, stagnation, banality, decadence, and other forms of "panic-in-slow-motion." In such moral fables, utopia represents an end-of-the-rainbow scenario. The elusive qualities of utopia have inspired a latter-day Situationist and self-described "poetic terrorist," Bey, to formulate his concept of the Temporary Autonomous Zone or TAZ. The point of doing so is to acknowledge that "paradise" is a highly mobile concept which, in order to flourish in its authentic and "unmediated" state, must resist pressures to stabilize it.

Bey defines the TAZ as

> an uprising which does not engage directly with the State, a guerilla operation which liberates an area (of land, of time, of imagination) and then dissolves itself to re-form elsewhere/elsewhen, before the State can crush it . . . . The TAZ is thus a perfect tactic for an era in which the State is omnipresent and all-powerful and yet simultaneously riddled with cracks and vacancies. (1991: 101)

As a heterotopic eruption into the political mediascape, Bey's utopia is explicitly dionysian. Some of its most celebrated moments include the Paris Commune, D'Annunzio's outlaw state of Fiume, pirate utopias, 1960s' be-ins, and—more recently—non-commercial dance parties or "raves." (Neither John of Leyden's New Jerusalem, David Koresh's Waco Compound, nor the Bible Belt's "freedom zones" qualifies as a TAZ on account of the violence and/or coercion that underpins them. Those, however, who have seen William Gozecki's astonishing film, *Waco: The Rules of Engagement* [1997]—which documents the American government's brutal response to the Branch Davidians—may feel that this *was indeed* a TAZ, and one so successful that it could not be tolerated by the authorities.)[23]

In many respects Bey's prescription for an "eros of the social" emerges from a more romantic (though highly qualified and politically engaged) Baudrillardian perspective; perhaps closer to Vaneigem. "Disappearance" is acknowledged to be a valid strategy, provided it is not complicit with that "silence of an ironic hyperconformity" that Bey sees as the inevitable end point of the Frenchman's philosophy. "TAZ-theory tries to concern itself with existing or emerging situations rather than with pure utopianism," he writes. "All over the world people are leaving or 'disappearing' themselves from the Grid of Alienation and seeking ways to restore human contact" (1995):

> As I read it, disappearance seems to be a very logical radical option for our time, not at all a disaster or death for the radical project. Unlike morbid deathfreak nihilistic interpretation of Theory, mine intends to mine it for useful strategies in the always-ongoing "revolution of everyday life": the struggle that cannot cease even with the last failure of political or social revolution because nothing except the end of the world can bring an end to everyday life, nor

> to our aspirations for the good things, for the Marvelous. And as Nietzsche said, if the world could come to an end, logically it would have done so; it has not, so it does not. And so, as one of the Sufis said, no matter how many draughts of forbidden wine we drink, we will carry this raging thirst into eternity. (ibid.)

However, as Mark Dery succinctly pointed out to me during an interview, because "the TAZ is *temporary*" and *"autonomous,"* it cannot claim to be politically effective. "The obvious problem with a psychopolitics whose challenges to the status quo are a return to Dionysian excess and abandon," he insists elsewhere, "is that consumer culture eats such challenges for breakfast" (38). Like the allegedly "transgressive" carnival, the TAZ can be viewed as just another liminal space in which to reactivate the prohibition and reinforce the social order.

Bey tries to address this criticism in his article-*cum*-footnote entitled "Permanent TAZs" (1995). While his writing abounds with concrete examples of immediatism or TAZs, he offers no practical advice on extending the utopian use-by date. What we get instead are abstract calls to arms, as when he states that the Permanent Autonomous Zone is constituted by "the long-drawn-out intensification of the joys—and risks—of the TAZ," and that "the intensification of the PAZ will be . . . . Utopia Now" (ibid.). Here we see how the ghost of Baudrillard's *America* hovers over all attempts to envisage a non-naive and post-Edenic utopia. The question becomes politically vital; Can we separate "permanence" from its seemingly intrinsic alliance with the status quo? Is the duration of time inherently oppressive?

Bey tries to reconcile political activism with Epicurean sensualism—a conflict that provided enough sparks to power the counterculture of the 1960s. He has a sharp eye and an even sharper tongue, which is quick to denounce the pseudotransgressions of the millennial spectacle. Sporting his Situationist affiliations, Bey equates the machinations of capital with those digital circuses that it both produces and consumes in a grotesque model of perpetual motion. Agreeing with Baudrillard that "in every spectacle there is the immanence of the catastrophe" (1993: 186), he encourages us to shun its attempts at seduction. He believes we have fallen into the habit of interpreting mere antisocial behavior as subversive radicalism, mistaking reactionary self-loathing for some kind of "authentic" creativity. It seems fair to say that Bey would have little patience with Paglia's theory that "paganism has survived in the thousand forms of sex, art, and now the modern media" (25), for he would seek its legacy in far less visible spaces.

There is a powerfully libidinal component to Bey's TAZ, mainly because unmediated human contact is its raison d'être. Here again we can detect a grudging affiliation with Baudrillard, who also maintains that "anything that bypasses mediation is a source of pleasure" (1993a: 70). In this respect, the TAZ resembles Sir Richard Burton's "Sotadic Zone," that transgressive imaginary space "in which androgyny, pederasty, and perversion held sway" (Showalter 81). It thus forms another dionysian blindspot where Pan can cavort for a while before Apollo once more slams on the cuffs and reads him his rights. (Like all such discourses, the TAZ is complicated by ethics, law, and other liberal notions protecting the rights of the individual.)

Bey's insistence on "immediatism" forces him to use his agile intellect in dealing with the technophilia of many contemporary subcultures, including those ravers, techno-pagans and anarcho-hackers who, significantly, make up the bulk of his readership. Cyberians often claim the Internet, virtual realities, multi-user dimensions, and other fiber-optic paraspaces as the TAZ incarnate. Bey, however, is more cautious in handling the double-edged sword of communications technologies:

> The TAZ agrees with the hackers because it wants to come into being—in part—through the Net, even through the mediation of the Net. But it also agrees with the greens because it retains intense awareness of itself as body and feels only revulsion for CyberGnosis, the attempt to transcend the body through instantaneity and simulation. The TAZ tends to view the Tech/anti-Tech dichotomy as misleading, like most dichotomies, in which apparent opposites turn out to be falsifications or even hallucinations caused by semantics . . . . [The TAZ] will use the computer because the computer exists, but it will also use powers which are so completely unrelated to alienation or simulation that they guarantee a certain psychic paleolithism to the TAZ, a primordial-shamanic spirit which will "infect" even the Net itself (the true meaning of Cyberpunk as I read it). (1991: 110-112)

Bey harmonizes the conflict by resurrecting the old Situationist strategy of *détournement,* which involves turning the detritus of the system back on itself. Encouraged to become thieving magpies—the "hunter/gatherers of the world of CommTech" (109)—we are reminded of William Gibson's oft-quoted maxim, "The street finds its own uses for things," including, of course, electronic hardware. Neither Bey's pagan affection for the bucolic, nor his neo-Victorian weakness for the simple pleasures of quilt making leads him to ignore the technologically informed agenda of today's subcultures.

According to Bey, then, we need to return not just to a material but to a "psychic technology." In this conjunction between the mystical and the mathematical we find another guru of dionysian revivalism, McKenna, and his cyberian disciples from the "trenches of hyperspace."

Civilization and Its Discotheques

> Panic doesn't have to be unhappy. I see it as ecstasy. It's just a mode of propagation by contiguity, like contagion, only faster—the ancient principle of metamorphosis, going from one form to another without passing through a system of meaning.
>
> Baudrillard (Gane, 1993: 104)

All discussions of technology rely—to varying degrees—on metaphysical metaphors, especially when referring to its unprecedented acceleration and obscure destiny. While this is a strong theme in the relatively sober writings of Heidegger, McLuhan, and Virilio, it is also the staple of drug-casualties from the 1960s. While I myself have suggested that Pan is the goat in the machine, some writers display an unwavering faith in the new divinity of technology, seeing human salvation as courtesy of the *machina ex machina*.

According to a Californian mathematician, Ralph Abraham, a "brief kiss" between starched mathematicians and patchoulied hippies in the late 1960s constituted "a fractal event, marking a point in human history from which the underlying shape or order of existence . . . could be inferred" (Rushkoff 24). He goes on to argue that

> the cyberian interest in the pagan, psychedelic, spiritual, and tribal is not in the least contradictory to the advances in computer technology and mathematics. Historically . . . renaissance periods have always involved a resurgence of archaic elements along with the invention of new technologies and mathematical systems. (ibid.: 25—paraphrased by Rushkoff)

For the Pop-anthropologist, Douglas Rushkoff, the cyberians of the 1990s marked the point where the "sixties bell curve finally touches down" (ibid.: 85). Abraham and others become part of his project, which is dionysian in so far as it seeks to take the "logic" out of the technological. He diligently documents anecdotal evidence for the dawning of an age which, although slightly less waterlogged than Aquarius, operates with the same utopian promise.

The Nietzschean promotion of pagan values against the corrupt dogma of Christianity has become a legacy for today's young misfits. In Rushkoff's analysis, the 1990s become a reprise of the 1960s, marked by a resurgence of dionysian excess. Both the orgiastic carnival of the Burning Man festival in Nevada (where a giant wicker man is symbolically torched in a modern-day potlatch) and the mindless catharsis of a Rave in Yourtown, USA, are symptoms of a global neopaganism that treads the razor's edge between commercial appropriation and a grassroots celebration.

Like Bey, McKenna agrees that we are playing clumsily with a new "psychic technology"—just as the apes do at the beginning of *2001: a Space Odyssey* (1968). In a sense, then, we are awaiting that symbolic jump cut that will connect our ancient past with our glorious future. "What is happening," McKenna informs us,

> is an overall transformation of humanity into an entirely different kind of creature. The monkey is being shed. And the thing that is made of language and of image and imagination, that has resided in the monkeys for so long, is now superseding biological evolution and, through culture, taking over the reins of its own form and destiny. And the chaos of our age, which is so troubling to us all, is nothing unusual at all. It is the normal situation when a species prepares to leave the planet. This is the chaos at the end of history. (32)

How McKenna knows what is "normal" when a species prepares to leave a planet is anyone's guess. The giveaway is to be found in one of the epigraphs to this chapter, where he states that the twentieth century "does not make any sense" unless it results in a "complete transformation of the species." This hunger for meaning exposes the latent fascist logic in his transcendental theory of humanity, which he shares with extropians, performance artists, engineers, UFO cultists and other proponents of body-loathing "CyberGnosis." Understandably, this is the point at which he parts company with the more "authentic" dionysian, Bey.

McKenna is thus the latest in that long line of people who view history as a unified, coherent, and harmonious plot, whose gross tragedies and infinite subtleties coalesce into a pseudo-Proustian tale of redemption and salvation. He aims to make "people . . . say, 'Now I understand! Now I understand why the pyramids, why the fall of Rome, why Auschwitz, why the H-bomb" (18). Each becomes a nodal point on the path foreshadowed by a religious and scientific urge to see larger forces at work—to see Heidegger's "destining" in action.

Nevertheless, McKenna tries to talk in dionysian terms when affirming states of intoxication and the libidinal influence of Pan. But he often slips into a strange kind of elitism—and an eighteenth-century spirit of evolutionism—when suggesting that drugs should be taken only by town planners, architects, and other visionaries of the future. The most reactionary aspect of his thought, however, is located in the structure of millenarian prophecy itself, and especially in his resonant definition of history as "the shock wave of eschatology" (41):

> Something is at the end of time and it is casting an enormous shadow over human history, drawing all human becoming toward it. All wars, the philosophies, the rapes, the pillaging, the migrations, the cities, the civilizations—all of this is occupying a microsecond of geological, planetary, and galactic time as the monkeys react to the symbiote, which is in the environment and which is feeding information to humanity about the larger picture. (ibid.)

This "something" at the end of time is the Eschaton, a necessarily ambiguous transcendental object at the end of history. Like the millennium itself, the Eschaton is a floating symbol, equally as seductive and opaque as Arthur C. Clarke's monolith in *2001*. According to McKenna, the means to reach it is as vivid and psychedelic as Stanley Kubrick's famous climactic sequence at the end of the film; in fact, it is much more so, thanks to the magic mushroom and other potent hallucinogens. The details of his own experimental epiphanies—which involve "self-transforming machinic elves"—are recorded in a volume of essays and interviews entitled *The Archaic Revival* (1991). Its mantralike message is firmly within the premillennial tradition of utopianism, although it displays some specifically Californian idiosyncrasies.

McKenna thinks that a general historical acceleration will cause enough cultural friction to make the human kernel "pop" suddenly and miraculously into a fluffy white angelic creature. Although this popcorn theory exists on the fringes of accepted philosophy, it is central to New-Age ideology. In combining elements of both Aldous Huxley and Timothy Leary, McKenna provides an example of that retrospective tampering with the meaning of history that Michael André Bernstein calls "foreshadowing." Such a rhetorical strategy tries to "explain" suffering and injustice as "inevitable" or "preordained."

McKenna insists that

> [t]he Aeon, eternity, and the millennium are accomplished facts, not an anticipation. Hence the mushroom stands at the end of history. It stands for an object that pulls all history toward itself. It's a causal force that operates upon us backward through time. It is why things happen the way they do; because everything is being pulled forward toward a nexus of transformation. (70)

Indeed, McKenna sees it "as a necessary chaos that will lead to a new and more attractive order" (160). This is not Bey's ever-present, creative chaos: it is a storm-before-the-calm, to be weathered in the sheltered workshop of a contemplative mind. A fascination with colored lights in the psyche morphs into the familiar dilution of dionysian concerns and the political apathy which accompanies it.

It is easy to dismiss McKenna on the grounds that his own drug-induced revelations are exactly that: the frazzled ravings of a sixties' refugee. But because his sermonizing has been picked up by the global network of cyberians—and most notably ravers—these ideas are filtering into the melting pot of allegedly anti-Apollonian philosophies. McKenna's sophisticated prodrug message, together with his perceptive observation that culture itself is the original "virtual reality," function as a Trojan horse for his more insidiously Darwinian narrative, which acknowledges National Socialism as its "negative" incarnation (205). McKenna thus concludes that "it's true that the earth is the cradle of mankind, but one cannot remain in the cradle forever" (66). Sci-fi fantasies of physical transcendence not only render the very material basis of human existence expendable, but continue the legacy of colonization into the virgin territories of the galaxy.

As in the cases of the Heaven's Gate and Aum Shinrikyo cults, millenarian ideas that filter through popular science-fiction can seduce people into a thanatic rapture, and lead them to direct their murderous impulses either toward the self or the other. (Shoko Asahara and his advisors used Isaac Asimov's *Foundation* series as a blueprint for their own sinister New World Order [Kaplan and Marshall, 29-30].) Some young people—and not so young—weaned on a steady diet of *Dr. Who*, *Star Trek*, *Star Wars*, *The X-Files* and many other apocalyptically tinged science-fiction shows, display an aesthetic affection for such inter-galactic trappings. Science-fiction is a convenient host for parasitical discourses associated with neo-imperialism, paranoia, alien-nation and world domination.

How else are we to explain the fact that McKenna's followers consist mostly of environmentally conscious and politically active techno-fans? Why do these subcultures empathize with the sinister subtext of McKenna's evolutionist agenda? It seems that his fusion of the futuristic and the archaic acts as a smoke screen to smuggle in his notion of the Transcendental Fungus. Perhaps I am overstating the significance of McKenna's peripheral gospel, however, his arguments demonstrate the internal contradictions—and seemingly eternal dynamic—between prophecy and immediatism, utopia and temporary autonomous zones, and transgression and transcendence.

According to McKenna, the revelation and panic of the UFO signals the eruption of Pan, "bursting through from the underworld" (60). Indeed, he even refers to Huysmans, describing *A Rebours* as

> an amazing novel about a man who is so sensitized to perception that he can't leave his apartments. He has his walls covered in felt and keeps the lights very low. He collects the [French Symbolist painter] Redon when nobody had ever heard of Redon. He buys turtles and has jewels affixed to their backs. Then he sits in a half-lit room and smokes hashish and watches the turtles crawl around on his Persian rugs. Let's all go home and do this. (77)

Yet Huysmans's pessimistic decadence lies on the far side of the spectrum to McKenna's spaced-out fantasies of a posthuman superrace. *The Archaic Revival* invokes the unifying notion of the Overmind. It thus continues the tradition of anticipating quantum leaps in human existence, and gestures mutely towards Ralph Waldo Emerson's Oversoul and Friedrich Nietzsche's Overman. McKenna's ascendant agenda is not so much a climb up Jacob's ladder as a tour through the magic faraway tree; the perfect scenario for a rave.

Because McKenna champions the shamanic "ecstasy" of drugs, his project is appropriated by technopagans, who either overlook or ignore his contempt for large-scale, bacchanalian gatherings. There is no doubt that McKenna's writings encourage this enormous "global tribe," which he insists is superior to the 1960s counterculture in all respects, not least in its organizational skills and longevity. But because he defines ecstasy as "the contemplation of wholeness" (13), he sees no point in using "ecstasy" and other synthetic drugs purely for fun. Instead of a TAZ, he seeks a durable launchpad for the soul.

"Ecstasy" literally means "a standing forth"—of the soul from the body, in the Christian tradition. Ravers often speak (although usually not in these terms) of the almost Bataillean continuity experienced at a successful dance party. Indeed, Bataille's ghost haunts many of these gatherings, reminding us that the morbid flavor of much "gen-x" pop-culture has infiltrated the rave. "We can only reach a state of ecstasy," writes Bataille, "when we are conscious of death or annihilation, even remotely" (1986: 267).

The cultural critic Simon Reynolds argues that certain postmodern notions are "tailor-made for rave culture":

> The concept of the "desiring machine," for example, describes the way that the sound system, DJ and audience combine to form a single mechanism generating euphoria without pretext or context. The Deleuzian notion of the "body without organs"—a notion sufficiently opaque to defy any ready textual summary—might be best explained through the polymorphously perverse rapture enjoyed by the raver on ecstasy, a sensuous but sexless bliss without climax. (35)

Anybody who has experienced the aphrodisiac, even orgiastic, effects of the drug ecstasy would question Reynolds's use of the word *sexless,* which certainly does not describe that female techno-pagan's testimony to the disturbing sexual power of the rave, which I quoted in my introduction. Nevertheless, his observation that the mode of the rave is generally "bliss without climax" is accurate. Unlike the traditional rock-concert, it often emphasizes a mantra-like "monotony," devoid of peak hit-singles or a pyrotechnic finale. All the fireworks explode in the head while the body is left bouncing like a marionette.

The many different types of rave are organized according to techno-music's various subcategories and aesthetic allegiances. An urban drum 'n' bass party in a disused factory is a completely different experience from the trance party held by neopagans in the forests of northern Australia or on the coast of India. Urban raves tend to be more streetwise, focusing on the production and distribution of the music and its related visual paraphernalia. At least in my experience, rural raves are usually held by technopagans, or by more spiritually inclined people, who follow a hotchpotch of holistic philosophies, including Zen Buddhism, Gaia and the Goddess, benign satanism, green politics, and New Age transcendentalism. However, in their overtly carnivalesque aspect, all raves, no matter how "sophisticated," leave themselves open to charges of a postmodern bacchanalia.

At one point, Rushkoff's book introduces the concept of "morphogenetic fields." These are accumulations of mystico-psychic traces or empathetic vibrations that influence cultural phenomenoa. London's morphogenetic field, he tells us, is more powerful than America's:

> London's pagan cultures have endured centuries of repression and distillation. Their phase-locking was probably achieved somewhere in the twelfth century. Symbols and even personalities from ancient pagan times still live in London house [music] . . . . While the English rave has a quality of medievalism, tribal energy, and Old World paganism, the American cyber disco is the most modern mutation of bliss induction, and uses whatever means necessary to bring people into the fractal pattern. (120-121, 125)

Australian technopagans claim that a hundred thousand years of spiritual connections between dancing Aborigines and their land have created morphogenetic fields that account for the special quality of Antipodean raves. Without going into the complicated politics of post-colonial corroborees, we can appreciate how this subculture, in constructing its own dubious dynamic between past and future, provides sociological evidence for the Maffesolis of this world, who believe in the power of the orgy and in the explosion of new tribal formations.

New Age travelers were among the most visible and victimized critics of Margaret Thatcher's Britain, which introduced Draconian laws (including one banning "loud, monotonous booming sounds") to eradicate musical gatherings. These TAZs became even more temporary when riot police were sent in to stamp out such dionysian frivolity. But while in England it became a game of "thump the mole" between state and rave, commercialism was also waiting to feed off the carcass.

It is a countercultural truism that Pepsi can destroy any transgressive impulse or "authentic celebration" faster than any police force. Nevertheless, Pan continues to dance in invisible spaces, one step ahead of his Apollonian nemesis. No less than the Pill or the Bomb, the amplifier (and especially the sampler/sequencer/turntable) has been a political catalyst in stirring D. H. Lawrence's "pagan mass" into a frenzied fusion, which the authorities perceived as a threat.

Nietzsche's *Birth of Tragedy* (1872) valorized the dionysian properties of music. In the rave, mosh, Burning Man, and other youth-oriented carnivalesque eruptions we see other philosophical seeds beginning to grow. What they will grow into, and whether they will be genetically engineered into something else, is a question worth considering.

After the Orgy (But Before the Test Results)

> We seem to be in some sort of temporal flux.
>
> *Star Trek Generations*

> [T]here is no closure at the end of the twentieth century—sooner a "closure-effect."
>
> Geoff Waite (1)

The tension that exists between orgasm-as-sacrifice *(petite mort)* and orgasm-as-insemination (reproduction, immortality) always depends upon the panic dynamic. Accordingly, those three zeros contained in the year 2000 began to acquire a pornographic gloss. In the phallic economy of apocalypse, each zero becomes either an orifice used in the game of political withdrawal, or a womb to return to in a mass movement of redemptive regression.

The end as such, at least according to Baudrillard, is an *illusion;* perhaps the fundamental illusion in a world structured on such mirages. Hence the dionysian embrace of such uncertainty principles as the imaginary, dreams, intoxication, trances, the unconscious, pataphysics, and chaos theory. Perhaps this also explains the immense cultural impact of cyberspace—Gibson's "conceptual hallucination"—a new social space that was a hypothetical playground before it became a corporate battleground.

Information technologies have become the millennial terrain of erotic-thanatic interactions. This historical juncture is as intense as the final level of a video game played throughout the centuries, an enigmatic virtual challenge on which all previous achievements are staked. Do we save the game now, and continue later? Quit while we're ahead? Or is it already too late? Such a trite metaphor at least captures the Western perception of history as a linear process of accumulation.

The scientific rapture of the intellect reveals and uncovers what is not yet known, and this knowledge follows an apocalyptic momentum. The word *Doomsday* recalls the Domesday Book, William the Conqueror's first attempt in 1085 to catalog the populace. According to a popular rumor of the time, the completion of this task would herald the end of the world, a recognition of the bureaucratic affinity between this census and the Holy book of Judgment Day. Perhaps the very act of recording names could lead to salvation. In this sense, the Last Days will be characterized *not* by the victory of anarchy over civilization but rather by the *triumph* of the Western quest to pierce and record the secrets of the universe.

Arthur C. Clarke's canonical short story, "The Nine Billion Names of God" (1967), is a parable of how the Enlightenment project will be completed in the information age. A powerful new computer program is commissioned by a group of Tibetan monks who wish to identify the true name of God. Those who do not believe that IBM software could possibly complete such a sacred task begin to descend by night from the mountain monastery, only to see the stars wink out one by one. The power of this image stems not only from our deep connection to scientific narratives of completion and exhaustion, but from Deleuze's insight that "[w]e are made up of fatigues as much as of contemplations" (77). (See chapter 1 of *Difference and Repetition* for his unique perspective on the orgiastic.)

Apocalypse is thus a grand label for completion and closure: the mystery simultaneously answered and gone. Groaning under the weight of accumulated knowledge, our episteme secretly desires a clean slate and a fresh start. "The accumulation of time imposes the idea of progress," Baudrillard notes, "as the accumulation of science imposes the ideas of truth: in each case, what is accumulated is no longer symbolically exchanged, but becomes an *objective* dimension" (1993: 146). In other words, science traps its self-manufactured truth within dead objects, amputated from the general economy of existence. It therefore mistakenly relies on surplus time and knowledge, which are as useless as those enormous silos of "emergency" grain, which rots in the United States while much of the world starves. Baudrillard thinks "we cannot hope for a . . . revolution at the end of this process of spiralling hoarding" (ibid.: 147).

The postmodern vision of apocalypse is thus not a battle between demons and harlots, but a conference of bespectacled computer programmers with identical pocket-protectors. As the enigma of Armageddon morphs into the spreadsheets of Silicon Valley, Truth is revealed not in a thunderclap, but in Bill Gates's monotonal whine. As Krishan Kumar puts it, "[c]atastrophe will be expressed in lines on a graph rather than in the imagery of the Book of Revelation" (211). Such is the "debased millenarianism" (ibid.: 212) of our own epoch, where seduction and fate yield to rationality and causality.

"Our Apocalypse is not real," Baudrillard declares, "it is *virtual*" (1994: 119). Unlike Neil Armstrong, history itself is "taking a fantastic step backwards by building the ruins of the future" (ibid.: 79). The end of the space-race heralds the end of the most impoverished, the most materialistic, and the most imperialistic form of transcendence that our scientific society could provide. Even "the end" has become a sort of satellite, like transcendence, orbiting the earth without being able to hit the escape velocity needed for release. Should any of these grand values—history, apocalypse, and transcendence—ever return to us, it will do so only in the manner of a battered Mir-like satellite, spiraling back to earth in a spectacular crash.

7

Conclusion: The Revelation Will not be Televised

Y2Care: Debugging the Millennium

> It all follows, so why seek complexity where there is none?
>
> Dolmance (Sade 96)

> Eroticism's too heavy a burden for human strength. The torment of orgies is inseparable from the agony of war as Jünger pictured it: in the morning you wake up under the table with the litter of the previous evening around you. This is a *given* for orgies, a condition without which they wouldn't exist.
>
> Georges Bataille (Davenport-Hines 329)

New Year's Eves are notoriously anti-climactic. This is because we insist that they hold the symbolic weight of a temporally significant transitional moment, a weight the actual experience of time passing cannot hold. Despite the conviction of the prophets of apocalypse, there is always a morning after. We are always already after the orgy.

The urge for fusion through confusion, and continuity over discontinuity—no matter how primal, infantile, or mystical its origin—is a dionysian theme now being remobilized by the media, who anxiously await a spectacle worthy of the occasion. (The pop-singer Jennifer Lopez provided a perfect example of this orgasmic anticipation in her video clip for "Waiting for Tonight," which lovingly depicted a group of millennial party-goers being drenched in the Derridean spume of giant champagne-bottles-*cum*-fire-hydrants.) All the media hype surrounding New Years' Eve 2000 helped create the anticlimactic wave that swept the globe with the millennial dawn, compounded and aggravated by centuries of this discursive foreplay. "Ultimate detachment is not the same as freedom" Walter Kirn had already warned, before noting that "escape is no substitute for liberation and rapture isn't happiness. The sound-and-light show at the end of time . . . seems bound to disappoint" (Dery 49).

Every cliché in history was forced to jump through the mesmerizing hoops of those three zeros in the year 2000. Computer scientists and corporate executives awaited the date with dread because they had a self-made apocalypse on their hands, known as the "millennium bug" or the Y2K problem. As if believing unconsciously in the Christian Millennium, computer programmers put only two digits in each silicon chip, making '69 stand for 1969 without anticipating the problems this could bring in the twenty-first century. Possible scenarios offered by self-styled experts included everything from minor inconvenience to total system breakdown, including nuclear dysfunction. One newspaper reported that "[t]he failure to program even vastly powerful mainframe computers to cope with a trivial change of date may be the biggest, most costly and absurd mistake in the history of the industrialized world" (Reeve et al. 53). We were told to brace for the Infocalypse, which would begin in New Zealand and sweep west across the globe with the dawning of the millennium. The Y2K problem was thus a perfect fable of modern myopia, a prosaic twist on the Frankenstein myth that our technology will destroy us. Suddenly the corporate demand for "Y2K compliance" became a warning to us all—upgrade or freeze.

The year 2000 (or more specifically 2001) was more than a date. It represented a future that was never supposed to come, or at least not so soon. Currently taking the first tentative steps into the third millennium, we find ourselves in the position of someone who has lusted after a sex object for so long that consummation seems undesirable because it will be inevitably disappointing. Not being able to resist, however, we try to postpone an awkward awakening: "after the national orgasm a sort of collective melancholy" (Baudrillard, 1989: 58). Or even worse, feeling a sharp twinge in our loins—the location of the Last Judgement (Brown, 1990: 49)—we realize we have all caught the millennium bug, a virus with the potential to seize the entire system.

And yet the Y2K prophecy—like all others before it—turned out to be a hoax, just another in a long line of anticlimaxes. "The worst of it all," predicted Jean Baudrillard, "is precisely that there will be no end to anything, and all these things will continue to unfold slowly, tediously, recurrently, in that hysterisis of everything which, like nails and hair, continue to grow after death" (1994: 116).

Barely a year into the twenty-first century, and it becomes increasingly clear that Jacques Derrida was correct in declaring that "all language on apocalypse is also apocalyptic and cannot be excluded from its object" (1984b: 30). With the sound of the clock still ticking loudly in our ears, we nurse this historical hangover and prepare for the next; patiently enduring the cultural equivalent of being too tired to sleep. What can we expect from such hyper-ennui? What, indeed, *are* we doing after the orgy?

Anybody more obsessed with origins would be driven to distraction in trying to determine whether the ur-myth of apocalypse stems from the sexual act, or history itself. I have tried to demonstrate that not only is it impossible to decide, but that it is misleading to separate the two. Although Camille Paglia thinks that "the sex act cruelly mimics history's decline and fall" (20), we could easily provide evidence for the contrary. For as Marshall McLuhan remarks, "[i]nstead of asking which came first, the chicken or the egg," we could entertain the idea that "a chicken was an egg's idea for getting more eggs" (1974: 20).

As a conceptual model, the orgasm mimics and invokes the anticipated millennium, being in equal parts both apocalyptic horror and divine bliss. As contingent constructions, both "sexuality" and "history" seem to require a climax. To promote a "nonorgasmic" and "antiphallic" model of history barely counters the fact that the drive for transcendence dictates much of what we call "culture." In the last couple of centuries, tales of salvation, redemption, revelation, transcendence and transfiguration have been incubated in sexual metaphors. Consequently, they are now saturated in the libidinal economy of our age, so that apocalyptic tension has become both terminable *and* interminable. In such a situation there seems little evidence to counter Baudrillard's claim that political solutions are helpless against the symbolic.

Like Michel Maffesoli, I resist the "tyranny of the ought to be," but have nevertheless felt compelled to identify those currents that sometimes hinder, and sometimes foster, the most pragmatic of utopian impulses. To live after the orgy is not to mistake the End of the World for that right-wing phobia, the End of Civilization as We Know It. Rather, it is to fully appreciate the paradoxical desire to be saved from salvation itself.

Antiapocalypticians like Donna Haraway, Lee Quinby, and Michael André Bernstein maintain that the power of self-fulfilling prophecies is evident in the myopic politics of everyday life, whether conducted in Congress, the library, or at home. The more we "foreshadow" the future in apocalyptic terms, the more we create the conditions for its arrival. If we are continuously portrayed as waiting for the thanatic asymptote to cross the line and land on our heads (like the nuclear witnesses waiting at the end of Thomas

Pynchon's nuclear rainbow, or the masses gazing up at the Genitron clock) then the chances of its actually occurring, sooner or later, increase. The apocalypse thus becomes apocryphal, spread around like an urban legend that then becomes "true." As Steven Shaviro remarks, "[o]ur incessant waiting for catastrophe to happen itself enfolds or embodies the catastrophic event" (1997).

This point is crucial, for who can be sure of the extent to which tales of fire-and-brimstone justice informs the vengeful policies of the current president of the United States? (Especially in the wake of the spectacular terrorist attacks on the twin towers of the World Trade Center; which themselves certainly count as "apocalyptic".)[24] Yet those who write off the apocalyptic mode as intrinsically fundamentalist and dangerous unwittingly confuse "the truth of the revelation" with "the revealed truth" (Derrida, 1984: 28). This point is equally crucial, for antiapocalyptic philosophies fail to take account of the imaginary politics inscribed in many end-time scenarios.

A glib example occurs in the movie *Ghostbusters* (1984), when the city of New York is under attack from thousands of poltergeists. Dr. Peter Venkman (Bill Murray) describes the ensuing chaos as "cats and dogs living together—mass hysteria!" Old antagonisms are dissolved in that moment of panic when we confront the possibility of Armageddon. A more apposite example is found in Alan Lightman's *Einstein's Dreams* (1994), a literary meditation on alternative time-space continuums. One chapter depicts the town of Berne, which has recently learned that the world will end in one month's time on September 26, 1907:

> One month before the end, businesses close. The Bundeshaus halts its proceedings. The federal telegraph building on Speichergasse falls silent. Likewise the watch factory on Laupenstrasse, the mill past the Nydegg Bridge. What need is there for commerce and industry with so little time left? . . .
>
> A barrister and a postal clerk who have never before met walk arm in arm through the Botanischer Garten, smile at the cyclamens and asters, discuss art and colour. What do their past stations matter? . . . (56, 58)

In this utopian apocalypse, "a world with one month is a world of equality." The point of saying so, however, is not to bring such a situation into being, but to remind modern amnesiacs that different attitudes to time call for different definitions of community. Such stories counter the limiting determinism of people like McLuhan, who believes that "[w]e look at the present through a rear-view mirror," and "march backwards into the future" (1967: 74-75).

Those who see the End in negative and absolutist terms may find themselves awkwardly aligned with the religio-scientific logic of capital, in which life is replaced by survival. Take for instance, Ishmael Reed's "psychic epidemic" Jes Grew, in his novel *Mumbo Jumbo* (1996). This "antiplague" (which grips the vitals of its ecstatic victims, and is linked directly to "a young comer named Dionysus" [165]) threatens Civilization as We Know It: no bad thing, given the miserable history of the term and its violent implementation throughout the world. In other words, it is not a matter of being "for or against" the apocalypse, mainly because only a handful of humans have any real influence over the matter, anyway. Instead it involves exploiting the ironic aspects of millennial exhaustion in such a way as to incorporate Dionysian insights, while avoiding the joyless trajectory of their conclusions (and here I'm thinking particularly of Baudrillard, and also of "fascoid" residues in sadistic neo-Nietzschean schools of thought).[25]

Quinby castigates Baudrillard for his "ironic apocalypticism," which she believes provides the breeding ground for an irresponsible apathy (xxii). In contrast, Richard Dellamora offers the "ironizing of apocalypse" as a discursive strategy *against* destructive logic, particularly by gay activists, who have a direct investment in the postorgy politics of libidinal millenarianism. Antiapocalypticians, therefore, remain oblivious to the irritating grain of truth in Baudrillard's observation that oppositional tactics become obsolete if based on the *political* rather than on the *symbolic* economy. While I admire their attacks on the ideological subtext of doom-mongering, I believe these people fail to acknowledge the inescapable fact that apocalypse has become the only postrevolutionary model of radical change for an entire generation. Although this is in itself unfortunate, the unstable properties of millenarianism allow for a theoretical space in which to address the future as a crooked continuum rather than as a final culmination. In short, libidinal millenarianism is both the *product of,* and *antidote to,* cultural fatigue.

The apocalypse, deconstruction, postmodernity, millennium, Eschaton—call it what you will—is motivated by the desire for a progressive future, a making new. These ideas often represent a utopia that is more pragmatic than programmatic, implicitly recognizing the fact that an exhausted epoch may not have the imaginative energy or inclination to resuscitate discredited utopian models. Such chronotopic figures are susceptible, of course, to market-oriented manipulation, but they are also open to the seduction of dissent. The apocalyptic tone cuts both ways because it is capable of being manipulated in the interests of opposing prophetic agendas. As Richard Dellamora puts it, "[o]racular utterance needs to retain 'enough apocalyptic desire' to motivate both the pursuit of social renovation and the continuing critique of 'the apocalyptic discourse itself'" (1994: 26).

Bernstein believes that "the literary excitement of imagining an apocalyptic breakdown of all social restraints is usually thrilling in direct proportion to its improbability" (1992: 39). While it may be true that media moguls, safe in their mansions, get some perverse thrill from reading Edgar Allen Poe's *The Fall of House of Usher* or watching Bruce Willis in *Armageddon,* others less fortunate may genuinely relish the social leveling-potential of apocalypse. Millenarian fantasies have always nourished those with the least to lose and the most to gain: the poor, the disenfranchised, the marginalized and the exploited. For every Heaven's Gate there is a *Public Enemy,* using the End for their own means (see their 1988 album "It Takes a Nation of Millions to Hold Us Back"). Bernstein's formula thus ignores the proliferation of nuclear movies and novels that emerged in the cold world era, not to mention the rash of fictional viral scenarios since the hysteria surrounding HIV AIDS and Ebola. Indeed, Hollywood's response to the terrorist attacks on Manhattan are yet to be fully gauged, but it would be an historical anomaly if the production studious did not channel the subsequent panic into mass forms of entertainment. Genuinely apocalyptic moments have been accompanied by apocalyptic stories that are no less "exciting" for being more likely. Indeed, they swell the profits of doom.

Antiapocalypticians therefore choose to ignore or devalue Derrida's insight that "[n]othing is less conservative than the apocalyptic genre" (1984: 29). Indeed, "apocalyptic thinking can open up spaces for the enunciation or utterance of hitherto silenced and marginalized voices" (Dickinson 230). We must therefore remember that the radical indeterminacy of time is not only the source of metaphysical anguish, but also the political site of potential tomorrows. It represents the refusal to limit future directions through prophetic or utopian foreclosures.

Perhaps, to defer to Derrida once again, we can glimpse the hither side of this modern conundrum in his notion of the "messianic without messianism," or rather, a "future-to-come" that avoids the temptation to totalize; to approach tomorrow "without *concluding in advance*" (1994: 37). Rather than disposing of the prophetic tone altogether, Derrida believes that it is possible to sever the eschatological from the teleological, and therefore recuperate and reroute the various passages of time. Such a strategy "strips the messianic hope of all biblical forms, and even all determinable figures of the wait or expectation; it thus denudes itself in view of responding to that which must be absolute hospitality, the 'yes' to the *arrivant(e)*, the 'come' to the future that cannot be anticipated—which must not be the 'anything whatsoever' . . ." (168). Thus, the "messianic is general" is, according to Derrida (and in contrast to someone like Quinby) something that "we cannot and ought not to do without" (ibid.).

The asymptotic approach of the *arrivant(e)* is also reflected in the subtitle of this study: "*toward* a politics of exhaustion." Such a proposition usually implies a desired destination or a predetermined telos. I would hesitate, however, in making such a suggestion when dealing with libidinal millenarianism. The future-to-come never really arrives, and yet in order to make some kind of cultural sense out of the present we must behave as if these proleptic traces are leading us to some expedient state. The question therefore becomes, What is this politics of exhaustion? Have I merely been documenting the exhaustion of a certain kind of post-Enlightenment politics? Or "politics" itself? Or is it that political responses are constantly reborn from the compost of previous victory banquets? From the ashes of extinguished enthusiasms? Or even from the emotional residues of fleeting affiliations?

Clues to the answers of such questions can be found in the work of the Italian theorist, Giorgio Agamben, who has adopted the prophetic power of Derrida's "to-come" in relation to his particular vision of a "coming community," based on an "*inessential* commonality" (1993). Agamben states that the "coming being" represents a particular ontic mode whose power lies is in its pure possibility: humanity "has to *exist* as *potentiality*" (ibid.: 1, 44). "To come" represents that which has not yet been brought into being: a "region that is beyond perdition and salvation" (ibid.: 6).

The coming community is, therefore, an ideal place to begin looking for a politics of exhaustion on the other side of the twentieth century (so long as we realize that the search is more important than the object it seeks). The coming community also represents a collective expression of its own sophisticated millenarian subtexts, not least in its linguistic gesture towards eternity (ibid.: 101-103). In evading essentialist notions of identity, affiliation, and other representable conditions of belonging, Agamben's strategy attempts to defy the all-inclusive meta-discourse of the nation-state. (The task at hand is to further unpack Agamben's metadionysian model into the current media-globalist climate.) Such strategic evasions have the power to defuse those apocalyptic scenarios that reinforce the social bond through a rejuvenation of State power and presence (as witnessed in the painfully obviously Benetton-*dénouement* [*outcome*] of Roland Emmerich's *Independence Day*).

The coming community, along with the libidinal economy through which it circulates, is a promise that can't be kept, according to its inherent condition. Once we have come, we are "spent" (and all exchange is temporarily suspended). Thus, even Agamben's postutopian vision stems from a sense of anticipation: something glimpsed within the slippage between coming and going. (Imagine if lovers announced their own climax with the phrase "I'm going.") Again it becomes clear that millennial time discursively dwells in the eternally liminal space between an *always after* orgy, and an *always almost* apocalypse.

As Agamben notes, "At this point there is salvation—but not for us" (ibid.: 102).

The Owl of Minerva Versus the Millennium Falcon

> The idea that to-morrow morning at half-past seven o'clock a monstrous, unsuspected event will suddenly take place; that on Thursday next a complete revolution will be accomplished at a single blow, that a revelation, a redemption, the advent of a new age, is imminent—this is frequently observed among the insane; it is a mystic delirium.
>
> Max Nordau (544)

> The more things change, the less they stay the same.
>
> Spinal Tap interview

From Rock-a-bye Baby to *Revelation,* apocalypse and redemption form part of the most enduring and pervasive dynamic in Western history. From the everyday apocalypse of our refrigerator's use-by dates, to the more profound nuclear and viral fears, the urge for some kind of spiritual or emotional salvation from the brink has led to what Mark Dery has called a "theology of the ejector seat" (8).

The influential philosophies of the Marquis de Sade, Bataille, and Nietzsche were all fabricated in times of perceived crisis or ending: the Terror, the Holocaust, the fin de siècle, and thus echo nightmarishly in our own ears. By returning to dionysian ideas from a jaded millennial perspective, we better understand how the thanatic asymptote attaches itself like a tapeworm to our most cherished myths, especially the myth of progress. As Haraway reminds us, "there have been practical inheritances, which have undergone many reconfigurations, but which remain potent" (1997: 33). Incorporating everything from Aum

Shinrikyo's telepathic helmets through F. T. Marinetti's machinic madness to Neal Stephenson's cyborgs, this inheritance adapts to each unique cultural splicing.

The erotic apocalypse is so fundamental to Western eschatology that "libidinal millenarianism" is not *one specific* form of millenarianism, but its fundamental structure and function. Moreover, it is the persistent link between the liminal and the libidinal that creates the conditions for its transmission between people, generations, and cultures. For just as liminal spaces (e.g., trains, hotels, and nightclubs) encourage the libido, so too do liminal moments (e.g., weddings, carnivals, and the apocalypse).

Libidinal millenarianism is thus the ideological wreckage created by the redemptive, goal-seeking conception of history after its violent collision with a more ancient, cyclic perspective on the passage of time. By belonging to or issuing from "nature," Pan stands outside history, and as such he plays an ambiguous and ambivalent role in narratives of the End. "Transgression itself is organized," Bataille notes. "Eroticism as a whole is an organized activity, and this is why it changes over the years" (1986: 108). To reclaim or reinvent a diversity of political futures (which themselves refuse the politically dubious premise of vigorous health and boundless energy) is thus an imaginative and existential challenge.

As Shaviro observes, the "sense of urgency and impending doom," displayed in postmodern culture, "is always being ironized, stylized, and indefinitely deferred" (1997). Herein lies the difference between our own millennium and those heretical eruptions that preceded modernity: our self-conscious and almost embarrassed sense of still being here against all odds and sense of decorum. The stubborn persistence of the human race in spelling Armageddon for everything—from other species to obsolete technologies, languages, and worldviews—is tantamount to hubris. Although every lunatic in an end-is-nigh sandwich board has been wrong so far, he or she represents a kind of twisted truth. As Walter Benjamin's angel of history foretold, the end is always nigh, and progress is always catastrophic.

I have been arguing that dionysian rhetoric, which traditionally has been viewed as apocalyptic, smuggles in certain ideas antagonistic to historical closure, whether presented as Armageddon or utopia (which are two sides of the same bad penny). As the Earl of Shaftesbury cannily observed, "[i]t was never surely the business of Poets in those days to call Revelation in to question, when it evidently made so well for their art" (7). The same could be said for our scientists, journalists, and other cultural engineers.

"I love not knowing the future," said Nietzsche (Bey, 1994). The same cannot be said of weather forecasters, investment bankers, stockbrokers, corporate-affiliated psychics, and other commercial prognosticators. The future, as Andrew Ross remarks,

> has been heavily populated by traditionally anti-progressivist interests. It has become the natural habitat of technocratic elites; a lucrative haven for financial speculators; an indispensable tool in the politics of crisis management; a professional training ground for militarists; the next frontier for free-marketeers; and the locus for "thinking the unthinkable," to use Herman Kahn's notorious phrase for describing the logistics of post-nuclear survivalism. (172)

The urge to "colonize the future" (ibid.: 181) is a mandate of apollonian political economics, explaining the dionysian wish to escape the hypnotic power of a simulation society. It also explains the desire to break that Saturnalian curse—the obligation to lead time-bound lives—in order to experience what Bey has termed the *clockless nowever* (1991: 4).

For the dionysian, Nietzsche reminds us, "[t]he 'kingdom of God' is nothing that one expects; it has no yesterday and no day after tomorrow, it will not come in 'a thousand years'—it is an experience of the heart; it is everywhere, it is nowhere" (1982: 608). Libidinal millenarianism thus gives a negative answer to the question, "Has anyone anywhere in the history of the world ever genuinely believed in the reality of life after death?" (Lanchester 93). Eroticism can therefore be construed as an ongoing charivari against the worst serial killer in history: the grim reaper himself.

Means to an End

> It's been a prevalent notion . . . . someday, somehow, before the end, a gathering back to home. A messenger from the Kingdom, arriving at the last moment. But I tell you there is no such message, no such home—only the millions of last moments . . . no more. Our history is an aggregate of last moments.
>
> Pynchon (148-49)

My final image was given to me by a woman who spent one New Year's Eve in a hotel room in Jakarta, Indonesia, watching the celebrations on television. At five minutes to midnight, the camera closed in on one of those analogue clocks found in countless institutions such as schools and banks. Apart from some muffled cheers from off camera, nothing happened at the stroke of twelve. The lens remained on the clock-face until someone remembered, ten minutes later, to cut to a different show.

In addition to providing a humorous pathos at this "technological lag" between different nations and economies, the face of that analogue clock reflects our thoughts and actions. As Frank Kermode puts it, what we hear as the "tick-tock" of a clock enacts "a tiny genesis and a tiny apocalypse," from the first tick to the final tock (1995: 250). Analogue clocks are diachronic: they show us where we have been and where we are going. But the digital clocks —of which the Genitron is the quintessential example—are synchronic. Each moment is severed from the previous one and the next.

Baudrillard reminds us that the twentieth century could

> do nothing more than count the seconds separating it from its end without either being able, or really wanting, to measure up to that end—the digital clock on the Beaubourg Centre showing the countdown in millions of seconds is the perfect symbol. It illustrates the reversal of the whole of our modernity's relation to time. Time is no longer counted progressively, by addition, starting from an origin, but by subtraction, starting from the end. This is what happens with rocket launches or time bombs. And that end is no longer the symbolic endpoint of a history, but the mark of a zero sum, of a potential exhaustion. (1997)

The whole of the twentieth century can therefore be viewed as fundamentally millenarian in its outlook, defying the received wisdom that "life on the brink of the millennium is psychologically and politically impossible to sustain" (Rowland 55). Indeed, as I have endeavored to show, the modern era (at least from the Marquis de Sade onward) has witnessed a mode of organizing and absorbing eschatological exhaustion, defusing it and deploying it in equal measure. Life goes on despite the end being nigh; and these two clichés coexist in their own asymptotic relation, constantly canceling out each other without ever colliding. "We 'live from the end,'" writes Kermode, "even if the world should be endless" (1975: 58).

Postmillennial events have conspired so that we find ourselves at a red-light district performance of *Waiting for Godot,* in which we await a transcendent but belated climax. To bring forward the end by pulling God(ot) onstage, to expose the ideological pulleys and levers that held the world of Oz in suspense, is a triumphant rejection of the apollonian order. It is the empowering, and ultimately *political,* recognition that "[a]ll the agencies of repression and control are installed in this divided space, in the suspense between a life and its proper end, that is, in the production of a literally fantastic and artificial temporality" (Baudrillard 1993: 130).

To defer the orgasm via genderless foreplay is merely to mimic the capitalistic Christian strategy of "tomorrow never comes." The historical subject suffers the risks and frustrations of a millennia-long coitus interruptus, a method discouraged by most health professionals on account of its unreliability. It therefore becomes paramount that we abandon the equation between progress and evolution, anticipation and salvation, and sexuality and satisfaction. In J. G. Ballard's terms, we need to invent a myth of the future which does not preempt, foreclose, or dictate its unfolding. We need a "predictive mythology" that is not a blue-print for the engineering of tomorrow, but "an operating formula by which we can deal with our passage through consciousness" (Revell 42).

If we are to change the apocalyptic graph we shall have to recode the thanatic asymptote. The orgy is over; long live the orgy. The desire for peak-experiences should not be conflated with the death-wish desire for transcendence. A palpable cultural wish for "something" to happen can occur within the space of the climax only if we deepen our understanding of libidinal millenarianism and its dionysian heritage. Erotic peak-experiences are followed by negativity only when we use them to distract ourselves from certain pressing realities. When the climax is simultaneously an anticlimax —as it was in the year 2000—we forget that it could be otherwise. For when the future is completely inscribed by the present, we are already history.

Notes

1. The Eschaton is an enigmatic name applied to a transcendental object which lies at the end of history. It is the last of the Last Things.

2. See also Aaron Lynch's *Thought Contagion: How Belief Spreads Through Society* (New York: Basic Books, 1996), and Mark Dery's warning against the Darwinian subtext of memes in *The Pyrotechnic Insanitarium: American Culture on the Brink* (1999), p.48-9.

3. Throughout this book I distinguish the upper-case "Dionysian" from the lower-case "dionysian." The former refers to discourses directly concerning the god Dionysus (as with Nietzsche), and the latter its generalization in more recent usage. The difference should not be overstated, however, given the inevitable overlap between these. The same is true of my distinction between "Apollonian" and "apollonian."

4. For the full behind-the-scenes pathos of this publicity stunt, see Gough Lewis' independent documentary film, *Sex: The Annabel Chong Story* (1999).

5. Traditionally, prophecy itself has been coded as feminine. Consequently, Derrida can refer to Hegel's disgust at "mystagogic metaphysicians" behaving like "musclemen," who "lately preach with enthusiasm a wisdom that costs them nothing, since they claim they have caught this goddess by the end of her robe and thus have made themselves her masters and lords . . ." (1984: 17).

6. Traditionally associated with the pastoral, Dionysus has ancient links with the technological. One of the earliest documented automatons is believed to have been built in the first century AD by Hero of Alexandria, a Greek engineer who is said to have designed a mannequin theatre "in which the god Bacchus sprayed wine from his staff while bacchantes danced" (in Dery 114).

7. Unless otherwise stated, all Maffesoli quotes in this section are from the 1996 edition of *The Time of the Tribes* (1988).

8. A good deal of present-day scholarship which celebrates the antagonistic strategies of subcultures and marginalized peoples conflates the transgressive and the subversive, thereby failing to appreciate the fact that, "transgression does not seek to oppose one thing to another" (Foucault, 1977: 35). See also Stallybrass and White's *The Politics and Poetics of Transgression* (Ithaca: Cornell University Press, 1986), particularly pp.17-8 and 201-2.

9. I employ the upper case when I am specifically referring to the reified and deified construct of "nature."

10. This should not be confused with masochism (which traditionally has been interpreted as merely an inversion of Sadism), for Bataille's self-destruction is based on a totally different, and less Manichean, paradigm. See Gilles Deleuze's "Coldness and Cruelty" in *Masochism* (1989), and also Leo Bersani's *The Freudian Body*: *Psychoanalysis and Art* (New York: Columbia University Press, 1986).

11. For the sake of consistency I use the contemporary spelling of "Dionysus" throughout this book; however, when quoting Nietzsche directly I use his spelling, "Dionysos."

12. Unless otherwise stated, all quotes in this section are from Wolfgang Schivelbusch's comprehensive study, *The Railway Journey* (1980).

13. Baudrillard, once again, feels the need to divide the history of the accident into three distinct stages: the "natural-unforeseeable" catastrophe of the pre-modern era, the "manufactured-foreseeable" catastrophe of the modern era, and the "pre-programmed-deliberate" catastrophe of the post-modern era (1994: 71). This chapter covers the transition from the second to the third stage of Baudrillard's model.

14. Coincidentally, 1996 marked the 100th anniversary of the world's first fatal car accident. On 17 August, Bridget Driscoll (aged 44) was hit on her way to a folk dance in South London. Witnesses described the offending vehicle as "coming at a great rate – as fast as a bicycle". The coroner was quoted as saying that such a death "must never happen again" (Watkins).

15. The narrator of *Crash* is provocatively named James Ballard. In order to avoid unnecessary confusion, I shall refer to this character as "James Ballard," and to his authorial persona as "J.G. Ballard" or simply "Ballard."

16. A far more benign virus, namely the "Jes Grew" anti-plague of Ishmael Reed's *Mumbo Jumbo* also transmits itself through technology and glossolalia, resulting in dancing rather than death: "Some plagues arise from decomposing animals, but Jes Grew is electric as life and is characterized by ebullience and ecstasy. Terrible plagues were due to the wrath of God; but Jes Grew is the delight of the gods" (6).

17. In Aldous Huxley's *Brave New World* (first published in 1932), the term of admiration reserved for women is "pneumatic." This cyborgian image must date from the invention of inflatable tyres for cars. Its textual precursor is T.S. Eliot's Grishkin, whose "friendly bust/Gives promise of pneumatic bliss" ("Whispers of Immortality," first published 1920).

18. In *Decadence and the Making of Modernism* (1995), David Weir draws attention to the ideological baggage which Darwin's work has been asked to carry: "The scientific neutrality of Darwin's 'descent with modification' was misinterpreted as progressive 'evolution' by the optimists, and as literal descent or decline by the pessimists" (xiii).

19. This continuum is acknowledged in a 1997 advertising campaign by Sony, which employs Izaak Walton's *The Compleat Angler* (1653) as a hinge between "artifice" and "hi-tech." Fish hurl themselves at a floating television monitor which plays a video of insects. The narration is lifted straight from Walton: "Is it not an art to deceive a trout with an artificial fly?"

20. All quotes from Maffesoli in this section are from this text.

21. For a more detailed account of Joachim's historical system, see Cohn, 1993: 108-9.

22. Unless otherwise stated, all Baudrillard quotes in this section are from the 1993 edition of *Symbolic Exchange and Death* (1976).

23. For more information on D'Annunzio's occupation of the italian town of Fiume, see John Robert Woodhouse's *Gabriele D'Annunzio: Defiant Archangel* (Oxford: Clarendon Press, 1998). For more on historical temporary autonomous zones, see Peter L. Wilson's book *Pirate Utopias: Moorish Corsairs and European Renegades* (New York: Autonomedia, 1995). For more on John of Leyden's New Jerusalem see Greil Marcus's *Lipstick Traces: A Secret History of the Twentieth Century* (London: Secker & Warburg, 1993). Bible Belt "freedom zones" refer to those fuzzy areas mainly dotted throughout the American South and mid-West, claimed by anti-Government para-military organizations as autonomous territory outside the jurisdiction of the State.

24. In an article entitled "Welcome to the Desert of the Real," circulated by email immediately after the attacks on Manhattan and Washington, Slavoj Zizek writes: "Now, in the days immediately following the bombings, it is as if we dwell in the unique time between a traumatic event and its symbolic impact, like in those brief moment after we are deeply cut, and before the full extent of the pain strikes us - it is open how the events will be symbolized, what their symbolic efficiency will be, what acts they will be evoked to justify." My claim, however, is that we have been dwelling in just this "unique time" since Sade, and most certainly since the bloodshot dawn of the twentieth century. This is the real meaning of the last pages of Pynchon's *Gravity's Rainbow*.

25. In their book *Empire*, Michael Hardt and Antonio Negri promote just such potential in the emergent formations of the "global multitude," which they believe "conceives the future only as a totality of possibilities that branch out in every direction" (Cambridge and London: Harvard University Press, 2000, 380).

Works Cited

Adler, Jerry. 'Far From Home.' *Newsweek* (7 April, 1997), 37-9.

Agamben, Giorgio. *The Coming Community*. Translated by Michael Hardt. Minneapolis & London: University of Minnesota Press, 1993.

_____. *Remnants of Auschwitz: The Witness and the Archive*. Translated by Daniel Heller-Roazen. New York: Zone, 1999.

Airaksinen, Timo. *Of Glamor, Sex and De Sade*. Wakefield: Longwood Academic, 1991.

Ballard, J.G. *Crash*, Herts: Panther, 1975. First published 1973.

_____. 'Ballard Responds.' *Science Fiction Studies*. 18, 1991. 329.

_____. 'The Car, The Future.' *User's Guide to the Millennium*. London: HarperCollins, 1996. First published in 1971.

Barthes, Roland. *A Lover's Discourse: Fragments*. New York: Hill and Wang, 1978.

Bataille, Georges. *Erotism: Death and Sensuality*. San Francisco: City Lights, 1986. First published in 1957.

_____. *The Accursed Share*. Vol. 1. Translated by Robert Hurley. New York: Zone, 1988. First published in 1967.

Baudrillard, Jean. 'What are You Doing After the Orgy?' *Art Forum* (October, 1983). 42-6.

_____. *America*. Translated by Chris Turner. London: Verso, 1989.

_____. *Fatal Strategies*. Translated by Philip Beitchman and W.D.J. Niesluchowski. New York: Semiotext(e), 1990.

_____. 'Ballard's Crash.' *Science Fiction Studies*. 18, 1991. 313-20.

_____. *Symbolic Exchange and Death*. Translated by Iain Hamilton Grant. London: Sage, 1993.

_____. *The Transparency of Evil: Essays on Extreme Phenomena.* Translated by Chris Turner. London: Verso, 1993a.

_____. *The Illusion of the End.* Translated by Chris Turner. Oxford: Polity Press, 1994.

_____. *The Perfect Crime.* Translated by Chris Turner. London: Verso, 1996.

_____. 'The End of the Millennium or the Countdown.' *ICA Archive*, Online. Internet. 26 May, 1997. n. pag. http://filament.illumin.co.uk/ica/Bulletin/talks/baudrillard/endofmillennium.html

Beachy, Stephen. 'AIDS and the Apocalyptic Imagination.' In Eric Liu, ed. *Next: Young American Writers on the New Generation*, New York: W.W. Norton & Company, 1994. 17-37.

Beaumont, Barbara, ed. *The Road from Decadence: Letters of J.-K. Huysmans.* Cambridge: The Athlone Press, 1989.

Benjamin, Walter. 'The Work of Art in the Age of Mechanical Reproduction.' *Illuminations.* 1992. 211-44.

Bernstein, Michael André. *Bitter Carnival: Ressentiment and the Abject Hero.* Princeton: Princeton University Press, 1992.

_____. *Foregone Conclusions: Against Apocalyptic History.* Berkeley: University of California Press, 1994.

Bey, Hakim. *T.A.Z.: The Temporary Autonomous Zone, Ontological Anarchy, Poetic Terrorism.* New York: Autonomedia, 1991.

_____. *Radio Sermonettes.* Online. Internet. 1994. n. pag. Available http://www.speakeasy.org/~ibbey/mo/sermonettes/index.html

_____. 'Permanent TAZs.' Online. Internet. 1995. n. pag. Available http://www.etext.org/Politics/Spunk/library/writers/bey/sp000128.txt

_____. *Millennium.* New York: Autonomedia/Garden of Delights, 1996.

Boyer, Paul. *By the Bomb's Early Light: American Thought and Culture at the Dawn of the Atomic Age.* New York: Pantheon Books, 1985.

_____. *When Time Shall Be No More: Prophecy Belief in Modern American Culture.* Massachusetts: Belknap-Harvard University Press, 1992.

Brecht, Stefan. 'Review: 'Dionysus in '69.' *Tulane Drama Review.* 13, 3, 1969. 156-71.

Brown, Norman O. *Life Against Death: The Psychoanalytical Meaning of History.* Middletown: Wesleyan University Press, 1970. First published 1959.

_____. *Love's Body.* Berkeley: University of California Press, 1990. First published 1966.

_____. *Apocalypse and/or Metamorphosis*. Berkeley: University of California Press, 1991.

Buck-Morss, Susan. 'Aesthetics and Anaesthetics: Walter Benjamin's Artwork Essay Reconsidered.' *New Formations*. 20, 1993. 123-43.

Bukatman, Scott. *Terminal Identity: The Virtual Subject in Postmodern Science Fiction*. Durham: Duke University Press, 1993.

Bull, Malcolm, ed. *Apocalypse Theory and the Ends of the World*, Oxford: Blackwell, 1995.

_____. 'On Making Ends Meet.' In Bull (1995) 1995b. 1-17.

Butler, Judith. 'Contingent Foundations: Feminism and the Question of "Postmodernism."' in J. Butler and Joan W. Scott, eds., *Feminists Theorize the Political*. New York and London: Routledge, 1992.

Cherry 2000. Dir. Steve DeJarnatt. Perf. Melanie Griffith and Ben Johnson. Orion. 1987.

Chidester, David. *Patterns of Transcendence: Religion, Death and Dying*. Belmont: Wadsworth, 1990.

Chua-Eoan, Howard. 'Imprisoned by His Own Passions.' *Newsweek*. (7 April, 1997). 36-8.

Clarke, Arthur C. *3001: The Final Odyssey*. London: HarperCollins, 1996.

Cohn, Norman. *The Pursuit of the Millennium: Revolutionary Millenarians and Mystical Anarchists of the Middle Ages*. Sydney: Pimlico, 1993. First published 1957.

_____. 'How Time Acquired a Consummation.' In Bull (1995). 21-37.

Coupland, Douglas. *Microserfs*. New York: Regan Books, 1995.

Cowley, Geoffrey. 'Viruses of the Mind: How Odd Ideas Survive.' *Newsweek*. (14 April, 1997) 14.

Crash. Dir. David Cronenberg. Perf. James Spader and Holly Hunter. Columbia Tri-Star. 1996.

Darwin, Charles. *The Origin of Species*. London: John Murray, 1859.

Davenport-Hines, Richard, ed. *The Penguin Book of Vice*. London: Penguin, 1995.

Deleuze, Gilles. "Coldness and Cruelty." In *Masochism*. Translated by Jean McNeil. New York: Zone, 1989. First published in 1967.

_____. *Difference and Repetition*. Translated by Paul Patton. New York: Columbia University Press, 1994. First published in 1968.

Deleuze, Gille and Felix Guattari. *A Thousand Plateaus: Capitalism and Schizophrenia*. Translated by Brian Massumi. London: Athlone Press, 1999. First published 1980.

DeLillo, Don. *White Noise*. London: Picador, 1985.

Dellamora, Richard. *Apocalyptic Overtures: Sexual Politics and the Sense of an Ending*. New Jersey: Rutgers University Press, 1994.

_____, ed. *Postmodern Apocalypse: Theory and Cultural Practice at the End*. Philadelphia: University of Pennsylvania Press, 1995.

Derrida, Jacques. 'Of an Apocalyptic Tone Recently Adopted in Philosophy.' Translated by John P. Leavey, Jnr. *Oxford Literary Review*. 6, 2, 1984. 3-37.

_____. *Specters of Marx: The State of the Debt, The Work of Mourning, and the New International*. Translated by Peggy Kamuf. New York & London: Routledge, 1994.

_____. *The Gift of Death*. Translated by David Wills. Chicago: Chicago University Press, 1995.

Dery, Mark. *Escape Velocity: Cyberculture at the End of the Century*. New York: Grove Press, 1996.

de Sade, The Marquis. *Philosophy in the Bedroom*. London: Velvet, 1995. Written in 1795.

Dickinson, Peter. '"Go-go Dancing on the Brink of the Apocalypse": Representing AIDS,' in Dellamora (1995) 219-40 .

Dionysus in '69. Dir. Schechner, Perf. The Performance Group. Theatrical Production. 1968.

Dr. Strangelove: Or How I Stopped Worrying and Learned to Love the Bomb. Dir. Stanley Kubrick. Perf. Peter Sellers and George C. Scott. Columbia. 1964.

During, Simon. *Foucault and Literature: Towards a Genealogy of Writing*. London: Routledge, 1992.

Eagleton, Terry. 'Back to the Future.' *New Statesman*. (1 May, 1990) 42-3.

Editorial. 'The Next Level.' *Newsweek*. (7 April, 1997) 28-35.

Elam, Diane. *Romancing the Postmodern*. London and New York: Routledge, 1992.

Eliot, T. S. 'Whispers of Immortality.' *The Complete Poems and Plays of T. S. Eliot*. London: Faber & Faber, 1969. 52.

Erickson, Steve. '2001: A Sex Odyssey.' *Details*. (May, 1995) 52-60.

Faurschou, Gail. 'Fashion and the Cultural Logic of Postmodernity.' In Kroker and Kroker (1988). 78-93.

Flaubert, Gustav. *Dictionnaire des Idées Reçues*. [*Dictionary of Received Ideas*] Online. Internet. 1999. n.pag. http://perso.wanadoo.fr/jb.guinot/pages/oeuvres9a.html. First published 1913.

Foucault, Michel. 'A Preface to Transgression.' In Donald Bouchard, ed. *Language, Counter- Memory, Practice*. Translated by Donald Bouchard and Sherry Simon. Ithaca: Cornell University Press, 1977. 29-52.

_____. *The History of Sexuality*. Vol.1. Translated by Robert Hurley. London: Penguin, 1990.

_____. 'Nietzsche, Genealogy, History.' In Paul Rabinow, ed. *The Foucault Reader*. New York: Penguin, 1991. 76-100.

Freud, Sigmund. *Civilization and Its Discontents*. Translated by James Strachey. New York: W.W. Norton, 1962. First published 1930.

_____. *Beyond the Pleasure Principle*. Translated by James Strachey. London: Hogarth Press, 1961. First published 1920.

Fukuyama, Francis. *The End of History and the Last Man*. New York: Maxwell Macmillan International, 1992.

Gane, Mike. *Baudrillard's Bestiary: Baudrillard and Culture*. London: Routledge, 1991.

_____, ed. *Baudrillard Live: Selected Interviews*. London: Routledge, 1993.

Gasché, Rodolphe. 'The Falls of History: Huysmans' *A Rebours*.' *Yale French Studies*. 74, 1988. 183-204.

Gegax, T. Trent. 'The Unkindest Cut of All.' *Newsweek*. (7 April, 1997) 39.

Ghostbusters. Dir. Ivan Reitman. Perf. Bill Murray and Dan Aykroyd. Columbia Pictures. 1984.

Gibson, William. *Mona Lisa Overdrive*. London: Grafton, 1989.

_____. "Burning Chrome." *Burning Chrome*. London: Harper Collins, 1995.

Gillespie, Michael. *Nihilism before Nietzsche*. Chicago: University of Chicago Press, 1995.

Gitlin, Todd. *The Sixties: Years of Hope, Days of Rage*. New York: Bantam, 1987.

Gleick, Elizabeth. 'The Marker We've Been Waiting For.' *Newsweek*. (7 April, 1997) 22-30.

Grant, Linda. *Sexing the Millennium*. London: Harper Collins, 1993.

Graves, Robert. *The Greek Myths*. Vol.1. Harmondsworth: Penguin, 1960.

Guattari, Félix. *Chaosmosis: an Ethico-Aesthetic Paradigm*. Sydney: Power Publications, 1995.

Hallock, Betty. 'Sex Champ: Annabel Chong.' *Giant Robot*. 6, 1996. 82-83.

Haraway, Donna. 'A Manifesto for Cyborgs: Science, Technology, and Socialist Feminism in the 1980s.' *Socialist Review*. 80, 1985. 65-107.

_____. *Modest_Witness@Second_Millennium.FemaleMan©_Meets_OncoMouse™: Feminism and Technoscience*. New York: Routledge, 1997.

Hayles, N. Katherine. 'The Borders of Madness.' *Science Fiction Studies*. 18, 1991. 321-23

Heidegger, Martin. *The Question Concerning Technology and Other Essays*. Translated by William Lovitt. New York: Garland Publishing, 1977.

Hillman, James. *Pan and the Nightmare: An Essay on Pan*. Dallas: Spring, 1988.

Huysmans, J.-K. *Against the Grain (A Rebours)*. New York: Dover, 1969. First published in 1884.

Jameson, Frederic. *Postmodernism, or the Cultural Logic of Late Capitalism*. Durham, N.C.: Duke University Press, 1991.

Juno, Andrea et al., eds. *J.G. Ballard*. San Francisco: Research, 1984.

Kaplan, David E. and Andrew Marshall. *The Cult at the End of the World: The Incredible Story of Aum*. London: Arrow, 1996.

Kermode, Frank. *The Sense of an Ending*. London: Oxford University Press, 1975.

_____. 'Waiting for the End.' In Bull (1995). 250-63.

Kingwell, Mark. *Dreams of Millennium: Report from a Culture on the Brink*. Toronto: Viking, 1996.

Kossy, Donna. *Kooks: A Guide to the Outer Limits of Human Belief*. Portland: Feral House, 1994.

Kroker, Arthur and Marilouise Kroker, eds. *Body Invaders: Sexuality and the Postmodern Condition*. Canada: Macmillan, 1988.

Kumar, Krishan. 'Apocalypse, Millennium and Utopia Today.' In Bull (1995). 200-26.

Lacayo, Richard. 'The Lure of the Cult.' *Time*. (7 April, 1997). 33-34.

Lamy, Philip. *Millennium Rage: Survivalists, White Supremacists, and the Doomsday Prophecy*. New York: Plenum Press, 1996.

Lanchester, John. *The Debt to Pleasure*, London: Picador, 1996.

Land, Nick. *Thirst for Annihilation: Georges Bataille and Virulent Nihilism*. London: Routledge, 1992.

Landon, Brooks. 'Responding to the Killer B's.' *Science Fiction Studies*. 18, 1991. 326-27.

Lawrence, D.H. *Lady Chatterly's Lover*. London: Penguin, 1994. First published 1928.

Levin, Charles. 'Carnal Knowledge of Aesthetic States.' In Kroker and Kroker (1988). 99-119.

_____. *Jean Baudrillard: A Study in Cultural Metaphysics*. London: Prentice Hall/Harvester Wheatsheaf, 1996.

Levy, Stephen. 'Blaming the Web.' *Newsweek*. (7 April, 1997). 46-47.

Life of Brian. Dir. Terry Jones. Perf. Graham Chapman and John Cleese. Handmade Films. 1979.

Lightman, Alan. *Einstein's Dreams*. London: Sceptre, 1994.

Lyotard, Jean-François. *Discours/figure*. Paris: Klincksieck, 1964.

_____. *Libidinal Economy*. Translated by Iain Hamilton Grant. London: Athlone Press, 1993. First published 1974.

Maffesoli, Michel. *The Shadow of Dionysus: A Contribution to the Sociology of the Orgy*. Translated by Cindy Linse and Mary Kristina Palmquist. Albany: State University of New York Press, 1993.

_____. *The Time of the Tribes: The Decline of Individualism in Mass Society*. Translated by Don Smith. London: Sage, 1996.

Marcuse, Herbert. *Eros and Civilization*. London: Abacus, 1973.

_____. *One Dimensional Man*. London: Ark, 1986. First published 1964.

Marinetti, F.T. *Let's Murder the Moonshine: Selected Writings*. Translated by R.W. Flint and Arthur A. Coppotelli. Los Angeles: Sun and Moon Press, 1991.

McKenna, Terence. *The Archaic Revival*. San Francisco: Harper, 1991.

McLuhan, Marshall. *Understanding Media: The Extensions of Man*. London: Abacus, 1974. First published 1964.

_____ . (with Quentin Fiore). *The Medium is the Massage: An Inventory of Effects*. New York: Bantam, 1967.

Merivale, Patricia. *Pan the Goat God: His Myth in Modern Times*. Massachusetts: Harvard University Press, 1969.

Milner, Andrew. 'Apocalypse Australia.' *Australian Book Review*. 153, 1995. 36-37.

Moore, Daniel. 'Bliss Apocalypse.' *Tulane Drama Review*. 14, 4, 1970. 52-71.

Natoli, Joseph. *Speeding to the Millennium: Film and Culture 1993-1995*. Albany: State University of New York, 1998.

Neville, Richard. *Playpower*. London: Paladin, 1971.

______. *Hippie Hippie Shake*. Port Melbourne: William Heinemann Australia, 1995.

Nietzsche, Friedrich. *The Birth of Tragedy*. Translated by Francis Golffing. New York: Anchor Books, 1956. First published 1872.

______. *Ecce Homo*. Translated by R.J. Hollingdale. London: Penguin, 1979. First published in 1888.

______. 'The Antichrist.' In Walter Kaufmann, ed. *The Portable Nietzsche*. London: Penguin, 1982. 565-656. First published 1895.

______. 'Twilight of the Idols.' In Kaufmann (1982a). 463-564. First published 1889.

Nordau, Max. *Degeneration*. Lincoln: University of Nebraska Press, 1993. First published 1892.

Nuttall, Jeff. *Bomb Culture*. London: Paladin, 1972.

Odell, David. *A Rushed Quality*. Online. Internet. 2001. Available http://www.blackjelly.com/arushedquality.pdf

Paglia, Camille. *Sexual Personae: Art and Decadence from Nefertiti to Emily Dickinson*. London: Yale University Press, 1990.

Pefanis, Julian. *Heterology and the Postmodern: Bataille, Baudrillard and Lyotard*. Sydney: Allen & Unwin, 1991.

Praz, Mario. *The Romantic Agony*. Glasgow: Fontana, 1960. First published 1933.

Preston, Richard. *The Hot Zone*. Sydney: Bantam, 1995.

Pringle, David. 'The Fourfold Symbolism of J.G. Ballard.' In Juno et al (1984). 126-37.

Pynchon, Thomas. *Gravity's Rainbow*. U.K.: Picador, 1975.

Quinby, Lee. *Anti-Apocalypse: Exercises in Genealogical Criticism*. Minneapolis: University of Minnesota Press, 1994.

Reed, Ishmael. *Mumbo Jumbo*. New York: Scribner, 1996. First published 1972.

Reeve, Simon et al. 'Countdown to Armageddon.' *The Australian*. (25 June, 1996) 53.

Revell, Graeme. 'Interview with J.G. Ballard.' In Juno et al. (1984) 42-53.

Reynolds, Simon. 'A Philosophical Dance Stance.' *The Australian*. (11 December, 1996) 35.

Rivers, Theodore John. *Contra Technologiam: The Crisis of Value in a Technological Age*. Maryland: University Press of America, 1993.

Robbins, Tom. *Jitterbug Perfume*. New York: Bantam, 1990.

Robotham, Julie. 'Chaos is King when the Chips are Down.' *Computer Age*. 20 August, 1996) 12.

Ross, Andrew. *Strange Weather: Culture, Science and Technology in the Age of Limits*. London: Verso, 1991.

Ross, Kristin. *Fast Cars, Clean Bodies: Decolonization and the Reordering of French Culture*. London: MIT Press, 1995.

Rowland, Christopher. '"Upon Whom the Ends of the Ages have Come": Apocalyptic and the Interpretation of the New Testament.' In Bull (1995). 38-57.

Ruddick, Nicholas. 'Ballard/*Crash*/Baudrillard.' *Science Fiction Studies*. 19, 1992. 354-60.

Rushkoff, Douglas. *Cyberia: Life in the Trenches of Cyberspace*. San Francisco: Harper, 1995.

Ruthven, Ken. *Nuclear Criticism*. Melbourne: Melbourne University Press, 1993.

Schivelbusch, Wolfgang. *The Railway Journey: Trains and Travel in the 19th Century*. New York: Urizen Books, 1980.

Schwartz, Hillel. *Century's End: An Orientation Manuel Toward the Year 2000*. New York: Currency and Doubleday, 1996.

Shaffer, Elinor. 'Secular Apocalypse: Prophets and Apocalypticians at the End of the Eighteenth Century.' In Bull (1995). 137-58.

Shaftesbury, Anthony, Earl of. 'A Letter Concerning Enthusiasm,' in *Characteristics of Men, Manners, Opinions, Times in Three Volumes*. Fifth Edition. Birmingham: John Baskerville, 1773. First published 1711.

Shaviro, Stephen. *Doom Patrols*. Online. Internet. 1997. n. pag. Available http://www.dhalgren.com/Doom/

Showalter, Elaine. *Sexual Anarchy: Gender and Culture at the Fin de Siécle*. London: Virago, 1992.

Sleep of Reason. Dir. Peter Jordan. Independent. 1994.

Sobchack, Vivian. 'Baudrillard's Obscenity.' *Science Fiction Studies*. 18, 1991. 327-29.

_____. 'Beating the Meat/ Surviving the Text, or How to Get Out of this Century Alive.' *Cyberspace, Cyberbodies, Cyberpunk: Cultures of Technological Embodiment*. Featherstone & Burrows, eds. London: Sage, 1995.

Springer, Claudia. *Electronic Eros: Bodies and Desire in the Postindustrial Age*. Austin: University of Texas Press, 1996.

Stableford, Brian, ed. *The Black Feast: the Second Dedalus Book of Decadence*. Cambs: Dedalus, 1992.

_____, ed. *Moral Ruins: the Dedalus Book of Decadence*. Cambs: Dedalus, 1993.

Stephenson, Neal. *Snow Crash*. U.K.: Bantam, 1993.

_____. *The Diamond Age*. London: Viking, 1995.

Strange Days. Dir. Kathryn Bigelow. Perf. Ralph Fiennes and Angela Bassett. 20th Century Fox. 1995.

Tabachnick, Norman M.D. et al., eds. *Accident or Suicide: Destruction by Automobile*. Illinois: Charles C. Thomas, 1973.

Thompson, Damian. *The End of Time: Faith and Fear in the Shadow of the Millennium*. London: Minerva, 1997.

Toffler, Alvin. *Future Shock*. New York: Random House, 1970.

Tuveson, Ernest Lee. *Millennium and Utopia: a Study in the Background of the Idea of Progress*. New York: Harper Torchbooks, 1964. First published 1949.

2001: A Space Odyssey. Dir. Stanley Kubrick. Perf. Kier Dullea and Gary Lockwood. MGM. 1968.

Vaneigem, Raoul. *The Movement of the Free Spirit*. New York: Zone, 1994.

Virilio, Paul and Sylvère Lotringer. *Pure War*. New York. Semiotext(e). 1983.

Virilio, Paul. *Speed and Politics*. New York: Semiotext(e), 1986.

_____. *The Art of the Motor*. Minneapolis: University of Minnesota Press, 1995.

Waite, Geoff. *Nietzsche's Corps/e: Aesthetics, Politics, Prophecy, or, the Spectacular Technoculture of Everyday Life*. Durham: Duke University Press, 1996.

Walker, John. 'Seizing Power: Decadence and Transgression in Foucault and Paglia,' *Postmodern Culture* 5, 1, Online. Internet. 1994. Available http://muse.jhu.edu/journals/postmodern_culture/v005/5.1walker.html

Watkins, Sian. 'We're Still Dying to Drive.' *The Age*. August 15, 1996. 4.

Weir, David. *Decadence and the Making of Modernism*. Amherst: University of Massachusetts Press, 1995.

Weiss, Allen S. *The Aesthetics of Excess*. Albany: State University of New York Press, 1989.

Wiesenfelder, Joe. 'The Information Superhighway (This is not a Metaphor).' *Wired*. 4.02, 1996. 126-129, 177, 180.

Wilson, Louise. 'Cyberwar, God and Television: An Interview with Paul Virilio.' *CTHEORY*. Online. Internet. 1994. Available http://www.ctheory.com/a-cyberwar_god.html

Wired for Sex. Dir. Laine Drewery. Canadian Broadcasting Corporation. 1996.

Wood, David, ed. *Writing the Future*. New York: Routledge, 1990.

Index

2000 (the year), ix, 2–3, 145, 148, 151, 168, 171–72, 182
2001: A Space Odyssey
  See Kubrick, Stanley
  See also Clarke, Arthur C.
Adamites
  See cults
Agamben, Giorgio, x–xi, 177–78
AIDS (HIV), 21, 112, 121, 126, 134–35, 140, 142, 176
  See also virus
alienation, 1, 30, 33, 46, 74–77, 81, 103, 110, 133, 149, 155–56, 159–61
aliens, 5–6
Anthony, Earl of Shaftesbury, 25, 27–29, 33, 88, 93, 179
apocalypse, ix–188 *passim.*
Apollo(nian), 7, 22, 24, 26, 29, 32, 101, 109, 122, 130, 132, 138–39, 164, 167, 181, 185 n.3
Applewhite, Marshall Herff, 1–2, 4, 7, 107
  See also cults; Heaven's Gate
A Rebours
  See Huysmans, J.-K.
Armageddon, 6, 15, 29, 56, 123, 129, 151, 158, 169, 179
Autogeddon
  See crash, the
arrivant(e), 176–77
artifice, 20, 30, 32, 60, 88, 102, 107–10, 130, 143, 150, 153–56, 187 n.19
Aum Shinrikyo
  See cults

Babel, 86–87
Ballard, J.G., 6, 20, 66, 68, 70–83, 87, 89–95, 97, 113, 125, 182, 186 n.15
  Crash, 20, 66, 70–83, 87, 113, 186 n.15
Bataille, Georges, 5, 6, 7, 20, 37–61, 74, 93, 121–22, 138, 143, 155, 166, 171, 178–79, 186 n.10
Baudrillard, Jean, xi, xv, 9, 12, 19, 21, 33, 35, 64, 69, 71–78, 83, 86–88, 92, 96, 98, 121, 133, 135, 141–70, 172, 175, 181–82, 186 n13, 187 n.22
belatedness (psychology of), x–xi, 103–04, 115
Benetton, 143, 177
Benjamin, Walter, xi, 81, 151, 179
Bernstein, Michael André, 22, 129, 164, 173, 176
Bersani, Leo, 138, 186
Bey, Hakim, 34, 97, 157–64, 180
Bigelow, Kathryn
  See Strange Days

Bin, Kimura, x
Bliss Apocalypse, 133–34
Bomb (the atomic), 21, 86, 124–29, 139–40, 163, 167
boredom, ix, 103, 110, 114, 125, 155
Boyer, Paul, 125–29
Branch Davidians
 See cults
 See also Koresh, David
Brecht, Stefan, 132–33
Brown, Norman O., 52, 73, 118, 123, 129, 131, 137–40, 142, 153
Buck-Morss, Susan, 81
Bukatman, Scott, 80
 on terminal identity: 69, 73–74, 85, 94
Burning Man Festival, 162, 168
Butler, Judith, 93

Carmageddon
 See crash, the
Cathars
 See cults
Cherry 2000, 20, 78, 89–90, 96
Chidester, David, 37–39, 52
Chong, Annabel, 9, 185 n 4
Christ, Jesus, 11, 16, 28, 41, 158
 anti–Christ, 53–57
Christianity, 11, 18–19, 27, 40–61, 101, 109, 112, 154–55, 162, 166, 172
Clarke, Arthur C., ix, 10, 163, 169
 See also 2001: A Space Odyssey
climax, 12–16, 30, 102, 107, 112, 134–36, 166, 173, 178, 181–82
 anti, ix, 21, 102, 166, 172, 182
Cobain, Kurt, 152
Cohn, Norman, 10–11, 45, 57, 131, 147, 187 n.21
cold war, the, 4, 129, 134–37, 140
coming
 community, 177–78
 ejaculation, 14–16, 30–31, 58, 87
 second, 12, 19, 104, 115, 150–52, 158

Coupland, Douglas, 31
crash, the, 64–98, 170
 Autogeddon, 78–82, 87, 91
 Carmageddon, 97–98
 Infocalypse, 78, 82–87, 172
 snow, 86–87, 94
 See also virus
Crash
 See Ballard, J.G.
Cronenberg, David, 73, 153
Cuban missile crisis, 129
cults
 Adamites, 13
 Aum Shinrikyo, 2, 11, 28, 165, 178
 Branch Davidians, 2, 28, 159. *See also* Koresh, David
 Cathars, 22
 Extropians, 76, 163
 Heaven's Gate, 1–7, 23, 28, 107–08, 111, 143, 165, 176. *See also* Applewhite, Marshall Herff
 Movement (Heresy) of the Free Spirit, 9, 22, 42, 44–45
 Order of the Solar Temple, 2, 7
 Ranters, 131
 Select Followers of Oklahoma, 6
culture, popular, 2, 20, 35, 37, 145, 151–52, 166
cyber
 gnosis, 161, 163
 punk, 7, 20, 32, 161
 sex, 31–32, 80, 88–96, 130
 space, 32–33, 69, 77, 82–87, 168 (*see also* Metaverse)
cyborg, 24, 70, 77–79, 86–90, 102, 108, 179, 187 n.17
 See also Haraway, Donna

D'Annunzio, Gabriele, 19, 159, 187 n.23
Daniel, Book of, 14
Darwin, Charles, 3, 45, 86, 100, 130, 154, 164, 187 n.18
death drive, 48–50, 74, 138
death fashion, 141–44, 151
decadence, x, 9, 11–12, 19–20,

23–4, 30–31, 34–35, 45, 49, 78, 97, 99–115, 118–19, 132, 138, 142–44, 147, 156–58, 165, 187 n.18
Degeneration
 See Nordau, Max
Deleuze, Gilles, 27, 144, 166, 169, 186 n.10
 and Felix Guattari 27
Dellamora, Richard, 21, 175–76
Derrida, Jacques, 14–16, 30, 87, 110, 172, 174, 176–77, 185 n.5
Dery, Mark, 159, 178, 185 n.2
Des Esseintes
 See Huysmans, J.-K.
Diana, Princess, 91–93, 154
Dionysian, ix–188 *passim.*
Dionysus in '69, 132–33
Dolmance, 42–46, 171
Domesday Book, 169
Dostoevsky, Fyodor, 26
Dr. Strangelove
 See Kubrick, Stanley
During, Simon, 39
Dylan, Bob, 12, 129
dystopia(n), 45, 80, 96, 113, 158
 See also utopian

Eagleton, Terry, 119
entropy, ix, 9, 54, 57, 104, 110–14, 149, 158
Eros, 6, 19, 20, 22, 29, 32, 37–61, 74, 97, 132, 136–38, 143, 153
escape velocity, 3, 70, 81–82, 149, 170
eschatology, x, 2, 15, 18–19, 30, 40, 56–57, 133, 138–39, 158, 163, 176, 179
Eschaton, 3, 125, 134, 163, 175, 185 n.1
Eternal Return, 12, 58–59, 150
exhaustion (cultural), ix–x, 9, 11, 22–23, 78, 100–101, 137, 158, 169, 175, 177, 181
Extropians
 See cults

fin de siècle, 26, 35, 60, 99–114, 119, 152, 178
 1890s, the 20, 118–19
Flaubert, Gustave, 76, 99
Foucault, Michel, 38, 40–42, 61, 110–15, 123–24, 129
Freud, Sigmund, 3, 6, 29, 39, 48, 66, 77, 112, 121–22, 138
Fukuyama, Francis, 149, 157
future shock, ix, 67, 101
Futurism
 See Marinetti, F.T.

Gasché, Rodolphe, 88, 105–08
Gates, Bill, 2, 169
 Microsoft, 63, 98
Generation X, 58, 112, 125, 146, 166
Gibson, William, 32, 70, 84–85, 161, 168
Ginsberg, Allen, 120, 129, 133
globalization, 23, 101
God (death of), 37, 40–42, 109
Grant, Linda, 43, 80, 130–35
Greer, Germaine, 118, 135

Haraway, Donna, 77, 91, 140, 173, 178
 See also cyborg
Hardt, Michael, 188 n.25
Heaven's Gate
 See cults
 See also Applewhite, Marshall Herff
Heidegger, Martin, x, 17–19, 97, 162–63
heroin chic, 142
Hillman, James, 25, 29–32, 123
Hiro Protagonist, 82–85
 See also Stephenson, Neal
history, end of, 3, 104–06, 112, 149, 157, 163
Huysmans, J.–K., 23, 30, 66–68, 76, 99, 102–114, 149–50, 165
 Des Esseintes, 30, 66–68, 88, 95, 102–114
 A Rebours, 20, 95, 99, 102–114, 149, 165

Iliad, The, 84
Infocalypse
See crash, the
Internet, 2–4, 13, 30, 33, 63, 69–70, 73, 84–87, 92, 98, 123, 161
See also cyberspace
See also Metaverse

Jameson, Frederic, 141
Jes Grew
See Reed, Ishmael
Joachim de Fiore, 13, 147, 187 n.21
jouissance, 13, 76, 123
Jünger, Ernst, 64, 74, 81, 171

Kadrey, Richard, 31
Kermode, Frank, 2, 13, 147–48, 181
Kerouac, Jack, 126–27
Kingwell, Mark, 31, 68, 142, 152
Koresh, David, 7, 29, 159
See also cults; Branch Davidians
Kroker, Arthur and Marilouise, 32, 142
Kubrick, Stanley, ix, 3, 136, 164
Dr. Strangelove 136
2001: A Space Odyssey ix, 3, 92–93, 162–64

Land, Nick, 37, 42, 48, 52, 57–60
Last Judgment, 19, 27, 43, 45, 56, 58, 104, 129, 172
Lawrence, D.H,. 19, 140, 156–57, 167
Leary, Timothy, 118, 140, 164
Levin, Charles, 144
libertine(s), 30, 39, 42–49, 78, 95
Lightman, Alan, 174
Luddites, x, 144
Lyotard, Jean–François, 53, 60

Maffesoli, Michel, 19, 33–35, 52, 121–23, 128, 156, 173, 185 n.7, 187 n.20
Manson, Charles, 1, 6, 22
Marcuse, Herbert, 52, 118, 127, 139, 153
Marinetti, F.T., x, 66, 70–71, 93, 102, 178
Marx, Karl, 3, 99, 120, 147
Marxism, 3, 86, 147
McKenna, Terence, x, 4–6, 31, 140, 157, 161–66
McLuhan, Marshall, x, 22, 31, 63, 71, 76, 89, 98, 143, 162, 173, 174
memes (memetics), 4, 185 n.2
Merivale, Patricia, 25–27
messianism, 2, 4, 18, 29, 131, 139, 146, 176–77
Metaverse, 84–88
See also cyberspace
See also Internet
Microsoft
See Gates, Bill
millenarian(ism), ix–188 *passim*.
millenarianism, libidinal, xii, 3–7, 13–15, 20–24, 27–30, 60, 95, 99, 106, 113, 124, 130, 142, 145, 148, 151, 175–182
millennium bug
See Y2K problem
Mondo 2000, 8
Movement of the Free Spirit
See cults

National Automated Highway System, 72
Nature, 29, 39, 41–48, 53, 60, 129–30, 186 n.9
against, 38, 43, 45, 53, 97
See also Huysmans, J.–K.; *A Rebours*
necrophilia, 46, 73, 125, 136, 141–44, 154
Negri, Antonio, 188 n.25
Neville, Richard, 117–18, 137
Nietzsche, Friedrich, 6, 11, 18, 20, 25–27, 30, 32, 35, 37–61, 70, 97, 104, 109, 112, 125, 132, 140, 143, 151, 162, 165, 168, 175, 178–80, 185 n.3, 186 n.11
The Birth of Tragedy, 53–57, 109, 168
Ecce Homo, 53, 57, 59, 104
nihilism, 7, 9, 16, 18, 35, 41–47,

54–61, 78, 83, 93, 104, 109, 125, 146, 159
Nike, 1, 143
Nordau, Max, 10–11, 65, 70, 93, 97, 99–101, 104–08, 113–115, 178
Degeneration, 10–11, 99–101, 113-14
nuclear
deterrance, 151–52
fear of, 29, 123–29
war, 29, 134–37, 157, 176, 178
Nuttall, Jeff, 122, 124–26, 131

Odell, David, xii
Order of the Solar Temple
See cults
orgy, 7–9, 32–35, 37, 110, 115, 121–23, 128, 132–33, 144, 182
after, ix, xi, xv, 7, 9, 24, 37, 95, 104, 123, 142, 144, 151, 153, 172–3, 178
ante-festum, x–xi
post-festum, x–xi, 19
Overman (*Übermensch*), 55, 60, 70–71, 140, 165
See also Nietzsche, Friedrich

pagan(s), 7–8, 33, 53–54, 75, 101, 107, 109, 56, 160–61
technopagans, 151, 161–68
Paglia, Camille, 12–13, 67, 110, 115, 118, 160, 173
Pan, 6, 12, 25–35, 75, 95, 97, 109, 156, 160, 162–63, 165, 167, 179
panic, 6, 12, 25, 81, 109, 128, 132, 134–37, 140, 152, 168
sex, 32–34, 142
Pill, the (contraceptive), 21, 124, 127, 130–32, 140, 167
Pixis Interactive, 32
pornography, 9, 16, 30–32, 40, 48, 74, 82, 88–91, 94–95, 132, 135–36, 150, 152, 168
postmodern, ix–x, 8, 30, 34, 89, 94, 104–05, 141, 143, 145–46, 150, 156, 166, 167, 169, 186 n.13
postmodernism, 77, 126, 144,
postmodernity, 20, 34, 57, 150, 175, 179
posthuman, 70–71
posthumanist, 74
potlatch, 51, 122, 129, 162
prophecy, 79, 114–15, 139, 147–48, 165, 176, 185 n.6
self–fulfilling, 111, 152, 156, 173
Pynchon, Thomas, 12, 152, 173–74, 180, 187 n.24

Quinby, Lee, 12, 173–77

Ranters
See cults
rave(rs), 13–14, 21–22, 34, 159–68
Real Doll, 90
redemption, x, 5–6, 22, 48, 82, 98, 106, 137–39, 163, 168, 173, 178–79
Reed, Ishmael, 175, 186 n.16
Reich, Wilhelm, 44, 123, 137–38, 153
repentance, 112–13, 150–51
Revelation
of St. John, 14–18, 54, 57, 87, 106, 157, 169, 178–79
as a general concept, x, 1, 3, 6, 12, 17–18, 59, 71, 91, 115, 138, 149, 165, 173–74, 178–79
Rivers, Theodore John, 17–19
Robbins, Tom, 29, 117, 134
Ross, Andrew, 180
Rousseau, Jean Jacques, x, 44
Rushkoff, Douglas, 162, 167
Ruthven, Ken, 136

Sade, Marquis de, 20, 37–61, 70, 97, 102, 104, 109–10, 119, 125, 143, 150, 171, 178, 181, 187 n.24
Salome, 110, 115
salvation, x, 5, 10, 18, 93, 97, 126, 139, 162–63, 169, 173, 177–78, 182
Schivelbusch, Wolfgang, 63–66, 186 n.13

Schopenhauer, Arthur, 58, 104, 138
Select Followers of Oklahoma
See cults
Seven Seals, the, 15–16
Shaftesbury (see Anthony, Earl of)
Shaviro, Steven, 96, 174, 179
Shoah, the, 21
Situationists, 22, 125, 154, 158, 160–61
Sixties, the (1960s), 6, 20–21, 29, 31, 54, 117–140, 145–46, 153, 156–62, 164–66
Snow Crash
See Stephenson, Neal
snow crash
See crash, the
Sobchack, Vivian, 74, 77–78
St. Augustine, 16
St. John
See Revelation, of St. John
St. Theresa (of Avila), 5, 39, 50
St. Thomas, 13
Stableford, Brian, 112
Stelarc, 70, 76, 140
Stephenson, Neal, 7–8, 20, 70, 82–88, 94, 179
The Diamond Age, 7–8
Snow Crash, 20, 70, 82–88
Strange Days, 20, 93–96
Swift, Jonathon, 127, 157–58

techné, 17–19, 97, 107
techno–music
See rave(rs)
Temporary Autonomous Zone, 34, 97, 102, 156–61, 166–67, 187 n.23
See also Bey, Hakim
terminal identity
See Bukatman, Scott
terrorism, 85, 148, 158, 174, 176
thanatic asymptote, 48–52, 95, 151, 178, 182
Thanatos, 6, 19, 20, 22, 37–61, 74, 97, 132, 135, 138, 143, 153
Toffler, Alvin
See future shock
transcendence, 3, 22, 37–61, 81, 109, 138, 156, 164–65, 170, 173, 182
transgression, 3, 22, 37–61, 81, 95, 142, 156, 160, 165, 179, 186 n.8

UFOs, 4–6, 163, 165
utopia(n), 3, 35, 45, 120, 137, 158–60, 162, 165, 174, 175–79
See also dystopia(n)

Vaneigem, Raoul, 9, 155–56, 159
Vaughan
See Ballard; *Crash*
Virilio, Paul, 50, 67–71, 81, 83, 85, 92–96, 125, 137, 162
virtual reality, 66–89, 92–96, 164
virus, 4, 30, 126, 172, 176, 178, 186 n.16
computer, 84–87, 89, 172
See also crash, the
See also AIDS (HIV)

Waco
See cults; Branch Davidians
See also Koresh, David
Wagner, Richard, 30, 56, 100, 109
Waite, Geoff, 20, 30, 32, 57, 168
Walker, John, 46, 61
Weir, David, 102–05, 187 n.18
Weiss, Allen, S. 43, 60
Whore of Babylon, xv, 14–15
Woodstock, 137
World, End of the, xii, 16, 22, 37, 79, 124, 155, 157, 159, 169, 173

X-Files, The, 1, 5, 165

Y2K problem, 172

Zarathustra, 11, 29, 35, 55
Zizek, Slavoj, 187 n. 24
Zoroaster
See Zarathustra